Not About Madonna

Not About Madonna

My Little Pre-Icon Roommate and Other Memoirs

~

WHIT HILL

Heliotrope Books
New York

Copyright © 2011 Whit Hill

All rights reserved. No part of this book may be reproduced or transmitted in any form or by any means, electronic or mechanical, including photocopying, recording or by an information storage or retrieval system now known or heretoafter invented — except by a reviewer who may quote brief passages in a review to be printed in a magazine or newspaper — without permission in writing from the publisher.

Heliotrope Books LLC
c/o SB Design
125 East 4th Street
New York, NY 10003

Photograph of Madonna on the cover and title page by Peter Kentes
Photograph of Whit Hill on the back cover by Robin Dodd
Designed and Typeset by Naomi Rosenblatt with AJ&J Design

For Dad, who has always been there.

For Helen, who stepped in, so gracefully.

For Al, who makes me dance and sing.

Contents

Author's Note	8

Part One

New Girl	15
Ballet	31
The Rube	43
Party Time	53
Star Trek Child	57
Snow Day	63
Candle	81
The Christmas Letter	85
Boppers	107
Little Slugger	121
Al Pacino/Mississippi	123
Diploma	141

Part Two

Soho	163
Cape Cod	185
Michelle	201
Truth or Dare	217
The Value of Their Hard Work	233
VH1	241
Calumet	263
Acknowledgments	281

Author's Note

In the fall of 1977, when I came to Ann Arbor to study dance at the University of Michigan, I thought I knew a thing or two. I had acted professionally in New York City, my hometown. I had posed nude for art classes. I had smoked marijuana. I had done "the bump" at a disco. My birth control device was always within easy reach. My mother had raised me to be a confident, smart woman in control of her own destiny, in control of herself. I was polite, assertive, and outgoing. I got good grades. I dieted. I was a very modern girl.

When I met Madonna Ciccone, my initial assessment, even as I watched her leg soaring into an effortless front extension, was that I had little to learn from any young whippersnapper from Michigan, safety-pinned earlobes or no. I felt no instant flush of warmth and trust the day we met, no recognition of a kindred spirit—in fact, all I recall feeling was an almost seismic wariness. But somehow, a few days later, she was my roommate. She moved into apartment 10A of University Towers, an ugly 60s-era monolith right on campus, and took the bed on the other side of a Formica partition. I never knew what hit me.

My new roommate was thin, quick, funny, irreverent, and very crafty. She was sexy on the dance floor and sexless at night in her socks as she complained about how boring Michigan was. And she saw in me, or purported to, things she lacked and wanted: serenity, New York City roots, a doting mommy. And so for that school year, we "studied" each other. I, in particular, felt as if I were her secret project. Any reluctance to play along was met with those half-narrowed eyes, a soft fluttering of kiss on my cheek, protestations of love and encouragement mixed with a tinge of whine. With her I climbed fire-escape ladders and clambered around on rooftops. With her I catwalked down steep railroad embankments to the Huron River where we swam naked with strangers. With her I flirted and hitchhiked and told lies and smoked pot and raced my heart stealing candy and magazines. Madonna, dare I say it, liberated my inner child. And that child was a juvenile delinquent.

On the flip side, she seemed fascinated with my life—my status as a pampered only child of divorced parents, raised in New York, well-schooled, and well-traveled. It seemed to blow her mind that my father, a respected actor and member of the Actor's Studio, played poker with Al Pacino every week. Sometimes, when my mother called, I sensed that Madonna was listening carefully to every word I said, trying to puzzle the errant justice that had taken her mother but spared mine.

If there was an occasional edge of competitiveness in our friendship—we were dancers after all, staring in mirrors all day, being judged for our thinness, artistry, and fearlessness—there was just as much support. There were many, many long and convoluted conversations in which we strove to build each other up, and to figure out men and life and dance and selves. And like college girls everywhere, I wrote it all down in a red, Pen-Tab notebook.

When she left for New York, I was quietly relieved. Knowing Madonna and loving her (for we had grown to be close friends) was a lot of work. For all our bonding, I never really trusted her. I drifted back to my old ways: dating wide-eyed college students who immediately made plans to marry and sequester me; sucking up to teachers; cultivating friendships with nice, interesting, normal women who did not straddle me on the dance floor. Madonna went on to New York, her goal to rule the world tucked safely in her bosom, her legendary $13 jammed in a fist that let nothing and no one get in her way. Cool.

If she hadn't gone all famous, I believe we would have kept in touch. I think about that sometimes, about the times I would have called her if I could have. When my first child was born, I wanted to tell her about it, but I didn't know where she was. When she married Sean Penn, it would have been nice to send her a chafing dish. A picture frame. I don't know. Maybe not. It is kind of strange though, knowing that any attempt at communication with her might now be perceived as having some kind of agenda. Whoa. No thanks.

Knowing Madonna didn't really change my life in any substantive way, but the reality of what she has become—that has been rather weirdly inescapable. She comes upon me at the oddest times: I turn my head in the checkout line and thar she blows, all blonde and shiny, and I peer into the face searching for the girl I knew. I stand on a street corner and her voice croons at me from a passing car. I listen for a memory of some ordinary thing she said: "Hey, Whitto, I'm gonna wear your scarf, OK?" Sometimes a person at a party gets that look and shyly asks me, "So ... is it true? What I heard about you? You were Madonna's roommate?" Sometimes I lie, just to get back to the onion dip in peace, to remain in the present. If pressed, I'll tell a few things: about what we did together, how different we were, her loneliness, her smartassness, her smile. That yes, she was a very good dancer, that she worked harder than anyone I'd ever known. That no, I am not surprised a bit at what happened. That, no, I do not long for reunification but that I do wish her every happiness.

My knowing Madonna has been like the world's largest, most persistent mosquito, or like a dissertation you were supposed to hand in years ago and just can't quite wrap your head around. Some years ago, I was driving back from a music festival with a guy I was in the process of breaking up with. It was one of those mutual things, so the mood was not too bleak. We were talking about Madonna—she was in the news for something or other and people were asking me about her again—and he suddenly said, "You should write a book." Well, that seemed like an idea. I wrote a few chapters and got bored, ambivalent, and busy. There were children to raise and rehearsals to run; I have been a performing artist my whole life. Plus, it seemed that in order to write about the Madonna "back then" I'd have to actually care about the Madonna she had become, to be somehow invested and amazed by her many accomplishments. And—how to put this—while I am interested in some facets of American pop culture, Madonna's particular niche never has really steeped my tea.

After a long hiatus, I gave it another go. The more I thought about it, the more I realized that the story of my knowing her has a lot to do with some themes I actually *am* interested in: women artists in America, fame versus nonfame, life versus life onscreen, and all the ways you can lose your mom.

As I wrote, I made every effort to be as accurate as possible while creating something people would actually want to read. My journals from my college years were enormously helpful to me, despite being mortifyingly boring and embarrassing. At times, the journals are quoted verbatim; other times, I have taken short, cursory entries and expanded them to tell a story with richer detail. Sometimes, for the sake of fluidity, I have changed the chronology of some minor events. I have also changed some, but not all, names. Conversations, of course, are recreated, except for those that I wrote down, or remember vividly. The Christmas Letter is included almost in its entirety, including Madonna's occasional misspellings and flights of punctuation. I think it is a beautiful piece of writing, just as it is.

So here's my dissertation. But first, I have a request:

Close this book and look at the title again. Read it out loud. Did you? Good. I just want to be really clear about what this is. If you are looking for the dirt on a prefame Madonna, there are quite a few volumes of literature out there that will meet your needs better than this one, that will tell you what you expect to be told. I am happy to share with you most of what I remember from that time—and quite a bit more—but it may not be what you are after. Madonna is a spoke in my wheel, a cog in my whirring factory. This book is a lot of things. And even though she's in it, this book is not about Madonna.

Whit Hill
Nashville, Tennessee

PART ONE

encourages me not to be negative, and to hug trees), buying a banana split from the Dainty Maid stand. I really want one too, but I had better not. After a summer of Jimmy, fried clams, and ice cream, I'm not looking forward to pouring my pounds into a leotard and looking in a mirror. I can hardly waste away by the time classes start in three days, but I can try.

The University of Michigan, Ann Arbor

Journal, September 8, 1977

Tired, of the bone variety. I miss everyone and everything even remotely familiar. I hate this room and this pretentious town and Tony and Joel and my fat self. I definitely have an eating disorder I think. Why did they ever let me transfer into this department anyway? Can I even dance? I don't know anymore. I more than held my own at Brockport State, but this is a "Real Place." I mean Christine Dakin went here and now she's a leading Martha Graham dancer. Today I was in the student lounge and I found this old Dance Department yearbook thing and there she was: Christine Dakin with big thighs. Now she's tiny and famous and incredible so I guess there's hope. Someone else famous went here too, but I forget who right now. I'm so tired. And sore.

Will someone tell me why I trusted T and J to find us an apartment? They have signed a lease on an apartment that is a sin against God. It is a perversion, a sickness, and a crime. And I must pay to live here, unless I ditch and inconvenience the only friends I have in this state, which of course I am too nice to do. And so I, for the next 9 months, am going to live in apartment 10A of University Towers in Ann Arbor, Michigan.

This is not my style. My style is old college house. My style is tattered sofa on porch and happy hippie housemates all cooking up vegetarian cuisine, and warm parties and cats and long talks about the arts around a late-night kitchen table. And wood, lots of splintered, well-trodden wood. And ripply windows looking out onto trees that tell me the time of year. Instead, I am to live in a 60s-era high-rise built for students too artless to care about their surroundings. Decidedly unfresh carpeting, and the view? Can I look out from my tenth-floor window and watch the leaves of Treetown change, watch the storm clouds and the protests and the sunsets? No. University Towers is built in the shape of a huge, angular

U, and apartment 10A is on the inside of said U. What do I see when I look out the window? I will go and check and tell you. OK, I'm back. I can see, across the fucking airshaft, the head of an Asian student bent over a desk, illuminated by a fluorescent reading lamp. If I press my face hard against the glass, I can see a distant triangle of sky.

Oh—and furniture is supplied! Black Naugahyde sofa and chairs in the living room, fake wood desks. Icky twin beds in the bedroom, head-to-head and separated by a fake wood-divider thing. I have already called maintenance and had them remove my bed. I will sleep on the floor in my sleeping bag and retain some semblance of myself. I will be that much closer to the earth.

So it's been 11 days since I've opened this book. Since Cape Cod and Jimmy and camping on that little island, a one-minute swim off Cotuit Beach. Oh, I miss you, Jimmy. Wish you were here, but you'd wither in this horrible little room, with no sky at all and the grim geometric view of windows and student heads. I cannot even get into the voyeuristic possibilities. Maybe later.

Today was the second day of classes: ballet, technique, repertory... not sure if I'm gonna be up to African too this semester, but have to decide soon. Tomorrow I hit my first academic: American Art and Architecture. Gotta squeeze in some stage tech requirements at some point, but right now I just want some rich, handsome man to appear at my door, take me to dinner, and promise me a life of socially-conscious work. Mixed with some minor luxury. Modern dance? What was I thinking? I am way too fat for this. Stop it stop it stop it. I love to dance. BREATHE. Ow, that hurts my abs. Ow ow.

And then there's the roommate issue. The guys are sharing one bedroom and I need someone to share mine. In 45 minutes, this woman is coming over to see the room and meet with me and the guys (who seem somehow very eager for her to move in). I am less than thrilled about this prospect and I'll tell you why. I have seen her from a distance and I am not impressed. This afternoon I was in one of the studios with Tony and he told me she was next door taking a ballet class and I peeked, and what is my first view? A woman half the weight of me—really maybe 95 pounds (OK not half)—doing a developée to the front (my worst extension) and it's way over 90 degrees. How can I live with someone like that? Oh, oh, oh, but I need a roommate. Shit.

Had a dream last night that I was lying on the side of this big, sandy-colored pyramid, just staring up at the sky. Somewhere in Mexico, I think. I could see blue-green mountains far away and knew that there were waterfalls in the mountains, even though I couldn't see the waterfalls. Then someone nearby called my name, really sweetly and gently. I arched my back really a lot to try and see who it was. Remember thinking—I've got to use this arch shape in a dance sometime.

Well, whaddaya know—my period. I'll bet she is too THIN to get periods. (I am sure I'll be finding out.)

Same night, 11:04 p.m.

Must get lots of sleep if I'm to survive tomorrow, but I'll take a moment to write the final chapter in "Whit Seeks a Roommate." At six sharp, Tony walks in with her (they'd just finished their rep class) and she sits on the sofa opposite me and we talk. She looks at the room and we talk some more. A lot of stuff about the department. The guys seem, how shall we say, "taken with her." I feel strangely distant and beaten. Here's this woman in black jeans and a white T-shirt that she seems to have cut holes in on purpose. She is beautiful in a way that terrifies me. She looks like Scarlett O'Hara, postwar—thin, stretched face, bony shoulders (the shirt drapes over one), hair quite dark, chopped off somehow, as if she did it herself with a knife. Her eyes are huge and green. She gets up and goes in the kitchen and gets herself a glass of water (my mug) while we talk. While they talk, that is. It's like she already lives here. I find myself studying Cheng's head across the way.

She tells us about herself. She's from some Detroit suburb, her dad works for some car company. This is her first real semester at the department and she has a scholarship. Christopher Flynn, the ballet teacher, is her best friend in the world; he got her into dance. They spend a lot of time together.

I stretch my face into a smile and really do try to be open-minded and friendly. While at the same time trying to remain true to my feelings of EXTREME ANXIETY.

I start thinking: OK. I don't like this woman, but if she moves in, will I then be friends with Christopher? He's so colorful and deliciously gay and brilliant. I love his ballet class (well, the one I've had so far), but await with some trepidation his sarcastic corrections. Some girl in the locker room showed me a blood blister on her inner thigh where Flynn pinched her to get her to turn out more. Will he like me more if I'm friends with his protégé? If I'm friends with his protégé, will he not pinch my inner thigh? Why am I having these thoughts? Am I at all like these people?

So then Cat Woman breaks a conversational lull and says, "Gee, Whitley, you don't look very happy right now. What's the matter?"

Fuck. I'm busted. I stammer something inane but more or less true and dealing with current fatigue levels. Then, "Yeah, sure, you can move in right away." She seems satisfied with this, but more than that, she seems interested too. She smiles at me and things lighten a bit. I think. I don't know. Then the phone rings. It's my mom, and I talk for a minute, tell her I'll call back. When I hang up, Tony and Joel have gone into their room to get something and she's over by the window, her face pressed to the glass, looking up.

And I have a new roommate. Get this: her name is Madonna.

When I get home from class the next day, Madonna is all moved in. Further expressing my outrage over the view situation, I have given her the bed with the window. She's got it all set up, neat as a pin, which isn't too hard 'cause she doesn't have a whole lot of stuff. There's bedding on the bed and a couple of books on the desk, but that's about it. No sign of her though, and I'm pretty relieved; I'm so sore from the first few days of classes that there isn't room in my brain for small talk and nascent friendship. I'm asleep when she gets in, late at night. I wonder groggily where she's been, who her friends are, if they will become my friends. If Madonna will become my friend.

I'm not very old, but already I can see a disturbing pattern in life and friendships. In elementary school I was "best friends" with Sarah Caldwell and Hani Lanin. We were proud, bratty, confident Manhattan urchins who ruled our little bit of turf—an area called Turtle Bay, on a slight rise over the East River. It's a historic area, or so the occasional grimy, ignored bronze plaque attests. Somebody got hanged here, across from Gristede's Food Mart. Some Revolutionary battle got fought there, in front of that Chinese restaurant. But my friends and I didn't think a whole lot about history. Blood and intrigue were soundly paved over and covered with apartment buildings in the 1920s.

Together, Sarah and Hani and I played "Mary Poppins" on rainy days when the wind would whip off the river and come bellowing down our street. We jumped with our umbrellas off the stoop of Sarah's brownstone, trying to fly. It almost worked. We had burping contests. We played endless rounds of Mystery Date, crammed into Sarah's tiny bedroom. We invented "roller butting," strapping one skate to our bottoms with a pillow and bathrobe sash, then propelling ourselves down the sidewalk with our hands, while our mothers drank gin and tonics on the front stoops in the fading light of a summer night. I fervently believed I would know and love these friends for the rest of my life.

Ah, but in junior high, I sort of lost track of those guys and found my really, truly best friend, Sharon Greenberg, who lived in a luxury high-rise between First Avenue and the river, just half a block from my little walk-up. Sharon was exotically Jewish and had two little brothers and a stack of romance and horror comics as tall as I was. Once, at an agreed-upon moment, she went out on her balcony and I put my head out my bedroom window at the height of rush hour. We screamed at the top of our lungs *and actually heard each other*. But Sharon moved away and I went off to high school and made other friends who I'm rapidly losing track of.

Friends are like ghosts, I think, rolling over in my sleeping bag, listening to Madonna quietly undressing and climbing into her bed. You gotta be in the right dimension to see them, but once you leave that place, they're gone. I've got lots of ghosts wandering around in my wake. Does this mean I'm a ghost to them, all those once–good friends? I'm certainly not trying to be. I've been thinking about this a lot lately. Who will I be ghost to next? From the bed on the other side of the Formica partition comes no kind of answer.

The next morning is Saturday. Of course the architecture prevents me from even guessing whether or not it's a nice day. I listen quietly with my eyes closed, wondering if my new roommate is up yet, and if I will have to deal with her anytime soon. I hear the door open and smell cinnamon.

"Whitley," she whispers. "Are you awake? I brought you some tea."

Well.

I open my eyes and stretch.

"Wow. Thank you. What's that?" She's holding a little dish of some kind of strange pellets.

"Corn Nuts. They're good. You can have them for breakfast."

"Oh. Thanks." I sit up and sip the tea and Madonna sits down at my desk and watches me. She's wearing old-man boxer shorts and a long white T-shirt. The Corn Nuts are good. Salty. They make me feel like a pilgrim. She reaches across and plucks one off my saucer.

"Wanna go to the co-op?" she asks as she crunches. "We need to buy food. The farmers market is today, too. And I know this really good thrift shop down on Fourth."

"Hunh. How far is it?" I ask. I am thinking of my calf muscles, which have hardened from the first week's classes to a gypsumlike consistency and threaten to shatter unless I'm careful.

"Oh, it's not far. Across the Diag, then a little bit more. Come on, it'll be fun. I'll show you around town. We'll sightsee."

The tea is good, too.

Gosh, it's a pretty day—sunny with a twist of fall. We walk down South University, past copy shops and bookstores. The head shops aren't open yet, 'cause it's only about 10:30 on a Saturday, but I can smell them anyway, a faint blast of patchouli. Down a couple of blocks is Central Campus, and Madonna steers me past Ulrich's Bookstore and onto the Diag, a pathway that cuts across over to State Street. We pass huge libraries and old brick buildings oozing with brains and facts and theorems and for a second I'm just so grateful I'm a dance major. A dance major with long hair on a sunny day and, if not a friend, then someone to walk around town with for a while.

"So, you're from, where? Detroit, right?" I ask.

"Nah, not really. I wish I was from Detroit. I have a lot of friends in Detroit." She sighs. "Rochester. I live in Rochester. It's a friggin' suburb. I'm from a suburb."

"Well, that probably means you have a nice house. A house with, like, a yard and rooms and stuff."

She looks quickly at me.

"Yeah, it had rooms. What do you mean?"

"Well, I mean it just sounds nice. Big. Normal."

"Well, it wasn't. It sucked."

She gives me a rundown. She tells me again what car company her dad works for, but I forget it again within five seconds, 'cause I don't do cars, and the idea of a person making cars is beyond my grasp at this point in my life. Or rather, the idea of a person making cars, while not secretly dreaming of being a dancer or an actor or a painter—that's beyond me. I can certainly understand that someone might *have* to be involved in the making of cars due to circumstances beyond their control. But as a chosen career? Whoa.

Madonna says she's got a whole slew of sisters and brothers and I feel a quick stab of jealousy, picturing late-night giggling and teasing and noisy Italian dinner tables.

"That's cool," I tell her. "I don't have any brothers or sisters."

She gasps and stares at me again. Two guys on bikes whiz past us. "You don't? You mean you're an only child?"

Now it's my turn to sigh. "You know, all my life I have had to tell people that I have no brothers and sisters and every time—*every time*—they respond by saying, 'You mean you're an *only* child?' What else would no brothers and sisters mean? Yes, I'm an *only* child."

Oh. I think I have teased her too soon.

"I can't even imagine what that would be like," she says, quietly. "Just you and your parents."

"Well, just me and my mom. Or just me and my dad. Not only am I an *only* child, I come from a *broken* home."

"Wow. Cool," she says.

"Yeah."

We've reached State Street and turn west down Liberty, past the old Michigan Theater. We peer in the darkened windows into old, rundown vaudevillian splendor. They actually show movies in here, Madonna says. We'll go sometime, she says. They have good popcorn.

"So," she ventures, "who did you live with?" Madonna turns and walks backward for a while, facing me as we talk.

"My mom. I lived with my mom for eighteen years—from the day I came home from the hospital to the day I left for college. Well, my dad lived there too until I was five and things got ugly and he moved out. My dad's an actor. Then it was me and my mom in this tiny one-bedroom apartment on First Avenue. Midtown. We shared a bedroom. Well, the bedroom was kind of L-shaped, so I had kind of an alcove of my own. It wasn't bad. Whenever I tell this stuff to people who grew up not-in-New York, you know, with houses and dogs and stuff, they always act like I've been all deprived, 'cause I had to share a room with my mom for eighteen years. But it wasn't that bad. The apartment was, like, 87 bucks a month so she had lots of money for us to do other things. We traveled a lot. Besides, we're best friends. She's not really like a mother, she's"—and I actually say this—"like a part of me. Like we're one person in two bodies. I know it sounds weird, but it's not. We have all this psychic stuff between us. Like, my first year of college at Brockport, I was suddenly sure I had a lump in my breast. I went to the doctor and everything. They acted like I was nuts, a hypochondriac. And then I found out that she was having a lump in *her* breast removed at the very same time—it wasn't cancer, but she was scared. And the point is, I just knew it; my body knew it. Anyway, she's amazing. You'll meet her. I'm sure she's going to come out here sometime and visit."

She turns around and walks regular, a few steps ahead of me. I can't see her face. I catch up to her at a corner and we wait for the light to change. She turns to me and she's kind of smiling at something off in the distance, the wind tossing the short chops of her hair.

"So what does your mom do?" I ask, after a pause. I, of course, will never assume that one's mom doesn't work outside the home. Madonna is so interesting that she's got to have an interesting mom.

"She's-dead-she-died," she says, too fast, and singsong—like a little kid repeating something she heard somewhere. "She-got-cancer-and-died. I was really little. But she died. And my dad married the housekeeper and now I have an evil stepmother."

Now, I normally have something appropriate to say for just about any occasion, but I sure don't have anything at this particular moment.

I think I tell her I'm sorry.

I think I tell her ... wow.

I think I tell her, "I bet she was beautiful, your mom."

And I think she tells me that she was beautiful, very beautiful.

And the light's about to turn red again, so we run, fast to the other side.

Of course, I am immediately plunged into flush-faced guilt. Have I hurt her feelings, blathering off like that about my most excellent, most definitely living, breathing mother? In fact, the truth of my mother is not so simple. My mother is my own, personal Faulkner novel, one that I, as an Only Child, get to carry around, pressed against my chest, all by myself. She is a good book, my mother, in that you never know what's coming. And you can't put it down.

My mother is a Southern belle. Raised poor, the daughter of a cotton farmer-turned-dairy deliveryman and his sweet, school-lunch-lady wife, my mother escaped as soon as she could and came north to become a famous actress. As a child, I spend hours gazing at her college yearbooks, the photos of her as Miss Personality one year, Miss Charm the next, and Queen of the College in her senior year. She wears billowing white antebellum gowns and white gloves. When she is not home, I furtively pull out the black notebook that holds her publicity photos and stare at them, trying to figure out just who this woman is: jaunty and laughing in Central Park, her head thrown back over a park bench. Or brooding and morose in another photo, her hair covered by a black shawl, like a character in the *House of Bernarda Alba*.

These pictures are just like it was: the expressions and costume changes of a long and masterful performance: epic, travelogue, soap opera, tragedy.

There are more pictures, too, in no particular order, ones that did not make it to film, but rest vivid in my mind ... .

I am four years old. My mother is doing summer stock again—Sweet Bird of Youth, or something like that—in a rundown vacation spot on the Jersey shore. We stay in a rooming house. I sit in the theater and watch her as she rehearses, or I play outside in the driveway. My mother suffers from stage fright. The day her play is to open, she becomes sick with fear. I remember a crowded, dirty clinic. Brown linoleum floors. They give her a shot of something. Then we are walking across a field, walking back to the house. It is hot. She faints in the field. I run to a nearby road and flag down a car.

I am twelve years old. My mother has stopped doing summer stock and stopped taking acting classes in the Village. She has thrown herself into being a schoolteacher and makes enough money to support us well in our tiny apartment. One day she brings home a bunch of travel brochures and we begin to plan a trip. We go to Rome, Athens, and Paris together. "You are sisters, no?" say the Italian men, flirting with my mother. She laughs and shakes her head. Sometimes at night I wake up in the hotel and she is not there. But I am not afraid. She is a wonderful traveling companion. She is fun and daring and lets me walk barefoot through any fountain.

I am eight years old, and terrified once again, because I do not know what is wrong. She is sitting at the kitchen table, her head in her hands. She has been there a while. For the life of me, I cannot figure out what I have done wrong. I pull up a stool and sit next to her.

"What's wrong, Mommy?" I ask again.

Her hand is quick, like a serpent. It flies across the table and slaps me hard across the face.

"You know what's wrong," she snarls at me.

I do not tell Madonna any of this, not yet at least.

She's right, the farmers market is great. This is my third late-summer/fall experience outside of New York City, and the novelty has not remotely worn off. Huge tables piled high with corn and tomatoes and shiny cukes. Fat farmers' wives with their baked goods. Friendly hippies with their organic ... things. Honey. Tie-dyed baby clothes. U-finish'em bookshelves. Boxes of puppies and kittens. I find it all so very earthy.

We buy veggies and bread and popcorn still on the cob, because Madonna is very interested in all forms of popcorn. I buy a cinnamon bun and we get frosting all over our faces. Then she leads me across the street to the co-op.

Now, counterculture food purveyors are distinctly fascinating to me. During my two years at the State University College of New York at Brockport, from whence I have transferred, I spent a lot of time in a church basement called the Crypt where earnest guitar players played songs that were *really good*. And if you volunteered to help clean up at the end of the night then you could eat your fill of vegetarian casseroles and strange, alternate-universe cookies. Now, here in Ann Arbor: a real, live hippie co-op food store, like the ones I've heard so much about.

The wooden screen door slams behind us and a guy looking at a bulletin board covered with flyers looks up quickly, then back at an announcement. *Room in a house. Lecture in Sufism. Nice dog available ... owner allergic and distraught.*

Sun fills the big front window and lights up motes of flour dust. Our feet slide on someone's spilt lentils.

"Oooh, it smells great in here. Like bread and cookies."

"That's the bakery. It's next door. We'll go there next. If you work an hour, you can get a free loaf of bread."

"But we just bought bread," I say.

"Well, we'll just have to come back next week. Look at this. I'm gettin' it."

It's a bag of something called Bear Mush. A wholesome wheat cereal. I don't object. We go next door to the bakery and get some pecan cookies to bring back to Tony and Joel, then head back into the sunshine.

On the next block, in another old storefront, is the thrift shop Madonna's mentioned. It's managed by the Methodist Ladies Organization or some such, and I'm not expecting much, just old lady religious-person clothing. Some years later I will grow to love old lady religious-person clothing, with Army boots, but not just yet, as my sense of irony is still developing. We walk in with our bags of tomatoes and I bump into a display of used sunglasses and nearly knock it over. Madonna cracks up and immediately starts trying on shades, mugging in front of the mirror. The lady behind the cash register ignores us, so I say hello overly brightly to make her smile, which she does, grudgingly.

I quickly figure out that there's nothing I like here, but Madonna is doing something amazing. Whatever she tries on looks great. A red wool, professorial cardigan. A cream-colored white '60s sheath. A man's flat, black hat. A baseball jersey. I put the bags down and close my eyes and pick up the first thing my hand falls upon, a blue and gray dress, and slip it over my head where it hangs on me like a backhanded compliment. I rip it off and put it back on the rack. Madonna's got a pair of men's brown pants on over her shorts and she's cinched them tight with a belt. She slips into a pair of brown wingtips and walks over to the mirror. I notice she has a very singular walk: heel-toe, heel-toe, heel-toe, very precise and in line. I think it would take effort to walk like that. She slaps the flat-top hat on her head and stares at herself for a moment. Then turns to me. "OK, let's go. I don't got no more moola, anyway."

Forty-five minutes later, we're back in the apartment, with all the windows open, 'cause it's suddenly hot as blazes. I put Earth, Wind, and Fire on the stereo as we put away the food and pretty soon, we're dancing around the kitchen, flapping open cupboards, slamming them shut, singing along. I realize I haven't thought about Jimmy and last summer all day long.

When the record is over, we put on Stevie—"Songs in the Key of Life"—and we find we know all those words too. The guys are out somewhere and pretty soon we're splayed out, stuck to the Naugahyde sofas as the first side of the record ends and the needle clicks itself up, over to the side, and down. I've always thought that sound, that click, makes everything that comes after it more silent.

And I realize that I'm in the same place on the couch as when she first came over to see the room, and she's sitting opposite me in the same place she was sitting, way back, two days ago.

"I'm tired," she says.

"Me too."

I'm looking at her, wondering whether or not to get up and turn the record over.

"What?" she says.

"Nothing," I say.

"*What?*" she says again.

"Nothing." And she gets up and goes over to the stereo. And I think this might actually be okay after all.

Ballet

The last exercise is a killer and I am ill-prepared to attack it, having just returned from a trip to the bathroom. (I caught myself in the mirror on the way out: burgundy-cheeked; hair in interesting frizzy mayhem; black leo and tights; faded gray T-shirt hiding most of midsection; holey, navy legwarmers. I feel safe, covered).

I dash down the cement steps and enter Studio D. The pungent smell of ballet class pours over me as I notice that in my absence, Christopher's let out all the stops and now imagines himself the ballet master of the Bolshoi, rather than the underpaid instructor in a Midwestern American university dance department (modern dance emphasis) that he is. His fantasy is secure. His cigarette dangles daintily, his accent grows vaguely European, pompous, exaggerated.

"Step throoooough, arms a la secoooonde, piqué—and hooooold, hooooold, place fourth, and ahhhup!" Christopher finishes his gazillion-count masterwork with his usual multiple pirouette flourish, ashes spinning wildly. He drops into a passable fifth and waves at the pianist.

All fine, except that I've missed the entire first part. I eye the door and opt instead for a quick study from the sidelines. I search frantically for Madonna, but she's off and running, paired with Mick, a big, sweaty guy who likes to stare at her. I watch and mark the steps by the barre. She's got it, not great, but definitely recognizable.

Madonna, in the last class of a rainy Thursday in November: her hair's pulled back via seven or eight plastic kiddie barrettes. She's wearing old, dark red tights (um, they're mine, I notice), some nondescript leotard, and a filmy, white T-shirt that flows as she leaps and runs. She's got a thin ribbon of elastic placed just under her breasts, *a l'empire*, which makes that humble shirt, peppered with holes in some earlier snipping frenzy, lovely as the shroud of a punk Giselle. I learn the combination of steps and don't flail too mightily. Actually get a "Yes!" from Monsieur Flynn, which makes my day.

The clock says 5:30—quittin' time—but Flynn says "Again!", so again it is. I feel a hand on the back of my neck.

"Hey, lady," says my roomie. I lean back into her thankfully, feeling her bones. We have become friends.

"C'mon. I'm sick-o-Micko. Let's do it," she says.

We hear the vibrant intro (Strauss, I believe, or Offenbach) and run to the front of the line. We charge into the space laughing, dancing with a fullness that defies technique but defines movement. Our fantasies leave Flynn's in the dust. She's slightly ahead, then I am. Her leg arcs higher, but my jump has more push. We hold the pose an extra beat, watching our sameness in the mirror, then polish off the turns, two each. Funnnnn.

We run to the wall and wait for the others to finish. I watch her watch the class. She leans her back against the barre, propped on her elbows, wrists dropped down, hips thrust out. Her feet in their dirty, pink Capezios are planted firmly, slightly turned out. But there's nothing casual about her. Nothing at all.

Lori's out now, eating up the phrase as if it's a nutritious snack. She's a solid girl, with a fresh, farmer's-daughter openness. She brings something pure into the studio whenever she dances. We know it, the teachers know it. Only she seems unaware as she slams into the final eight bars. (She never looks in the mirror).

Madonna has a problem with this. I recall our latest Lori-dissection, about a week ago, between classes, in the dim back hall.

Madonna (hands making white knuckles on the banister): "Whitley, that's it. I am absolutely sick to death of Lori French and the way everyone in this shit-ass department seems to think she's some kind of god. Do you know what Susannah just did in class? Do you know? We were working that really hard jump-fall combination, the one I've been BUSTING MY BUTT on outside of class and she stops the whole fucking class and says, 'Everybody, watch Lori. She's got the dynamics down. She's really punching out the counts, blah, blah, blah ... and she makes us all stand around like some kind of cretins or something and watch Lori do the whole fucking thing ALONE. Excuse me, but when I watch her all I see is THIGHS and that insipid smile of hers. You know, I'm not spending all this money and time in this department to watch Lori French jump around with a piano. Shit ..."

Me (agreeing on many of these points but feeling strangely loyal to Lori who, after all, is making every effort to be my friend these days): "I know. I hate when they do that. It's so humiliating and stupid. But Lori ... I dunno, I like her. I do. There's something so real about her, innocent. And she likes you, too. She told me so. She wants you to be in her comp piece, but she's too scared to ask you."

Madonna (not listening past my fourth sentence): "And I was doing it so good, too. I got right out in front of Susannah and she didn't even notice. I did it way better than Lori and she didn't even notice …"

Me: "Madonna."

No response, but her knuckles are no longer white.

Me: "Madonna, it's not worth it. Really it's not."

She looks at me long and hard. She sighs. We go sit in the lounge for a while and I give her part of my sandwich.

Class is over and my reverie is interrupted by the drenched presence of a hulking Mick.

"Hey, Madonna," he says, sweating out the words.

He ignores me pointedly, has consistently ignored me since he hurt his back when he tried to lift me in repertory class.

"We're hitting Bicycle Jim's in a bit. Wanna come? Plus, there's this French film over at Lorch Hall that I really want to see. I think you'd like it. It's about these two women—in France, um, yeah … I think it's French, but now I'm not so sure, maybe Spanish … but anyway, they're on this kind of quest, you know like an Aboriginal walkabout kind of thing, but in France and—"

"Gee, Mick, Whitley and I have plans. Sor-ry," says Madonna, looking him right in the eye.

A particularly big glob of salty ballet water is hanging on the end of his nose. I wonder if it's going to fall off anytime soon.

"Oh, well, OK," says our boy.

"C'mon, Whitto," says Madonna, a bit too loud. "Time for shower. We gonna sauna, right?"

The University of Michigan Dance Department is tacked on, like an architectural afterthought, to the Central Campus Recreation Building, a boxy monolith erected to the quest for fitness and the elimination of fatness. The buildings adjoin, but the students aren't allowed direct access. Faculty have keys to the many interior doors between the two buildings. Students don't. At the end of a long day, there's something inherently stupid about bundling up, going outside, walking about fifty feet, turning a corner, and then entering the same building. By now, we're resigned to it though.

"Jeez, I need heat. My hip's fucked up again," mutters Madonna.

We dress slowly. For some reason, there's no one else in the dressing room. It's quiet in here, only the hum of the building. This morning—it seems like years ago—it was bitterly cold, too cold for November, so I stack on the layers. Leaving the dressing room, we pass a bunch of nonmajors looking confused.

"Which way is Studio D?" they ask.

We tell them and head for the door, glancing at audition and job notices. "Ypsilanti Community Players seek choreographer for *Damn Yankees*." "Life Drawing Models Needed (Dancers Preferred.)" "Subjects Sought for Study on Eating Disorders. Call Jim at ..." Same old stuff.

I feel Madonna's arm snaking through mine as we near the door. I'm used to this by now and welcome the closeness. It took a little getting used to, my roomie's almost Victorian protestations of affection: The afternoon she kissed me right on the lips on South University before darting off to class. The notes left on my bed. The sudden hugs as she passes me in the hall. There's nothing particularly sexual in all this, just sensual and warm and familial. There's a faintly apricot hue of mother/daughter to our ways and I see no reason to fight it. I understand why I feel this way, why she needs this, and don't mind a bit. She can be so very sweet. She can also be a pain in the ass.

"Oh, Whitleeee, I'm so tired," she says softly.

"Me too, love," I answer. "You know, you looked really good in that comp showing today. Why didn't you tell me you had those cool lifts with Ken?"

" 'Cause I didn't want anyone to see me get dropped on my skull, that's why."

"No! Did he drop you? I thought it was supposed to be like that, you know, some kind of movement allegory about abandonment, that kind of thing."

"Uh-uh, nope," laughs Madonna. "I was hanging on with my nails by the end. Almost pulled his tights off. I could hear him grunting a little. It was great, actually."

"Well, I couldn't tell. Everyone seemed to like it."

"Hmm. I mean why didn't he drop Lori? She weighs a ton more than me."

We're standing in the vestibule near the outside door when I notice that all Madonna's got on is her jean jacket. Her bag's bulging with sweats and sweaters.

"What's this? Mad, put your stuff on. You're gonna freeze your butt," I scold.

There is a moment of silence. We look at each other.

"I'll wait here for you. That way only one of us gets cold," she says. "You go around and come through the basketball courts. The door on the far side opens out right there."

She gestures through the window to a giant steel door with no doorknob, behind some stunted shrubbery and cedar chips, just steps from where we stand. The door says "No Admittance." Madonna kisses my cheek.

I stare at my roomie and think about this. I don't want to walk through the basketball courts. I don't want to risk the ire of the Rec Building Security Staff. I don't want to sneak around. I don't want to.

"I don't want to," I say.

"C'mon, Whitley, Pleeeeze. It'll be fine. No one'll notice. Just do it, alright?"

Madonna makes herself look slightly pale and wan and I feel myself starting to buckle inside. *Besides,* I think to myself, *I need to start taking a few chances. What's the problem here anyway? Just a simple favor for my best friend who has a bum hip. Time for some risks, Whit. Get-it-together. OK? Yes . . . .*

I smile a heavy smile and head out into the night. It is unbelievably cold. I hate Michigan. Sharp, tiny snowflakes like fiberglass particles zing against my cheeks. Near the corner, I look back and see Madonna silhouetted against the glass, as if frozen in greeting. She's watching me. Even from this distance, I can see her fingers move, a tickle of a wave. *Yeah, yeah,* I think.

I haul open the door of the Rec Building and show my ID to the bored work-study student. I wander down the hall, listening for the sound of thudding basketballs. I open a door and step into a brightly lit gym and survey twenty or thirty male humans dribbling, shooting, bonding. I Do Not Belong.

When I was eight, my dad took me to see *Fantastic Voyage*, and it was my favorite movie until it was supplanted by *2001: A Space Odyssey* two years later. There were ever-so-many scary aspects to *Fantastic Voyage*, but by far the scariest was the fact that the tiny submarine containing Raquel Welch and random others was, in fact, a *foreign body* that would eventually be detected and horribly consumed by *white corpuscles*. This minor trauma seems to have ignited a low-burning fear of not belonging.

The guys stop for a moment and take me in—my hair twisted like a bun-head ballerina's, my dance bag slung over my shoulder, a determined expression on my face. The door in question is directly opposite me: about six miles, by my calculations, and getting farther away by the minute. I (foreign body) will have to walk right through the game to get there, or hug the wall and circumnavigate this global gym. I pick the long way around and start walking as if this casual stroll makes all the sense in the world. Keep your eyes on the door, Whit.

I'm halfway there, just under a net. The guys are on the other end of the court yelling things and bouncing their ball. Suddenly, I perceive Imminent Nearness of Males and look up to see both teams (corpuscles) running at me full force. I mean, *what'd I do?* I think. *Why are they all running at me?* I quicken my step, trying to maintain relative coolness and keep my mind on my goal: the door behind which Madonna Ciccone waits in confident, neobeatnik, bum-hip glory.

The men stop just shy of me and focus on throwing the ball through the little net. I have never understood this. I reach the door. It reads "Emergency Exit Only—Do Not Open," but open it I do, anticipating sirens and floodlights and concertina wire to descend on my sorry self. Nothing happens.

Madonna sees me from her foyer haven and sprints across the woodchips to me.

"Alright, Whitley!" she says, oozing gratefully into the warm gym. The men's sneakers squeak on the floor like tortured mice.

We start back across the gym where we are immediately intercepted by a burly security guard (BSG).

"Fuck, Madonna! I knew this would happen! They're gonna take our IDs away! Shit! Why couldn't you just walk around with me?" I spew furiously. I think spit actually comes out of my mouth.

Madonna stops and looks at me curiously.

"I told you, Whit, my hip's buggin' me and I gotta keep it warm, remember?"

BSG asks to see our IDs and looks us over. I feel like a criminal, picture the expressions on my parents' faces when the call comes from the president of the University of Michigan regarding my expulsion. Madonna has this wide grin on her face. Her eyes never leave him.

"Ladies, that door is clearly marked 'Emergency Exit Only.' You simply cannot use it to come in and out."

I jump in.

"I know, I'm sorry. I really am. I didn't know it was that big a deal. I mean, yeah, I can see now that it's clearly marked. It's just that we're dancers, uh, in the Dance Department next door? And it's, uh, such a drag to walk all the way around when … but you're absolutely right and it won't happen again, it's just that …"

At the same time, another part of my brain is wondering exactly from which side I inherited this gene that regulates the all-important "Lameness of Response"? Jesus! I shut up.

BSG continues yammering and I can see Madonna getting a trifle impatient, swaying from foot to foot, snapping her gum.

Suddenly she erupts: "I'msorryI'msorryI'msorryI'msorryI 'msorryI'msorryI'msorry, OK?"

He looks at us carefully one last time and smiles a little. He's young, with acne scars, but pretty blue-green eyes and red hair. Good cheekbones, too.

"OK," he says, handing us back our IDs. "Don't do it again."

"We won't," says Madonna. "We'll be good." She smiles a supreme Madonna smile, lowering her eyelids a bit. Click. He's hooked. He smiles back.

"You'd better be …"

"I will. Bye." Madonna's walking backward toward the door, still smiling. Then I hear them talking a little. I stride ahead, angry and embarrassed. I head for the saunas and am almost undressed by the time Mad arrives.

"Aw, don't be pissed Whitley," she says, watching my face. "He was really nice, didn't you think?"

"Yeah, uh-huh," I say, throwing my stuff into a locker.

I put a towel on a bench and sit down on it, naked, enjoying the warmth of the room, the sound of women talking, laughing, washing—all those little rituals of kindness to self.

Madonna kicks off each battered Adidas and worms out of her jeans. She has on the same T-shirt she wore to class and it clings softly to her. As she lifts it over her head, her ribs stand out away from her body, each sharply defined. *God, she's so thin,* I think. The bruise on her tailbone is as dark as ever. I ask her about it and she twists, naked now, to see herself in the mirror. It's something of an obsession for me, her bruise: a mark of favor from the gods of the dance, only bestowed on those devoted enough to be very, very thin, to do endless sit-ups after class. I will never be marked in this way.

This is mostly because I have an ass. A rather pronounced one. An efficient, muscular cushion to protect me from dance floors and hard chairs and slings and arrows. Unfortunately, in the late 1970s, assness is a liability. Flat is all the rage, especially in my chosen universe of dance. I am not flat. My butt sticks out, high and proud, like it has something to say. Like it has business to attend to. Once, at a party in high school, my friend Clayton announced to me and a group of my friends that I had the ass of a black woman. That he said this admiringly was lost on me. I was furious and hurt that he would even mention my ass in public and never forgave him.

But I am also perhaps hyperaware of my ass because mother is so bizarrely focused on it. The fact that she, a supremely flat-assed, Diane von Furstenberg wraparound dress-wearing sylph could have spurted forth from her loins a healthy, round-buttocked specimen blew her dainty mind. I remember once, when I was a child, she told me that I could decrease the size of my ass by *banging it against the wall*. This seemed strange to me, and it was stranger still when she helpfully demonstrated the technique, then had me try it. Always eager to please, I banged my butt dutifully against a wall in our apartment for a few days then checked for results. Nothing. After a while, she stopped mentioning it.

Point being, at this moment in my maturation, it is difficult for me not to compare my unfashionably round and muscular back end to Madonna's Acme-ass, so flat, chiseled, and unprotected that the simple sit-up could render it wounded.

I lean back against the cold metal of the locker and close my eyes. The after-image of Madonna's bruise floats in the darkness like an accusing eye. I wonder if I have the passion to hurt more than I already do; to be poor for a long time, to scrape by in New York for fifteen years, endlessly auditioning, showcasing in lofts, coming home to a shared room and a black-and-blue tailbone. No, I will never be marked in this way.

We walk slowly to the sauna and yank open the sticky, wooden door. There are two women sitting on the upper benches; they've been there awhile. I spread down a towel and lie on my back with my knees up, as I always do. I know exactly what's coming. It's the same every day.

Madonna sits quickly, butt right on the hot wood, then sighs loudly and looks at the other women.

"This is just not hot enough, no way," she says.

I keep my eyes closed and hear her get up, slam open the door. Just outside is the thermostat; she proceeds to turn it up as high as it goes.

I peek through my lashes. Both women start stirring. One looks annoyed, the other bored and unaffected. They leave in silence. Madonna immediately sprints to the top bench and lies down. She slowly unfolds one leg to the ceiling, digging into taut hamstring and quadricep muscles with her fingers. Then she works her foot carefully—flex, point, release. She repeats it all with the other leg, then rests, breathing easily. I doze and sweat.

"That Mick, man, I don't know about him," says Madonna.

"What don't you know, sweetie. Did you sleep with him ever? I've been meaning to ask you."

"Yeah, Whit, I have to say that I did, in fact, sleep with him. Once, when I first got here. I mean, he was so persistent and I was into it, sorta, for a while."

"Well?"

"Well, it was like being battered—bang, bang, bang ... shit—like guns or logs or something. I really hated it. I just lay there and waited for it to be over. It's just not supposed to be like that, is it? I mean I keep waiting for something different and good and fun, but all that stuff happens in the beginning when you're having a ball looking in their eyes and giving them little kisses and watching them dance and stuff. That part's great. I could just do that forever, just pull them in. Then you get in bed and it's like this mechanical thing that's nothing like all the stuff that came before. I don't get it." Her words are slow and tired.

I don't have anything to say. But I try.

"Well, I guess you shouldn't sleep with Mick anymore. Besides, he has the flattest, ugliest feet in the world, plus he hates me."

"Oh, my little Whitley, you're so wise," Madonna laughs quietly. "Sometimes I just watch you in class and I'm so glad and happy and thankful that I get to come home to you every night and talk and eat popcorn and soup and stuff..." I see her face across the hot darkness, her Cheshire Cat smile lingering, then fading.

Now I have never caught Madonna watching me in class, but I can pretend and besides, I'm feeling very warm at this current moment and my basketball court anger is seeping steadily into the cedar plank. I flash back briefly to this morning and remember her bony arm slipping around my neck for a quick squeeze when she passed me in the hall before Comp. I notice my heart doing that little opening thing that happens every now and again. I don't fight it anymore.

Later, we push out of the building and find an inch of snow on the ground, the first of the year. It's coming down hard, but we're so warm, we're steaming. My eyes tear up, making the streetlights dissolve into streaks and luminescent smears.

I am very happy.

We stop on the pedestrian bridge over Washtenaw Avenue while I fumble in my bag for gloves. Madonna's wearing a thin, dark green woolen scarf, wound many times around her head. The ends of her hair whip in the wind. Her breath comes in small, steamy blasts as she waits.

"C'mon, Whit, let's go," she says, with that bit of whine that's somehow a declaration of something more dear. She crams one hand into my pocket, where my hand finds and covers it. We walk home, taking our time, not talking much, knowing our tracks will be covered in only a minute or two.

    I am very happy.

The Rube

Damn, this is a good one.

I'm in Christopher's class, at the barre, grinding through yet another tortuous *fondu* exercise. Somehow, I'm the only person left; everyone else has gone to a football game or ... I'm not sure, some event that has something to do with toasters. It's just me and Christopher and the accompanist, a young woman with long, dark hair and wearing only a man's pajama top.

Christopher's smoking a long, long cigarette—it's more like a pointer, really, which he uses to correct my placement. He's smiling broadly and cheerfully, saying, "Ya, ya," in a Scandinavian sort of way. I notice that the floor is littered with seaweed and sand in swirling patterns, as if a tide has just come in and gone out and as I notice this, I can feel my legs getting lighter and lighter. They are, in fact, surrounded by seawater. I am surrounded by seawater, up to my neck (the studio is gone, and Christopher, and the pianist ...) and my right leg unfolds, extending like an endless petal in time-lapse photography and I'm totally loving every minute of it. There's no pain, no burning in my supporting leg, just weightless perfection and schools of tiny fishes frisking about. The pianist's pajama top floats by.

"Whitley, get up."

This cannot, must not, will not be a dream.

"Whitleee. Whitley, my little mumbling cabbage, you must rouse yourself. Now."

I open my eyes. Inches from my face are two pale, bony shins sprouting from a pair of sweat socks filled with feet. Views like this: one of the perks that come with sleeping on a mattress on the floor. This is my wake-up call, courtesy Madonna. I get many of them, some agreed upon, some not. This one, I'll admit, is contracted. My clock says 9:14 p.m. and I guess it really is time to start dressing for my first trip to the Rube.

"Whitley, are you awake? If I go take a shower will you go back to sleep?"

"Most definitely. It's night. People sleep at night. And besides, I was dreaming about the perfect extension."

"People dance at night. And you already are perfect, you little shit, so get up."

I sit up. Why do I sleep on the floor anyway? Aren't there more comfortable ways to make manifest one's vague spirit of rebellion?

I hear the water running in the bathroom. Out in the living room, Joel has Bach's Partita in D minor playing once again but we all love it. Whenever it's on, the odd convergence of personalities in this apartment seems to make more sense. It's our bonding music.

I go through my dresser, drawer by drawer, rejecting every option. This is my first trip to the Rubaiyat—Ann Arbor's renowned gay bar. This is, in fact, my first trip to any gay bar. "Going out dancing" has always had its terrifying aspects and my experience to date has consisted of gingerly jumping around on a crowded floor, willing my fingers away from my ears, and trying to avoid the flying spittle of a football player.

You'd think I'd like this, right? I'm a dancer. I dance. But in a studio, you're working, you're striving against something—the constraints of your body, the sluggishness of your mind, the constant desire *to stop this nonsense and just lie down for a minute.* In a studio, you're an artist, a character, an important feeling embodied in movement. In a studio, there is a teacher in charge in case things get out of hand.

But dancing in a bar is different. Dancing in a bar is sex. Dancing in a bar can lead to not being terribly well-behaved and other things that terrify me. It is giddy freedom and flirtation and alcohol. It means being myself in public, when I have absolutely no idea who I am. But more than these, it means being part of a group of people who are all doing the same thing. I hate that above all things.

Remember Bernard Marx in that book *Brave New World* that everybody had to read in high school? Remember how on alternate Thursdays he was obliged to attend Solidarity Service where he and eleven other Alphas would dance in a circle, chanting, "Orgy-porgy, Ford and fun ..." until rapturous, Ford-infused unity was achieved? That's how I feel about going dancing. Everybody looks ecstatic, but inside aren't they all really saying, "Am I doing it right? Am I?"

I think about this as I rummage for clothes, how I really have to get over these "limitations." How there seems to be some kind of mischievous logic at play here. Here I am in the metro Detroit area, about to be indoctrinated into the local dance ritual scene by a genuine daughter of Ford-dom (or is it GM?). I am a novitiate, and I must dress the part with care.

But I can't find anything that defines the sloppy/sexy/artsy image I wish to convey. I pull out an old, white, button-down shirt, purloined from my mother's wardrobe for a possible costume. It's unbearably ugly. I'd look like secretarial help in this, so I throw it on the bed with the other outcasts. Finally, I settle on a red Alvin Ailey T-shirt with the neck cut out, a pair of jeans, and my white jazz shoes, nicely scuffed.

I'm attending to hair duty when Madonna comes out of the shower, wrapped in a towel, and looks at me.

"Is that what you're wearing, Whitley?"

"Yes."

A brief silence. Then she moves past me and starts opening her own drawers. She quickly steps into a pair of men's underwear (independently of each other, we've discovered the comfort of well-worn, cotton men's briefs). She pulls on her torn black jeans then turns around topless to look at my bed.

"Are you gonna wear that shirt? Could I wear it?" she asks, pointing to the "Take-a-letter-Miss-Jones" oxford.

"You can't be serious. You want to wear that? It's my mother's. It's awful."

But she's already slipping it on and POOF, that Madonna clothes-transformation thing happens, just as I knew it would. Damn. Impressive.

Madonna buttons the shirt up to her breastbone then rolls the sleeves up to the elbows. The bottom of the shirt hangs to the middle of her narrow thighs. She takes one side and tucks it in, leaving the other side long. I feel like I'm watching a painter at work, or a sculptor, someone who can effect radical, visual change with the unstudied, unaffected competency of a child at play.

Then she abruptly sits on the floor, in that narrow space between bed and desk, and puts on her own grimy Capezios.

Together, we put on makeup. These days, I'm using a tiny bottle of lip stain—some kind of deep-red juice that does its work on your index finger as well as your lips. But Madonna and I both like it very much. The color is just lovely, very dark red. We blot, carefully, head to head, peering into the bathroom mirror. I run a brush through my long hair and it crackles with static.

"Come on, Whitley. We've gotta get there. It gets really crowded around 10:30, so we've got to hurry."

I call a cab while Madonna puts the final touches on her look for the night. Heavy black eyeliner is next, then a dangly earring on one side and a safety pin on the other and we're ready to roll. We ride the elevator with a couple of Saudi engineering types who absolutely do not look at us in any way. As the doors slide open, Madonna burps loudly and sprints out.

The cab's waiting. We could've walked, but there's a light rain and besides, it's getting late. I'm already starting to have a good time. We look pretty interesting, M and I. I notice that I feel proud to be seen with my roommate. She's got a buzzy little energy working inside her tonight and I'm getting hits off it. I actually feel like dancing in a gay bar. This just might be fun.

"You nervous, Whitto?" she whispers in my ear.

"I don't know if nervous is the word. What's gonna happen? Are you going to stick with me? I bet we get there and you immediately disappear and leave me to the lesbians."

"Oh, that would be fun. You'd like that, I bet. You are nervous!"

She rolls down the window and yells, loud, to a bunch of sorority types standing on a corner, "Hey! Whitley's scared of dancing! She's scared of dancing with girls!" Then she rolls up the window and turns to me grinning. "Of course I'll stick with you. You're my date. I don't want to dance with anyone else. You're gonna dance with me whether you like it or not. It'll be fun. Everyone'll watch us."

"No one will watch us, stupid. Why would anyone watch us?"

"I don't know, they just always do, that's all."

"Will there be drugs?"

"Sure. And everyone will think we're lovers and all the straight men will gaze in unrequited awe. Now will you stop worrying and get out your money. All I've got is enough to pay the cover."

I pay the cabbie and crawl outside. Madonna opens the Rube door for me, a blast of throbbing music pours out onto the quiet street and quite suddenly I want to run after the cab, drive home, get in my bathrobe, and listen to that partita again.

It's that bar smell inside. Smoke and beer and sweat, mixed with flashes of expensive men's cologne. The dance floor's at the back of the club; you have to pass a long bar and a wall of booths to get there. A snarling Asian man in a too-tight suit checks our IDs and lets us pass.

We stop at the bar and get drinks: two Perriers with lime. Madonna digs quarters and nickels from her change purse, makes a big show and manages to meet the dollar price tag. For a bit we stand at the bar sipping, glancing lightly at the people in the booths who are glancing back at us. Tables of handsome men, their shirts half-unbuttoned to reveal gold chains and nice chests. Groups of women, wearing knit sport shirts and utilitarian haircuts. Madonna stands very close to me and I like it.

She shouts in my ear: "Whitley, why are gay men so pretty?"

"And smart and interesting?" I yell back.

"Yeah, you got it. Why?"

"It's one of the mysteries of the universe, sweetie."

I've thought about this quite a bit lately. Sometimes when a beautiful gay man walks past me and I just have to stop and stare, it's like a sunset, or a V of geese. It's like God having a good dream. And the unattainability is the very best part. I don't understand all those Christians. What's unnatural?

As if in response, the cosmos immediately propels past us a chiseled boy-man, his face surely pilfered from a Roman statue, but probably warmer. We mouth silent screams at his retreating back and clutch each other in laughter. This isn't so bad. Yes, I'm definitely having a good time. You see, it's the end of the '70s, and all is sweet and innocent and hopeful.

We take our drinks with us, snaking through the crowd to the back of the club. The dance floor is slightly sunken; it reminds me of a pit intended for a cockfight, but the vibe's friendlier. There are only a few guys out dancing, looking somewhat sheepish and tentative. Step-together, step-together. The basics. Mad slips her hand round my wrist and pulls me down the two steps to the sticky parquet floor.

The music's loud and gut-stirring: Donna Summer wailing out

"MacArthur Park." We charge right to the center of the space and I consciously blur my eyes and start moving as creatively as I can, not looking at Madonna. Don't get me wrong, I know how to do this. Me and rhythm go back a long way despite an Armenian/WASP genetic fusion that might result in any number of odd dance-floor proclivities. I firmly push back thoughts of Bernard Marx and peek through my lashes at the woman opposite me.

Just by dancing, Madonna's made herself the vortex of the room. There's nothing unusual about what she's doing—it's how, it's the intent, it's the charge. Any flung arm, any sudden thrust of her bony hip pulses with extra energy. Madonna's a complicated person; I've known that from the start, and her dancing mirrors that. Feet on the downbeat, hips on the backbeat, head and hands sprinkling pops and tiny crashes that shatter upon release. Every now and again, she spins tightly—one, two, three times around, like an ice skater. But when she comes out of the turn, her eyes lock again on mine. They dominate, like an irresistible drone that draws lemmings to the cliff.

Her eyes close and her head falls back. Her hair is damp now; dark strands cling to her forehead. She's doing this thing with one shoulder now, circling it round and round. Her shirt (my shirt, no, my *mother's* shirt) has slipped down on one side and what is revealed is a sexy anatomy lesson, precise and alive. Head still thrown back, the line from chin to breastbone cries out for a tracing by an inquisitive thumb.

The head climbs slowly up and this time her eyes are open. She looks at me and smiles, red lips over white teeth.

Why the hell is she looking at me that way? (God, she's beautiful.) What am I doing here? (God, this is fun.) Why is everybody looking at us? (God, make it last, make it last…)

Madonna keeps moving closer to me. I assume she's just getting caught up in the moment and is becoming forgetful of the basic rules of human proximity. It's OK. I take another deep breath and flash on how relaxed Europeans are about casual public touching. So what if she's from Rochester, Michigan? Madonna's as European as they come, quite the gamine, I've often thought. I close my eyes and get swept away by the music, the lights, the attar of impending sex that sweats through the room.

I feel someone's hand against my face and open my eyes to see Madonna's arm reaching out to me like some kind of misplaced umbilicus joining us together. Uh, what's going on here? Right on cue (she must've known it was coming), the music flips into one of those percussive instrumentals that I do like so much. She's got her gaze stomping right into my eyeballs and I'm stomping right back and I'll be damned if she's gonna stare me down. Somehow, her face is getting closer and closer and her hips are, uh, really going at it and gee, mom, it's just dancing and what the hell is going on and suddenly Madonna's got her thigh between my legs.

OK. Madonna's got her thigh between my legs and it's not just occupying negative space, it's really cramming in there, and pressing rhythmically and Jeez-O-Pete this is more than a little fun and what'd I just say and does this mean I'm a lesbian now and WAIT-JUST-A-COTTON-PICKIN-MINIT—where are the other dancers? Everyone else has stopped dancing and is standing on the side watching us, and it's official: we are making a spectacle of ourselves. I take a deep breath, one of many I'm taking at this particular time and keep attempting to look cool and sexually voracious and divinely confident. I peek at the watching crowd. Oh good. They've bought it.

I wait 'til the end of a particularly throbbing measure then pull away into a couple of turns along with a big swoopy kick to the side for effect. Madonna pops off another spin, this time kind of low to the ground (she's varying her usage of spatial planes, I note, recalling comp class theory).

We dance for a long, long time, until our shirts stick to us and euphoria becomes the norm. People eventually join us on the dance floor; pretty soon, it's a mob scene, which I find I am actually able to tolerate even though we are a group of people all doing the same thing. We stay 'til closing, drinking water and wine and flirting outrageously with anyone at all. But we stay close together, a unit, filling our chatter with private jokes and double entendres, laughing and feigning mystery. I'm surprised at how wholesome it all feels. The pairings that are underway all over the room have a friendly air. I feel like I'm swimming in a petri dish—watching grinning, hopeful little organisms skim and veer like dragonflies, searching for a happy roost.

When we get outside, the streets are quiet and still. The noise of the bar lingers, echoing in my head like the roar of a seashell. The rain has stopped and the air feels good so we decide to walk home. Besides, we've spent all our money.

"Madonna, that was so fun," I say. "I'm so tired, but I don't know if I can sleep."

"You'll sleep, Whit. You always do if I remember correctly," she says. "Do you want to get up early with me and do a warm-up at the studio? I was thinking of getting there by nine 'cause remember we have an 11 o'clock rehearsal for Carol's piece."

Now I have a very different plan for the following morning. My plan involves sleeping until 10:30 then going out with Madonna for a bean sprout omelette at Steve's Lunch, then arriving for rehearsal late and digesting just to teach Carol how indecent Sunday morning rehearsals really are. I tell her this.

She looks at me. "Whitley, you know I have to warm up really good. My hip's still bothering me and after slamming myself up against you all night at the Rube, I'll probably be kind of sore." She smiles.

"Oh, I don't want to talk about tomorrow morning, OK?" I shout. We're on Huron Street, heading east and my words bounce off the side of City Hall, which stands dark and quiet. Only a few cars pass us.

"OK," says Madonna.

She puts her arm around my waist and we giggle as we try to synchronize our steps. I have an idea.

"Do you know this old kid rhyme? Did you have this in the blighted Midwest? You step, 'Left, left, left my wife and 48 kids, Right, right, right in the middle of the kitchen floor …'" She picks it up and we're off. And there just has to be a camera behind us filming, locked on two girls dancing down the street, laughing and stumbling, getting farther and farther away until they can no longer be seen. Fade to black.

Party Time

I get baptized in the holy waters of Madonna's "attention thing" one day late in the fall when Liz, the head of the department, invites all the dancers over to her house for a swimming party. Liz and her husband have a pool.

Madonna and I are very excited about this—a true mingling of the faculty and the students. We will eat good food, dance to funky music, swim in improvised bathing suits, talk about art with our teachers, and perhaps improve our chances for excellent grades.

Liz lives in a beautiful contemporary home off of Geddes Road, not far from the Dance Building. It's a splendid fall evening, so Madonna and I walk there, past Strickland's Food Mart, past Forest Hills cemetery, and on up the hill past the Arb, yapping all the way. We have gotten to the point where we can pretty much talk about anything. And I am quite aware—and happily so—that Madonna has revealed herself to be perhaps the smartest person I know. That she is a good listener is part of her smartness. She seems genuinely curious about things, me included. I'd have to say I'm flattered. I actually write in my journal one night, "We are getting along swimmingly." Right-O. We are such jolly-good British club members, Maddy and I. Pip-pip or whatever.

But my joviality tonight is a bit of a ruse. Parties like this can be iffy for me—too much forced conversation, exhaustive smiling, and hair-tossing. I'm really making an effort to change and having Madonna for a cohort helps. Whenever I try to weasel out of stuff like this, she nags me mercilessly. She should win some sort of fishwife prize.

And for the first half-hour or so, it's pretty fun. I have to say, it's nice to arrive together, for us to be seen as a unit—roommates. Friends.

And then … click.

It's hard to say if it's something she actually does, my roomie, or if it's just that I suddenly notice it: the way she becomes the focus of the room. I can't fault her for it—what happens is utterly organic, like the way cats watch canaries, the way stars move across the sky, the way people are interested in sex. And the attention spurs it on. At once, she is in her element, laughing, flirting, cussing, dancing at the center of a small crowd in the middle of an ordinary living room.

Why does it even bother me? No one's excluding me. These

people are my friends. I dance with them every day. But suddenly there's a hungry vibration in the room that I don't understand. I don't like it and, worse, I don't know why. Is it not having siblings? As an only child, I never had to claw for attention. Indeed, if I get any more attention from my mother, I think I'll implode.

Someone has a joint out in the yard so I go out there and hit on that, but the pot's so strong I can't handle it. I find an empty bedroom and lie down 'til the world comes back together.

And out in the living room, it's her cute little destiny, stretching its wings.

Star Trek Child

I have a life besides Madonna and our hijinks. I have a life so full of wanting and feeling and imagination that it threatens at all times to drown me. It's always been this way, so I'm not particularly alarmed when, for example, I see some lady on the street and automatically construct an elaborate history for her that moves me to tears.

One day, I go for a walk and wander into a nearby residential neighborhood, where fraternities and sororities stand side by side with gracious professor houses. Suddenly, a white kitten comes darting out from under a bush and stops short when he sees me. We eye each other for about forty-five seconds. He won't let me touch him and soon disappears behind a shed, but I am completely and totally sure it is a sign of something wonderful headed my way, or at least a friendly hello from some deceased ancestor.

On Tuesday and Thursday mornings I have my American Art and Architecture class in ivy-covered Tappan Hall. Just next door is the Museum of Art. I have always loved museums and take to stopping by after every one of those classes to feel the quiet of the marble halls in the pit of my stomach and gaze at their token Monet.

Do you remember *Night Gallery*? Anyone who took TV seriously in the early '70s, as I did, will remember that show: three extra-creepy short stories per episode, and each dealing with a painting. Rod Serling, the whole bit. Well, I stand in front of that Monet so long every time I visit the museum that the guard staff begins to post a sentry in that particular gallery to make sure I don't start slashing or drooling or worse. What they don't know is that while I'm staring at that misty view of the river flowing past the tiny town of Vetheuil, I'm wishing so hard to be magically transported there that I fully expect to succeed.

Other nineteen-year-olds rebel by doing blotter, playing "chicken" on the train tracks, and whacking mailboxes with baseball bats. Not me. I choose to defy the laws of time, space, and dimension. Unfortunately, despite my very best efforts—staring at the painting, closing my eyes slowly then opening them again—not a whole lot happens.

This, of course, started way back. Perhaps it's the lot of the *only* child, this constant, manic imagination. Left alone while my mother went to acting class or therapy, I had plenty of time to build entire towns out of folded paper, towns with streets and parking lots and cars and people, all listing and weightless but *there*; time to capture and name and attempt to train cockroaches, as I had no pet; time to fashion the linguist Noam Chomsky out of an empty eggshell and some construction paper, as a surprise for my mother when she got home at night. She had kind of a thing for Noam Chomsky.

I looked forward to bedtime not because I was tired and needed to rest my mind from the day's relentless creative, verbal, and artistic output, but because it gave me an opportunity to play my favorite game: Star Trek Child. Once the lights were out and my mother had shut the door and was safely watching Johnny Carson out in the living room, I became the Only Child on the Enterprise—the orphaned daughter of two low-ranking but well-loved officers who had been tragically killed by Klingons in a manner that for my purposes was left vague.

I had the run of the ship, my own miniskirt uniform, my own lonely quarters festooned with dolls and souvenirs from every galaxy. But sometimes I would fall mysteriously ill and have to be carried to sick bay by Captain Kirk, my head flopping back off the crook of his elbow. And Bones would give me painless, hissing shots that would make me "come to," and I'd smile weakly from my glittering pillow and be fed warm, white soup. Other times I'd be kidnapped by aliens and the Captain and Spock and Bones would all have to come and rescue me and there would be more running around with me in their arms, and passing out, and coming to. And soup.

My inner life took some strange twists and turns. One night we had company—some friends of my mother's from the school where she taught. The adults were drinking their martinis and I was pilfering the olives when suddenly I got up and left the room. I went into the bedroom and shut the door. I lay down on my bed and spread my legs and pretended that a pioneer midwife was delivering my baby. I was about six and did not even know what a midwife was. But it was all-consuming and I brought my cold plastic doll tenderly up to my flat little breast and nursed and cuddled it.

But that was a long time ago.

These days my private eccentricities even take me out of doors. Not far from the abomination high-rise where each night I lay my weary head, is the Arboretum—the Arb—a tract of land owned by the University. It's a beautiful place filled with tall, tall pines, rolling meadows, and rocky paths. Whenever my busy schedule allows, I put on a long skirt, belt it tightly at the waist, then go to the Arb and ramble about in the woods trying to find a dimple in the time/space continuum through which I can step lightly into the last century. Again, I'm unsuccessful, but I do find places in those woods where I can see no building, no electrical wire, no other person. And in the space between the planes that fly overhead, I find a peace that approximates history. I sit down on the pine needles and drink it in.

Once and only once do I try to explain to Madonna the joys of attempted time travel and communion with cats. I have this idea that we can borrow some really authentic costumes from the theater department and go to the Arb early in the morning, you know, maybe with woven baskets, and walk the paths like we're actually on an errand? But though she's polite about it, I get the feeling she doesn't think it would be particularly fun, so I let it drop.

The rest of my free time is spent cultivating, nurturing, and honoring my relationship with my mother. Being away from home for a couple of years, being exposed to other girls my age, has given rise to a growing suspicion: that perhaps my mother and I are a tad too close. I have never rebelled, I notice. I have never told her to fuck off, as I hear other friends tell their parents on occasion. I never slam down the phone in anger. Anger? How could I be angry at my mother after all she has done for me? I'm all she has. I decide that I am not ready to examine this inkling in any meaningful way.

And so we write to each other with alarming frequency and talk on the phone at least every other day. Why? Because in life there's an awful lot of stuff that requires approval and/or absolution from one's mother. For sure, there's plenty I don't tell her, but then the not telling elicits all kinds of roiling misery, which gets duly recorded in my red notebook.

Here's an example:

Talking to my mother is like confessing, it really is. And probably the reason I feel shitty now is because I didn't tell her about (_____insert perceived transgression here). I'm such a fucking masochist. If I told her, she'd get upset, then I'd get hurt and defensive, and we'd both get hurt and angry and somehow an understanding would be reached though neither of us had said quite what the other wished to hear. And we'd both cry but soon stop. And I'd hang up the phone feeling strangely purged...

It's actually amazing that I get any schoolwork done at all with all the weeping and discussing that has to be fit into each day. But really, she's my best friend, my mom.

Snow Day

I remember before I even open my eyes that today is Saturday, and the delight this awareness heralds sits on my chest like a warm cat. I hear Madonna rummaging around in the kitchen, humming something, making too much noise, trying to get me up. The room has an icy look, a different light, and I know what that means.

"Good morning and has there been a snowstorm?" I call out sleepily.

"Good morning and shit yeah, there's been a snowstorm," answers Madonna, (clatter-clatter). She appears in the doorway, working on a piece of gum already. "Look outside, Whitley. It's still really comin' down."

"I don't need to look outside. I'm so warm and tired and it's Saturday, right? I'm not dreaming?"

"It's Saturday, but get up. We're going to the studio." She turns and goes back in the kitchen.

"Not me, I'm not," I holler to her back. "I have plans."

"What plans?" (Clatter.)

"I'm gonna finish 'Beneath the Wheel' and then do last Sunday's puzzle. I haven't even started it yet and we get a new one tomorrow. So I'm definitely busy."

"Oh, c'mon, Whitto." She's entered the whine register now. "Look, you have all weekend to read and be a bum. Let's go work out. None of them jokers will be there. We'll have the place to ourselves and we can do all kinds of things we're not supposed to do. And we can make up phrases. Maybe we can make a whole dance together and surprise everyone at the next comp showing. Come ooooon. Be in a duet with me, pleeeeze."

I lie very still and wonder about it. Hesse and the *New York Times* versus pliés and Madonna.

Ann Arbor seems a ghost town. A few plows clunking by, an intrepid student now and again. No children with sleds. I'm not certain there are any children in Ann Arbor. I certainly never see any. No dogs with frozen spittle and panting glee. Just frat houses gilded in white. The snow is very deep and everywhere. It's hard walking—big wind—but we're laughing and cussing and I'm feeling a tad self-righteous as we reach the Dance Department door and yank it open.

There's a big wall-unit heater in the vestibule and we lean against it gratefully, loving the fact that howling Arctic winter is just on the other side of the glass where we're not. Warm, warm. We peer down the fluorescent-lit hallway looking for any sign of life but all is still, as if maybe even we aren't really here. Wasn't there an *Outer Limits* about that? I get that empty-building feeling in the pit of my stomach.

I decide to say "C'mon" first and thus appear eager to get started with actually working out on a Saturday.

"C'mon, let's get started."

We climb up to Studio A on the second floor. No need to hit the dressing rooms; we strip down and change into sweats right in front of the bank of windows that looks out onto a small parking lot and a boxy apartment building across the way. The walk has made our muscles cold and I wonder if I will ever be loose and stretched out again. I start on the floor, rolling around, cheap and easy full-body massage. Madonna's facing the barre, seems to be looking out the window, then remembers why she's here, grips the wood, takes a couple of steps away and bends over, as if trying to pull it right out of the wall. A very effective hamstring stretch. She ripples her back gently a few times then stands up in first position, heels together, tailbone dropped down, neck long. The first plié sends her knees straight out over her feet—wide, wider, then slowly up. As Christopher has reminded us a thousand times, the simple plié is a lot more than just a knee-bend.

"Don't think of dropping doooown. What you're reeeally doing is separaaaaating your knees," he likes to say, sometimes dropping to the ground and crawling through the negative-knee space of some hapless freshman from Grand Rapids. "You want to grow taaaaller with each plié, taaaaller, taaaaller ..."

So Madonna does her pliés, separates her kneeees, and grows taaaaller while I roll around on the cool, smooth wood floor. No one's talking. Outside, the wind roars. I think of Siberia and wish for tea. And maybe some hot, savory corn muffin dripping with butter.

I join Madonna at the barre. Second position, demi-plié, stretch, relevé, heels down, demi, stretch, relevé, heels. Then grand plié, knees opening wide, almost a squat, feeling tendons sliding over each other, with little pops and mutters. Fourth position, left foot about eight inches in front of the right, both hips squarely placed, facing front. Two demis and a grande, two and a grande. Then fifth, feet smashed together, the connection traveling right up the legs to the crotch. Demi, demi, grande, go slow now, slow and controlled. Don't drop your weight at the base of the plié. Keep lifting out of it, lifting out (growing taller), 'til you replace the heels and rise through the demi to that delicious, solid stretch, knees tight together. Relevé once more to finish, hearing someone's old Chopin, just a fragment, arms *en haut* and hold, hold, hooooold ... Outside: wind, snow, maybe Omar Sharif.

We turn and do the other side, which means she's got her eyes on my back now. (Open to fourth position and demi ...)

"You know, you keep opening your hips out every time you straighten, Whitley. Did you feel that?" she says, a little breathless and concentrated.

"Hmmm," is the only way I care to respond to this. I hate it when she does that and one day I'll tell her so. I tell her this, instead: "When I was a kid I had this ballet teacher who used to say, 'Think of your hips in fourth position as two headlights, shining down the dark road! Don't let them turn unless the road turns!' but for years I thought she was saying 'head lice' and was so confused ..." (point, close fifth position ...)

I hear her snicker behind me.

"Whit, did I ever show you my aging ballet teacher impression? Wait, close your eyes."

I turn around and shut them.

"OK. Open." her voice is strangely tight.

I bust out laughing. Madonna's got her eyes open wide and her lips pursed and has somehow made every tendon in her neck stick out about an inch, like subcutaneous pencils. She's the victim of a very, very bad facelift.

"Get that leg higher! Higher!" she squawks, then drops down giggling, rubbing her neck.

We finish an abbreviated barre and mosey onto the floor for a quick stretch.

Snapshot: Madonna as yogi, in the plow position. Head, neck, shoulders on the floor, hips up high and legs slung back behind her. Her feet tread the floor like this, press, press, using her elbows to support her back. Her T-shirt flops to the floor, revealing that bruised spine, a row of slight plums. She's chatting idly, not knowing I'm watching all this, getting it down for use in some book in the misty future. She peeks at me as she talks, turning her head to the side. Green cat's eye, half hidden by scrunches of faded shirt.

I've brought my cassette player and the Bach tape, a collection of sinfonias (basically, the instrumental breaks in the cantatas), which everyone in the apartment adores. Madonna and I play a game I've imported from Brockport—"bop and leap"—taking turns making phrases of movement and stringing them together. Kind of like "I packed my grandmother's bag and in it I put ..." but with jumps and skitters and falls. After thirty minutes or so of this, we have a good phrase of movement to dance in unison, then in canon. Everything fits together nicely and we're sweating and feeling at one with Bach and each other. Just a coupla undergrad white-girl innocents emoting to classical music. Could be anywhere, anytime, but damn, it does feel special, and with all the snow—mmmm.

"I'm done," I say, flopping down to the floor, breathing heavily. Madonna walks her walk about the room, cooling down racehorse-fashion. Heel-toe, heel-toe, heel-toe. It's the walk of someone whose passion is making the exactly right footprint, every step she takes. Madonna crosses the studio (heel-toe) and drops beside me.

"Zeet lounge, then shower?" I ask.

"Definitely zeet," she answers, wisely.

We gather our mountains of stuff—coats, clothes, cassettes, boots—and wander through deserted studios to the back staircase, where the elevator is. There's a faint smell of chlorine from a pool on the other side of the wall. Off in the distance, industrial sounds; we're in the guts of the building. Madonna pushes the elevator button and we wait for the grinding sound that signals its arrival, then get in. Zeet Lounge, please, Operator.

Zeet lounge is on the third floor, where no one goes. It's nothing, really, but a small, dark storage area filled with odd, almost unrecognizable U-M jetsam: broken lab animal cages, sheets of drywall, ladders, light fixtures with parts missing. But, to the select few who know about it, it's privacy—a secret, quiet, if dingy, haven from vast wooden and mirrored expanses that we are obliged to fill with glorious movement. And "zeet," of course, is weed. It's a term coined by Trudy, a grad student with a modest wild streak, who dispenses joints with a smile. It's not a daily ritual, or a nightly one (more about that later), but it's something Madonna and I do enjoy on occasion and Zeet Lounge is the place to do it. One tiny barred window reveals gray sky, a bit of apartment building, snow. Maybe there's a light but we don't look for it. Dim is right for Zeet, makes the joint's orange glow seem so friendly. No one in the whole world knows where we are and this is good. We sit down on the floor and lean against some boxes.

"So, what's up for the rest of the day?" I ask, between drags. "I'm gonna make coffee and read and read and read." I exhale carefully, watching to see if I've actually managed to get any smoke into me. I am not a graceful smoker. I am clumsy and cough a lot.

"Well, you can read or you can hitch out to Arborland Mall with me," she says. "We can (fffffuh) go to Kroger's and check out the candy. It'll be a big, warm place where we can run around." She blows out daintily.

"Sounds good. I like to hitchhike, but I never do it alone (fffffuh). Too dangerous," I say. (Exhale. Dainty cough.) "And do you remember about Maria's gamelan thing tonight? I'm going and you should too, I think." (Huge, old-person-with-tracheotomy-style coughing fit.)

Indonesian music is big in Ann Arbor. There's a world-renowned gamelan ensemble that it's very cool to like. An elaborate, subtle gong show that, for me, treads the line between mesmerizing and sense-dulling. But I'll try again. After all, fellow dancer Maria is performing, and it's free. And if you stand in the back it's easy to ditch early. Madonna nods, mid-toke. She'll be there.

"Are you going with Colin?" I ask.

"No. I don't think we're going out any more. "

"What happened?"

"Nothing. I don't know. It wasn't really 'going out' anyway. We just kinda kissed a lot."

There is a long silence. The smoke wafts and curls.
"Do you like gamelan music, Madonna?"
"Not really."
"Mmm."
Takes us a while to get out of Zeet Lounge.

We walk to the corner of Washtenaw and South University and wait there with our thumbs sticking out. Little blasts of blowing snow now, no big deal. Madonna, bundled in jackets and sweaters and scarves, looks like a tailor from the Lodz Ghetto. All you can see are her eyes through a slit in the knitting. She catches me looking and squints.
"What?"
"Nothing."
"Why are you looking at me like that?"
"I'm not. I'm not looking at you any way at all."
"Well, why aren't you, you little shit? Why aren't you looking?"
She laughs and flicks snow on me.

We catch a ride with a taciturn businessman in a big car. He seems pleased to be ferrying these two nimble artistes. We get to the mall and gambol in empty Kroger's, dancing in the aisles. We get a bunch of cookies from the bakery counter, eat them as we shop, then stuff the baggie with the price tag behind some soup cans—a technique I learned from my last roommate, back in New York. Carol was from a wealthy Washington, D.C., family, and believed that, in addition to cookies (if consumed in store) it also was okay to steal tampons and spermicidal jelly, but only those items. To her, the risk of detection and subsequent handcuffing was preferable to placing those items on the checkout counter in front of a zitty-faced boy who would then actually have to touch them as he moved them through.

We laugh and eat candy and flirt with the help. I do a line of fast-spinning chaîné turns down the entire detergent aisle. We spend about five minutes doing contact improv in front of the meat counter, interpreting the Muzak. Madonna reaches deep into a frozen food case with her left leg in a stunning, near-split arabesque. A toddler in a blue snowsuit sits in his cart and watches her, wide-eyed. His mother mumbles "Excuse me ..." as she reaches past Madonna for some waffles. We buy margarine 'cause Madonna likes margarine. The time flies by.

It's not so easy to get a ride back. It is now ferociously cold and the snow is blowing all over the place and I'm starting to wonder if we'll be walking three miles home when a huge semi pulls up. Hmmm. Truck drivers. Two of them. Where will we sit?

Turns out it's a husband-wife team, so in love it's just about sickening, but they're friendly and fun, if partially toothless.

"Climb on in! Don't worry, I'll move over," calls Big Mama. Madonna and I grin at each other and clamber up that little side ladder gizmo. The cab is warm and homey—and so high up. Suddenly I can see why people like to drive trucks.

"So, where you gals headin'?" says cheery Truck-Drivin' Man, as I settle myself partly on Madonna's puny lap. ("Am I squishing you?" "Shit, yeah, girl, but I don't care ...")

"Um, we're just going down Washtenaw a couple of miles. You can let us off right before it turns into Huron. Do you know where I mean?" I say.

"No problem. You gals students at the U?"

"Yeah," says Madonna, "We're nursing students. We're gonna be nurses."

"Well now, how about that! My sister is a nurse down in Austin. The things she sees, and the crap she has to take from those docs—and the patients, too ..."

"Yeah, I know," I say. "We've been warned. I can't take that at all, so I've pretty much decided to go into veterinary nursing. It's just as noble a calling, I think."

Big Mama looks at me intently and nods in approval. I go on.

"But Brenda here, she's going all the way. Tell them Bren."

Madonna doesn't miss a beat.

"Yeah. I'm gonna be a nurse overseas. I'm Catholic and I might be a nun-nurse, but I haven't decided for sure. My parents really want me to, but I'm not sure Jesus has called me to be his bride," she says seriously. She sighs. "But there's plenty of time to decide. Right, Ann-Marie?"

I'm about lose it at this point, but pull myself together by digging my fingernails into my hand. That always works.

"Are you both Christians?" I ask the couple.

They look at each other and smile.

"We know the Lord, I guess, or try to, best we can."

"Yeah, Christ's great," says Madonna. I nod.

And so we talk about Christ and life on the road and the accident they almost had in Baltimore and how to not get stuck in the snow (put weight in your trunk). I wonder if Madonna and I will ever own cars. It is a merry time and they drive us almost to our door. I am having a wonderful day.

Back at the apartment, we thaw our feet and Madonna gets busy in the kitchen making popcorn. I put on Laura Nyro and curl up on the couch with last Sunday's puzzle. The guys are out.

"Ask me something," she calls out.

"OK, let's see … A five-letter word for a European blackbird."

"Shit, I don't know."

"I'm joking, Madonna. That's a crossword joke."

"Well, I don't do them, except with you. Really—ask me something."

She sits down beside me with the bowl.

"Yemeni capital?"

"Don't know."

"Bishopric?"

"Don't know that either."

"Come on, isn't that a Catholic thing?"

"Is it? 'Bishop … Yeah, I guess it is, but I still don't know," she says.

"How about 'Immediately.'"

"'Immediately' … Does 'Right away' fit? 'Pronto?' 'Stat?'"

"Wait. 'Pronto' could be it. Yeah. That's it, thanks."

"I got one. I can't believe it," she says. "How'd you get good at this stuff? Besides being naturally brilliant."

"I'm not naturally brilliant," I say, not entirely believing myself, but committed to the dancer's requisite self-denigrating response to all compliments, true or false.

"Well, how'd you get good at it? Did you go to puzzle classes?"

"Nope. My mother loved doing them, and my godparents, who

lived across the hall, loved doing them."

Madonna says, "Tell me about them. Tell me again about your mom and being a kid in New York and stuff."

"Hmm. What to tell?"

I stop to fill in an easy one.

"Well, in the summers it just gets unbelievably hot, because of all the buildings and streets and sidewalks baking in the sun and holding the heat. And, of course, we didn't have an air conditioner. We just had fans. And sometimes we just had to give up. My mom and I would walk up to around 59th and Third, near Bloomingdale's, and find some theater that had a couple of movies and just stay in there all day until it was cool enough to go back outside. Or sometimes we'd do this thing called 'beach' on the roof of our building. She'd fill up a plastic pail with cold water and we'd get beach towels and snacks and sunglasses and books and go up on the roof and sunbathe. Well, she'd sunbathe. Mostly I'd just stand in the bucket of water and convince myself it was refreshing. And I spent a lot of time leaning over the parapet and watching all the cars and people. Looking south I could see the United Nations. East to the East River and west to the Hudson. I could only last about fifteen minutes up there, but she'd slather on the oil and lie there for hours. She was really into being tan. I've told you she's from Mississippi? Yeah … And it smelled so good up there. Like … tar. And river water."

Outside, howling furies of snow. You can't even see the other side of the airshaft.

"What else?"

"What else? Well, on Saturday nights we had this little ritual. We would always go out to the little paper store down on First Avenue, between 53rd and 54th streets. It smelled so good there. The smell would even come outside and hover around the papers. Newsprint and ink and candy and tobacco. I loved that smell. And I would get to pick out the *Times*. It was like picking out a fish or a cut of meat for dinner; each one seemed slightly different. One might have a crinkled front page, or some mud on it. One might look kind of ruffled, like someone had been reading it and put it back. You definitely didn't want one of those. The paper had to be … I don't know, virgin, I guess. Untouched and perfect. So, finally one would kind of call out to me. My mom would get impatient 'cause sometimes I'd want one near the bottom of the pile, but I always got the one I wanted. And we'd carry it home like a new baby. A new, virgin baby paper ready to be opened. I'd get lots of ink on my hands. Sometimes we'd stop at the deli and get a pint of Häagen-Dazs. Chocolate."

"Then what," asks Madonna, dreamily crunching popcorn.

"Sometimes, my mom's boyfriend would come over—he was this Jewish ex-millionaire … didn't I ever tell you about him? No? Well, his name was Hank and he was really tall and had very white fluffy hair and he just lived to spoil us. He would come over with smoked fish and bagels and kumquats and some other exotic stuff and we'd read and eat 'til midnight. And we'd always fight over the "Arts and Leisure" section, of course. Or the *Magazine*. In my later teen years, I would make myself at least scan the other sections of the paper before heading for the puzzle. I don't know. Crosswords are so … right. Everything has its place. They're beautiful."

"And you ate kumquats with your mother?"

"Well, yeah. I mean, that's not all we ate. We ate regular stuff too."

"But you'd do the puzzle together and eat kumquats. On Saturday nights?"

"Well, yeah, I guess. When we had kumquats. What do you mean?" I ask.

"It just sounds so nice to me," says Madonna.

The stereo reaches the end of side one and shuts itself off. Outside, moaning wind. We sit quietly together.

Then Madonna does something.

She puts the popcorn bowl on the floor and reaches across me to turn out the light. Then she lies down and puts her head in my lap, right on top of the Sunday puzzle.

"I'm tired," she says.

"Do you want to sleep a bit? You can, you know. It's fine."

"OK."

"Madonna?"

"Mmm?"

"I'm sorry about your mother."
"I know. Thanks."
"You miss her, huh?"
"Yeah, I do."
"I miss her too. I miss her for you."
"OK."

Hill Auditorium is massive, almost a breathing, pulsing presence in the center of the campus, right next to the famous Bell Tower. On this particular night, it's glowing in snow and starlight. Groups of students, huddling together, laughing and hooting, tramp up the great stone steps to the doors, which are rectangles of gold against the dark. Madonna and I are so cold we're running. My eyes, as always in cold, stream tears that bend and smear the light. We started this journey only a few blocks ago, laughing and frolicking, but now we just want to get inside, fast. We join the throngs and file in.

The stage is set for something wonderful. Huge gongs hang from what I guess are gong-racks, beside drum-looking things, xylophones, exotic pillows, and mats. There is a festive, anticipatory air and this, plus the warmth, pricks my frozen face.

We find seats near the front, on the aisle, and the lights go down.

Forty-five minutes later, I'm tired of having Madonna's leg flung over mine. I'm tired of the serious, concentrated air of the twenty or so musicians, and I'm getting really tired of this music—oh, even though, yeah, it's actually quite beautiful—and so complex! I struggle for a while with the impropriety of leaving. Maria hasn't danced yet (her part doesn't come 'til near the end), and I do want to be supportive of her and I most especially want to like this heady stuff, but the problem is I just don't. I'm tired and bored and I want something to drink.

I whisper my plan to Madonna but she wants to stay. I throw my coat over my arm and wait for a musical lull, but none comes, so I decide to look like I'm just going to the bathroom and take off up the aisle. In the back of the theater I'm pausing to put on my coat and gloves when I hear a soft voice.

"Leaving so soon?" whispers Colin, of the clever poetry and lush lips. His golden curls flop languorously over his brow.

"Hi! Yeah, this is so beautiful, but I'm just too tired."

"Are you alone? Come stand with me over here and listen to just one more, then you can go. Don't give up too soon."

"Uh, Madonna's down in Row H. There's an empty seat next to her, if you want it," I say, not sure why I'm saying it. (All this, of course, furtively whispered.)

"Oh. No, I'm happy here, I think. I like standing here."

And so we stand, and Colin whispers interesting facts about Javanese culture. We find ourselves making "gong" puns ("I'm gong crazy." "I gong take my eyes off of you,") and giggling a bit. Colin stands very close to me and I like it.

I'm trying to top his last groaner when he interrupts.

"Ms. Whitley."

"Uh, what?"

"Wouldst thou care to join me at Drake's for a warm beverage and perhaps some sweet comestible?"

"Oh, but Madonna's down there. Is she waiting for you? There's an empty seat. You probably—"

"Do I need to repeat my question?"

"Yeah, would you?"

"Drakes, you, me, now …"

Hmmmmmmm.

"Sure."

Drake's is living history. It's a time-warp candy store a half-block from Hill. The owners, Mr. and Mrs. Tibbals, have owned it since the thirties and haven't changed a thing since the day it opened. There's a pressed-tin ceiling, painted shiny black. The counters and booths are all covered with layers of drab green with black accents. Along the walls are shelves jammed with jars of ancient candy—licorice squares, marzipan, candy canes. Does anyone really eat this stuff? But there's also a kitchen, of sorts, from which blue-smocked clerks (all U-M students) serve hot tea and slightly odd sandwiches, which, despite their ordinariness (tuna, cream cheese, BLT) seem to have been run through a molecular transport machine the Tibbalses have hidden in the basement. The stuff's good, just … odd. The tea's safe, though, as is my favorite: dark chocolate with nuts, measured out of a jar by a bored English major.

Colin and I scribble our orders on a pad and take a seat in a high-topped wooden booth. There are few people there and it's quiet. We chat about the gamelan concert, classes we're in, how he doesn't like where he lives, favorite writers—usual first date stuff, though this, of course, isn't a date. I go pick up our order. I notice myself trying to stuff back a grin. What am I doing here having fun with this man?

"Look …" I say. "They've left the door to the Martian Room open. Let's go up."

This must be my twentieth trip to Drake's and, until now, the door to the Martian Room has never been open. I've begun to believe that there really is no Martian Room at all. We gather our cups and peer through the doorway. We see dark steps going up and a warm light on the landing. Stealthily (we're not sure the Martian Room is actually, officially open) we ascend.

It's 1947 at the top of the stairs. Wild, retro-futuristic wallpaper, wigged-out lighting fixtures, and the sense that Biff and Edith and Frank and Midge have just left for the pep rally. We slide into a booth, giggling.

We chat about the gamelan concert, classes we're in, how he doesn't like where he lives, favorite writers—usual first date stuff and of course this is a date. A date with the man Madonna's been kissin' on for I don't even know how long.

"So," I ask softly, and for no good reason. "How long have you known my little roomie?" Colin looks away for a moment, then blows into his tea and sips it.

"'Known' in what way?" he smiles.

"In any way," I say. "When did you meet her?" I am feeling brave. This way, if she turns out to care about this little rendezvous, I can truthfully say that we spent the entire night talking about her. Which, of course, is what she would like. I am being thoughtful.

"It was—when?—about a year-and-a-half ago, I think. During the summer before I started school. I was working as a janitor at the hospital. I had this cool red ten-speed and I had ridden down to the Diag on a break and she was there, dancing on the grass with her sister, talking to everyone who passed by. And, I don't know, we just became ... friends. We'd see each other for a while, then she'd leave town or I would. What has she told you? About me?"

"Not much, really. Mostly that she likes to kiss you. That you both like to kiss."

"Yes, that would be the case."

"But it's not much more than that."

"No, not really."

A pause. Raucous laughter from downstairs.

Colin says, "And why are we talking about Madonna?"

Later, making snow angels on the Diag, Colin falls into a drift with me and we kiss. Warm mouths, icy faces, dark buildings all around, and the last few snowflakes of the storm.

I shut the door softly. The apartment is dark. I grope my way into my room and begin to undress. Tomorrow morning I will tell my roommate about what I've been up to. With Colin. Who is very, very attentive and nice and fun and never said a word about Madonna the whole time after that. Tomorrow morning I will tell her. She won't mind. Why should she?

Madonna's light clicks on.

Her head peeks out from behind the headboard partition, a sleepy smile across her face.

"Hi, my little Whitley."

Uh-oh.

"Hi. How was the rest of the concert? Why aren't you asleep? Did I wake you? I tried to be quiet."

"The concert was boring. You were right to leave. But I'm glad I stayed. And no, you didn't wake me. I've been waiting for you. I have to talk to you about something. Guess who I saw at Hill Auditorium? And guess who that mysterious person left with?"

I wrap a blanket around me and take a deep breath. I go and sit on her bed. She turns onto her back and throws her arms behind her head, looking at me slyly.

"Look, Madonna. If you don't want me to see him, I won't. I really didn't think it would matter to you. You told me it was pretty much over between the two of you and he said the same. We just went to Drake's then walked around in the snow then went back to his place for a bit and then I came home. That's all. Do you mind? You mind. I can tell."

There's a long silence during which I can't bring myself to look at her.

"Oh shit," I sigh.

"Whitley, Whit, look at me," she says.

I look and she's grinning wide, laughing slightly.

"My little Shitley, are you talking about Colin? Did you go out with Colin?"

"Uh, well, I guess I did. Isn't that what you …"

"You went out with Colin? After the concert?"

"Yes."

"He kisses nice, doesn't he?"

"Madonna, I …"

"Doesn't he? Doesn't he kiss nice?"

"Yes, he does."

"Did he take your face in his hands when he kissed you?"

"No. I don't … He … Madonna, I …"

"Now can I please tell you what I wanted to tell you?"

I look down at her.

"Go ahead. I'm listening."

"I kissed a woman tonight."

"You what?!" I am so glad she has changed the subject. And to this.

"After the concert a bunch of us went out to the Blue Frog. There was hardly anyone there, but we danced awhile. Guess who I danced with? I mean it. Guess."

"Madonna, I have no idea."

She tells me the name of a woman who plays drums for some of our classes. This woman is gorgeous, big and strong, with eyes that drive into you like dark bullets. She has great, calloused hands and wears amazing clothes. I've never spoken to her. She's always seemed so … so Gauguin, confidently hefting her conga up onto her shoulder at the end of class, grinning her sexy, toothy grin at whoever looks back.

"Well, are you going to tell me about it?"

"I don't know if I should. After all, you're probably screwing my boyfriend. What's next?" she says, teasing. I think. I'm pretty sure.

"Fine," I say getting up from the bed. She grabs my wrist and pulls me back down.

"I don't know how it happened, but we ended up in her room. She lives in a dorm, Whit! That amazing woman lives in a dorm! I almost couldn't believe it when she took me there. And we were just sitting around, talking, and she suddenly lies down on the bed and looks at me. And, I don't know, next thing I knew, I was kissing her. Or she was kissing me. I don't know … It was so fine. Her mouth was so soft and full, but strong, too. I loved it. "

"Then what?"

"Then I just got up and left. We didn't even talk about it."

"Did she take your face in her hands when she kissed you?"

"Yes, she did. It was very sweet. But then I felt funny and just wanted to be home in my room with you. But of course you were out fucking around with Colin. Oh man, who can you trust?"

Now I know she's joking with me. She reaches up and turns out the light. I get up and lie down on my ascetic floor-bed.

"You don't really mind, do you Madonna?"

"I really don't mind, Whitto."

For a bit there's silence. Then I hear her turning over.

As I'm drifting off, I hear soft whispers coming from the other side of the headboard. I think. I don't know. Maybe not.

Candle

Journal, December 3, 1977, shortly after midnight

Best, best time of night, just me and the little red book. This morning seems to have happened three weeks ago. Up early and out by 8:15. Had just enough time to stop at the Bagel Factory for coffee and an egg bagel with cream cheese—breakfast perfection. Then to Tappan Hall to kneel at Prof. Hunter's font of wisdom. I keep thinking that American Art and Architecture before the Civil War should be a fascinating and romantic class. Tappan's filled with wood and stained glass and creakiness. Hunter's beard bespeaks eccentricity but the whole thing's just too dull for words. I hate it when he shows one slide for the whole class. Just turn it off already ... Then in Ballet Christopher said it! He actually said it! (I've heard rumors of this and thank God he didn't say it to ME). He goes over to this freshman and pinches her stomach—hard, it looked like—and says, all English-style and very dramatic, "Suck it in ... or preferably, looooose it ..." It was delicious. Modern was OK. Liz said "Good!" to me once during the across the floor combination, then made fun of the fact that I was wearing a big T-shirt to hide my butt. Jeez, you just can't win. I must try harder to lose weight. Oh, and I'm starting to feel like an employment agency. On the spur of the moment I went around the corner to Miller's Ice Cream and got myself a little job, scooping cones, and as soon as I come home with my first carton of free chocolate almond, Maddie decides she wants to work there too. And then Joel. But that's cool. The more the merrier. Last night Joel came home with six cans of soup, a package of frozen fish patties, and two cartons of ice cream. We'll never have to shop again. And then, I call up the Art Association, across town, to find out about modeling for life drawing classes and pretty soon Mad's trying to score some high-paying nekkid time. I don't think she's ever posed before. I hope she knows what she's getting into. It can be weird dropping the robe that first time, plus you gotta watch out for the creeps who hang around after class. But if she wants—

"Whitley."

—to try it, there's more than enough work to go around. I'm gonna pose for this private drawing group that meets in some lady's house. They pay 8 bucks an hour, which sure beats scooping ice—

"Whitleeeeee."

A voice from the other side of the Formica partition.

"Madonna. What?"

"Can you just stop writing and go to sleep? I can't sleep when you do that."

"Madonna, are you saying that you can hear me writing? I'm using a ballpoint, for Chrissake."

"Well, that, plus the light is bothering me. It really is. And I have to get up early."

"What if I cover it up like this." I put my scarf over the lamp. "Is it bothering you now?"

"Yes it is. It casts shadows."

Pregnant pause.

"OK. Just a minute. Let me finish this thought."

"Whitleeee. I'm tired. Can't you finish it in the morning?"

Journal, December 3, 1977,

a few minutes after the previous entry

Suddenly pissed. Signing off. More later.

Journal, December 4, 1977, 11:30-ish

I'm not sure what to do with this idea for yet another "flat dance." "Icon" was so two-dimensional and I really liked it that way; it made sense, given the nature of the friezes I took the shapes from. Is this a phase I'm going through, or a rut? Oh, God, I've only made three dances and I'm already in a rut! This is silly. I should just make the dances I feel compelled to make and be thankful I feel compelled to make any at all. But it's such a responsibility! I need to express myself, but at the same time I need to watch myself carefully and be sure I'm not: 1. copying other work, 2. being lazy, 3. going for cheap effect at the expense of artistic integrity. I want so badly to be good at this. More and more I sense that my direction involves choreography, rather than just dancing someone else's vision. Anyway, this is all stuff to think about. Repertory auditions are coming up soon and I'm starting to get really nervous about them. What if I don't get into a good piece? What if everyone gets in a good piece but me? I have simply got to stop thinking this way. It serves—

"Whitley."

—*(Oh fuck, I think I woke her up) no purpose at all. So, what else? Got a nice letter from mom today. It was quite long, a lot of stuff about the kids she's teaching. She took them all to the Fashion Institute last week. Sixty-seven kids on the subway. I don't know how she does it. She's one special lady. I'm so lucky to have her—*

"Whitleeeee."

"Just exactly what is wrong, Madonna? This amount of light can't possibly be bothering you. Jeez, I can hardly see to write. I'm using a fucking *candle*!"

"I can smell the smoke."

The Christmas Letter

"Whitleeeeee…"

I whirl into our room, drop my dance bag beside the bed and start ripping off clothes. After Ballet, Modern, Comp, and Rep, I am fragrant, tired, and in need of a shower and a prone position. My back hurts and my hip hurts. I've been fighting tears since 3:00 when I looked particularly spastic in Susannah's across-the-floor combination and she pointedly said absolutely nothing to me. Her silence might as well have been a loud, sarcastic shriek in my direction.

"Whitleeee, hi."

"Hullo, Mad." I go over and sit on her bed, put my arm around her and squeeze for a second. Then resume stripping off layer after layer. Naked—the guys are not home—I head for the bathroom.

"Um, oh, I forgot to tell you that Cape Cod guy Jimmy called," she calls after me casually.

"Huh? When? Did he leave a number?" I stumble back in and lean against the door. "When did he call? Just now? Where's the phone?"

"Hold on, hold on! He called yesterday. Yeah, I think twice yesterday and, hmm, maybe a few days before that I think."

"He called three times? Jimmy called me three times and you only now just told me?"

"Relax, Whitleee. He didn't really leave a message. He just called. So are you going to that movie?"

Livid. Angry. Pissed-off. Furious. Hurt.

I don't say anything more to her. I go and take a shower. When I come out of the bathroom she isn't in the apartment any more.

I don't know why I am still interested in Jimmy, the tree-hugging, bad painting-producing, mango peel-masturbating boyfriend of last summer. I think it is because I like the look of his abdomen which is ridged with the offhand sculpture of youth. He does not exercise, particularly, he just looks like he does. I call him immediately, hair dripping down my chest. He tells me that he's been trying to get a hold of me. He keeps reaching this Madonna girl. Why haven't I called back? Am I seeing someone else? It's OK if I am …

I answer a lot of questions, then he tells me the reason for his call. In return for painting a bad acrylic painting of a rich travel agent's Cape Cod summer house, he's been given a trip for two to the

Bahamas over Christmas vacation. All-expense paid. Airfare, nice hotel, transfers, the works. Do I want to go with him?

I want to go. Suddenly, Jimmy's bad qualities dissolve into visions of tropical sunsets, swimming buck naked in turquoise waters with friendly fish, communing with coral, performing modern dance combinations on the sand ... I want to go. I don't even need to think about it.

I go to my movie. When I get home, around 12, Madonna's already in bed with the lights out. I lay down on my ascetic floor-bed and am similarly out. Next morning, my usual wakeup view: Madonna's shins.

"Whitleee, get up. I'm sorry about not telling you Jimmy called. Now get up, OK?"

"OK. Just tell me from now on. It's important to me. I mean how hard is it to ..."

"OK, I said I was sorry and I am sorry. Jeez." The shins pad out of the room.

The shins pad back into the room.

"What did he want? Get *up.*"

"Huh? OK. What?"

"What did Jimmy want? Is he coming out here?"

"He invited me to go to the Bahamas with him. Over Christmas break. I'm gonna go, I think. I need to get outta town."

"Shit, girl, you're lucky. Shit. The Bahamas."

The shins get to the door, then come back in. She lies down next to me on the floor. I can see the pattern of her sheets on her thin cheek.

"Christmas break? You're gonna be gone the whole time? I thought you were gonna be here part of the time."

"Well I was going to be here until I go to Mississippi for the big family Christmas at my grandparents', but now I guess I'll leave early, do the beach thing, then go directly from Boston to Columbus ... I'll be back right after classes start. I'll miss like the first day or something."

Silence.

"Uh, what are your plans, Mad. You going anywhere on the break?" Of course I already know the answer to this.

"I don't have any fucking plans. I'll go home for Christmas day if I can get a ride. The rest of the time I'm gonna work double shifts at Miller's. I think I can get a key to the Dance Building and work out. Plus Gay might teach some. There oughtta be some good parties for New Year's too. It sure is gonna be quiet around here though. You little *shit*, going to the Bahamas." She turns over and kicks me with her bony knee and we both laugh.

"I'll bring you back a lousy T-shirt that says I brought you back a lousy T-shirt," I say.

"You better." She grabs my blue teddy bear and holds it to her. "And I'm keeping Snuffles while you're gone. He'll keep me company. In fact, I'm gonna take him now, so's he can get used to me."

I agree to this plan and we get up and go get coffee and bagels across the street.

Speaking of coffee and bagels, food has become an interesting focus between Madonna and me. We've even taken to calling each other "My Little Bowl of Farina" or "My Little Serving of Wheat Cereal." We have also, after much research, devised the perfect meal. There are four variants of the perfect meal:

Diet Vernor's and popcorn
Diet Vernor's and Corn Nuts
Diet Cream Soda and popcorn
Diet Cream Soda and Corn Nuts

We take great pleasure in the perfect meal. We talk about it and plan it. We don't have it every day. It's for special occasions, but we manage to have a lot of those. I know. It sounds like a dancer-anorexia kind of menu, but you don't have to worry about that. I am in absolutely no danger of succumbing to any sort of weight-altering practice. I supplement the perfect meal with salad-bar orgies and plenty of Miller's ice cream. The perfect meal just makes me feel more like a dancer. It's kind of an accessory.

Madonna, on the other hand, certainly looks anorexic. She might weigh 100 pounds. I don't know. She seems to really like being skinny, but she also doesn't really like to talk about it. I, of course, am so jealous of her ridges and bruises, that there's not much room for concern. An outsider might regard Madonna's love of the perfect meal with suspicion, but not me. Nobody who works that hard can be starving. That girl gets calories from air.

In the next few weeks, we work and dance and write and dance and go to classes and dance. We scoop ice cream until our arms are coated with brown and white and pink and green. My hatred of our apartment stirs me to action. Trudy (purveyor of zeet) and her roommate, have a very nice old house in Burns Park. Wood trim, ripply windows, funkiness—just what I want. They have an extra room Mad and I could share, with a slanty ceiling and a view of a quiet backyard. Deep down, I don't think my roomie really cares all that much where she lives, but she wants to keep living with me. It's also cheaper, which is of definite interest to both of us. We start to feel hopeful and put an ad in the paper to see if some bozo wants our rat-hole apartment (though we don't word the ad quite that way). Joel and Tony aren't pleased. What if they get stuck with someone kind of right brain and uninteresting? There could be definite image ramifications. But M and I don't care. We'll move to quaint Burns Park and learn to bake bread and do old house kinds of things. All we gotta do is find just the right sort of sucker who actually likes internal-U views of people studying and no sky at all.

Maddie also starts talking about this guy Steve who works at the Blue Frog, a club over on Church Street. He's black and very beautiful, she says. She really likes him. We make plans to all go out dancing somewhere, but we never get around to it. The day of my departure approaches and through the haze of papers I have to write ("The Saint Matthew Passion—a Critical Response," "American Crazy Quilts," and—really—"What is Thought?") I notice that M is getting a little grumpy. I find myself reassuring her with hugs and little gifts: gum, jellybeans, the loan of my ultrawarm sheepskin coat while I'm gone. The afternoon I have to leave, she's nowhere to be found. I drag my bag to the Union and catch a shuttle to Metro Airport.

Jimmy meets me in Boston. It feels so good to be out of Michigan, anywhere different. The air feels deeply familiar; I can smell the sea. I hug him long and hard. He's been traveling the world and looks great—just back from a month in Africa—and is full of stories I can't wait to hear. I notice a guard slipping down, a guard I didn't know was up. What it is, I realize, is this: little Maddie is a thousand miles away.

Jimmy does not know her. Jimmy will not notice her. His attention is mine.

This feeling lasts about ten minutes. Waiting for the flight to Grand Bahama Island, Jimmy, in a soft and caring voice, confesses to me that he hasn't been traveling alone, that he has several girlfriends he takes with him on these excursions, that it's really okay, he loves me a lot, he loves all of us, and what harm is there in loving many people, in having an open heart, in sharing love, don't you see?

Well, I'm a bit put out by this turn of events, but I'm not about to give up a perfectly good trip to the Bahamas—and where else would I go?—so when I finish losing my lunch in the airport bathroom and wipe my eyes and blow my nose, I get on the plane with Shitwad and fly gamely out over the ocean.

I don't have a very good time. For once, I am delighted that my period touches down at the precise moment that the plane does, 'cause I sure don't want to have any sort of fun with this man, and now I have a tidy excuse. The hotel is uninteresting, but the weather and water are warm. We have bad conversations and pathetic sex until I'm so disgusted I just don't care any more. I'm just grimly determined to have some kind of fun while making him feel as uncomfortable and guilty as I can. After all, I'm on vacation. Whee.

We hitchhike over the island and sneak onto the grounds of an expensive resort. Under cover of darkness and with a storm coming in, we find refuge in a golf shed and spend the night there having more intensely unpleasant discussions about our relationship, my period, and our lack of sex. In the morning we are briefly arrested by the hotel police—a large amount of golf equipment has been stolen during the night. But the authorities, not finding any golf equipment in our backpacks, escort us to the gates and wait there, watching us until we find a ride. I am secretly exhilarated by this turn of events. I did something *wrong*! There appears to be hope for Little Miss A-For-Behavior yet.

And a few days later, I say good-bye to Jimmy at Logan Airport and hope I mean it. I certainly think I do. Dipwad. And through it all, all I can think about is, I can't wait to tell her about this. I can't wait.

The layers of angst fall away as my plane lands at the Golden

Triangle Regional Airport in Columbus, Mississippi. My mother is waiting at the gate, a scarf protecting her artfully fluffy blonde hair from the winds of the runway. My grandfather stands next to her, wearing his feed-store cap and an old denim jacket. They wrap me in their arms. "Oh, Anna," says my mother in her breathy Eastern Standard English. She has always called me by my middle name. And there is not a shred, not a DNA strand left, of the accent of her youth. "Oh, Anna."

"Hyah-now," says my grandfather. "Let's go, folkses."

His accent is simply him. It is beautiful and historic and rich. Why does she have to be ashamed of it?

We climb into his old blue Valiant and drive beneath a cold sky, past fields of last season's cotton, red clay, and scattered cedar trees, to the small green house where my grandmother awaits with her special traveler's meal: hot soup and corn bread. To me it is a house from which love pours through the cracks in the windows. It overflows. Maybe there's strife, stuff hidden, secrets, and bad decisions, but all I feel here is peace and a deep connection to distant ancestors who seem to hover over the dining room table as my grandfather bows his head for the grace he has said thousands of times.

"Forgive us for our sins, oh Lord. Accept our thanks for Christ's sake. Amen."

Now this is Christmas.

Late at night, I crouch in the hallway by the ancient gas heater and call Ann Arbor.

"Madonna?"

"Whitley—where are you?"

"I'm in Mississippi"

"Mississippi? Where the hell's that?"

She laughs. I whisper-laugh. It is so incredibly good to hear her voice.

"It's been so boring here," she whines. "Hey, I got my period! As soon as you left. And there wasn't no friggin' Tampax."

Maddie hasn't had a period in a very long time, for obvious reasons. She's gonna get that weird fur soon if she doesn't start eating more.

"Yeah, I got mine too. Perfect timing."

I tell her about my stupid vacation. Shame that's been dammed back for a week comes burbling out and suddenly I'm crying in the dark, on her conceptual shoulder.

"Did you get … that feeling? What we talked about?" she asks.

(That Feeling is something Madonna and I have spent a fair amount of time deconstructing: the weird stomachache you get when you know some guy *expects* you to have sex. Even if you kind of want to, the fact that he expects it makes you immediately part of this universal sisterhood of reluctance. Women in the rice paddies. Women in the Amazon. Women in Siberia. Me and Maddie in the Dance Department. We are all one in those moments, liking, perhaps, the flirtation and the foreplay, not so sure about all the fluids and the soreness and the ineptitude of the men and the danger of the babies. Society doesn't help. So it's the late '70s and we have this newfound and hard-won freedom to have all the sex in the world … now what? It's all very complicated.)

"Yeah. Yeah, I did. It was even more specific though. There was this point," I sniffle, "when we got back from hitchhiking around and we were back at the hotel and we were going up to our rooms and I had this sudden, awful feeling, a really old, kind of feeling, like …" (I hesitate) "like a memory from a past life or something. It was a feeling of the Inevitability of Sex, like I knew that he was expecting it from me. Like a husband or something. It made me sick. Do you know what I mean?"

I can hear her chewing her gum but she's listening.

"Yeah, I know," she says softly. "There's something fucked up about all this … this … How everybody's expected to fuck all the time and half the time you don't really want to. What an asshole. I hate him. If you don't hate him yet, I hate him for you."

I thank her for hating him for me. Mad changes the subject and tries to cheer me up.

"I just got back from doing that church dance, you know, that thing I was working on with Fran. Why? Whitley. Why do I get myself into situations like this? All that work and we had to wear these hideous costumes that totally hid the movement and at the last minute we had to perform it in this little, tiny area. And working with Fran is like working with a stiff piece of cardboard. I just kept wishing it was you the whole time."

Now I know that Maddie actually likes Fran pretty well, and I take this with a grain of salt, but it's nice to be needed and I don't argue. I do find the image of Madonna doing liturgical dance to be somewhat pleasantly surreal, and we sit in silence for a moment while I picture it.

She says she's been hanging around with Mark, the friendly hairdresser guy, a very fun and nice person with the best red hair in Michigan. Also, that things with Steve are heating up. I press for details but she's reluctant. I wonder for a moment if someone else is in our room.

"Guess what?" Madonna whispers.

"What?"

"I got a surprise for you."

"Really. What is it?"

"Well, if I tell you it won't be a surprise, now would it," we both sing-song together.

"You'll see." She yawns. "I gotta go, Whitto. I got class in the morning. I been taking class everyday except Christmas Day. You'd be proud."

I am impressed. The massive Christmas dinner silently digesting in my belly expands slightly, and I think of all the pliés and battements I have not done in the past week. I feel fat.

"I am proud of you, Maddie. Love you, dear."

"I love you too, Whit. Bye. Come home soon!" she whines cheerfully.

I hang up. I really do love my Little Bowl of Bear Mush. I just needed a bit of distance to remember it.

Three days later, I turn the key in the lock at number 10A, University Towers. There's no one home. I drag my bag into my room and there, sitting on my bed, is the surprise from Madonna Ciccone. Six sheets from a legal pad. Different pens for different days. Her life, her heart, for a little while, all for me.

Here it is. Well. Most of it.

Oh my Whitley, I miss you so much already—you have left bits of yourself everywhere but they make me want to be able to touch you even more—come home soon.

I just received your phone call and am elated to hear from you. You don't sound far away at all, like your in the next room. Lucky for you you're in Cape Cod cause as soon as I hung up yours and my favorite— Ken called. He said he wanted to speak to you before leaving to Penn. (How touching) Why do I love you so?

I had a dream last night that I won the ice cream scooping championship and then I became a poet and wrote beautiful poetry.

Egads, Whitto, I had a period today and wouldn't you know all the Tampax were demolished by that nasty pipe under the sink.

Had rotten terrible nightmares—I was sweating and afraid people were trying to get me and hurt me. I was alone and scared. Couldn't sleep and had no Whitley to cry out to.

I had a dream that I stumbled on a native land while exploring w/with friends and the natives came and said they wouldn't kill anyone if they could take me as a wife and slave to the head native. They put me in a hut but when there was a big commotion outside I escaped and my father was waiting with a car to take me away. I also dreamed that I swallowed alcohol thinking it was water and started spitting up blood everywhere.

Oh, Annie-Fanny—more horrid crazy dreams. Mark spent the night—we splet (slept) apart of course. We gossiped all night. Who slept with who, ect.etc. Went to dinner at Geof's with Tony—ate like a Queen (pig)

I've been eating so much lately you will mistake me for the chair when you come home and sit on me. Snuffles has been kind. Went to the Blue Frog to see Steve. He is prettier and nicer every time I see him. He is a musician. We danced. We are having a rendevous tomorrow pm. Hurry home sweet pea!

Gee Whit—since you been gone we don't get any mail at all.

Trudy keeps callin and buggin bout this friggin apartment. She says we should put another ad in the newspaper. But I say if they haven't called by now they're not gonna. Besides I ain't got no moola. Then she says, well I'll lend it to you. Well I'm not gonna let Trudy Mitchell manipulate me so I just told her no—besides I'm really havin' second thoughts about moving in with them 2. She really bugs me.

What a beeeeeeyoooooutiful day it was today (Fri. 23). Class with Gay was great. Mark and I drove Tony to the airport (Mark's car). Sun was firing away, sky so blue, and me so happy. OH I WANT MY SWEET, WARM LOVING WHITLEY BACK. COME HOME MY LITTLE CABBAGE HEAD.

Anyways. Steve is a musician in a band called "The Cost of Living." They play only original music and Whitley they are really fine. NO SHIT! Steve plays drums very well. You've got to see him sometime. They performed at the Roadhouse, a bar-nightclub outside of A2. Steve came and picked me up with the rest of the band and I went out and listened to compositions that are all worth recording. They're so good and it's great to dance to. Not like monotonous disco. He came home and slept w/me in my virginal bed. We couldn't really make love (although we both wanted to) 'cause I had no birth control. I've really gotta get a diaphragm. But he's wonderful and soft and warm and kisses good too. And I'm thrilled to be liking someone so much. (My first thrill was you.) Well I'm a-goin home today. Until then MC & Ho Ho Ho Ho—I love you I love you I love you.

Gee Whit, I'm a real mess. It's Tues. afternoon—class is over with. I reinjured my leg in my hip socket. Gay says I probably have tendonitis and that I should get x-rays and anti-inflammation pills.

Whoopee—I got home last night. Boy was I glad. If I had to sit around one more day doing nothing but eating Xmas cookies and listening to my little brother scream I'd go crazy. I did have a few enjoyable moments visiting old friends, but for the most part I was tense and anxious. Wondering what you're doing as always. To aggravate things more I have rent to pay in two days with only $50.00 to my name. Joel and Tony have left me no money. The electric bill came for $20.00 and I have no money to pay that. To top off all of that—I'm trying desperately to get *a diaphragm and Health Services are closed till school opens so I called Planned Parenthood. The only thing I can do is come in tomorrow night and be very very late for work at Millers (can I find a sub? No!) or wait till the next opening in the middle of January. Will Steve and I practice celibacy until then? Not only that but it's going to cost me $35 and I absolutely haven't got a cent. I'm all mixed up. I don't know what to do. I wish you'd call and tell me what to do. Oh Whitley, I need you right now.*

Oh Whitto Baby, what a day—what a night. So much to say—so much to write. After walking 3 miles in the blizzardy snow—feet like frozen turds, tears streaming from eyes, and 3 hours of anxious waiting, insistent probing, measuring, questions, urine, blood, & yes, no, yes, no lubricating jelly.

I received a diaphragm, a bill for $35 and a strange feeling in my stomach as Steve came to pick me up. I had that same feeling you did before you went to the Bahamas—Jimmy expecting sexual fulfillment and a lot of other things you weren't sure you could give him. A very scary feeling. Now that I had my diaphragm we could fuck all the time—I haven't an excuse not to. Do I want to fuck all the time? Boy this subject really causes me a lot of anxieties. As it turns out we did sleep together and we did make love and it was much better than I thought it would be, but not good enough to make me want to do it all the time like every other seemingly normal person wants to do. Not only that, but I'm liking Steven more and more each day. He is very good and good to me. Very sensitive and aware and intelligent, and he dances good and so far there are no bad points against him. Guess who followed me home last night? Willie! I'll explain that later.

Millers is gettin to be a real bore. We're gettin a new manager and she's gonna be a lot tighter than the previous half ass system. No more rip offs. It's colder than a witches tit and you're a lucky bitch to be where it's warm. I miss the hell outta you girl. But I've got lotsa new books to read so they'll have to do till you come back. I've realized how much I've grown to depend on you for a listener, advice giver and taker and general all around most wonderful intimate friend in the whole world. I miss the hell outta you girl. The rent's due tomorrow and I ain't got it—only

¾ and your check—nuttin from Tony or Joel. I don't know what to do. I wish one of them jerkoffs would call. I'm generally scraping the garbage can for food & money. But that doesn't bother me one bit as long as I got popcorn. Later, darlin'...

Forgive me for neglectin' my literary duties to ya. I'm also so sad after you call me. I never know quite what to say because I feel like I really have too much to say and besides I don't want to hear you, I want to see you and inevitably after we hang up I have found that I've forgotten to say at least a hundred different things. No matter. You will be home soon.

My NY's Eve parties were incredibly exciting—I think because I didn't expect much from any of them. Jeff came and picked me up in his Audi (borrowed) and we went to Maureen's (Boorsville, USA) stayed and danced awhile but the people there were so dead and uptight that I could've done a striptease act on the table and they would have merely nodded their heads. Went to a very chich party (Mark's friends). There was a doorman in a tuxedo. He took our wraps. We were led into a room with a table boasting oysters, clams, mussels, salmon, chicken liver paté, caviar, raw vegetables, creamy rich dips, and chocolate cheesecake. Oh oh oh my taste buds were aroused. Next was a table laden with Chamagne glasses all filled to the brim with the appropriate New Year's drink. The next room was large and spacious (wood floor) where we all commenced to dance in the New Year. Music was perfect for dancing. When the clock struck 12 we all poured champagne on each others head—everyone hugged and kissed— mucho fun—and oh, how I danced and danced and I must say amazed and entertained quite a few people. Jeff was quite intoxicated so I took over the driving the rest of the evening. We hopped from one party to the next stayin' for a while eating, dancing, then getting bored and leaving. By this time we had acquired Mark and my sister. I remained straight (in mind) the rest of the PM.

It was quite entertaining to watch everyone get plastered—although Willie had given me some speed earlier in the day, but I don't believe it had any effect on me. Came home at 5:00, went to sleep, and was awakened at 12:30 by Steve who drove me to Detroit to have dinner at his Grandma's and see a movie: Close Encounters—I loved it. I cried at the end, and if you haven't seen it—SEE IT ... Signing off for now. P.S. I snooped in Gay's grade book. You and I both got an A- in her rep. That cunt only gave me a B+ in her modern class. The only one to get an A was Lori French (I'm jealous of her. Should I be?) Oh come home and make me feel secure. UOY EVOL I

Hey there most loved and missed friend that is sooooooo far away. It is the absolute coldest it's ever been in A2 and I do not, do not want to get out of bed. After this vacation it's gonna be hard trying to make it to a 8:00 class. Fortunately I'm not in it alone. But if I have to beg you out of bed every morning, well forget it! Anyways, as usual I had only a few hours of sleep, either 'cause I stay out late or 'cause Steve spends the night. Last night I went dancing at the BF w/Linda. I've been using your ID to get in everywhere (you left it in your coat pocket). Well, I sure had a good time. Mark came later and Steve was working so we didn't have to worry about drinks. People were not shy in expressing either disgust or delight in the way Linda and I were dancing. We were verbally accused of lesbianism several times. Boy, it sure was fun. This little African man (rubber body) came and challenged me to a dance. Whew! We put on a show. I spent the night at Linda's and we ate popcorn all night and talked about being crazy and sleeping with men and diaphragms, etc. It was lotsa fun, but I always wished it was you the whole time. Well, I gotta go. The winds a-blowin and it's time to get dressed for class. YUK! I DON'T WANT TO DO ANYMORE PLIÉS. I JUST WANT TO BE NATURALLY GOOD. Miss your lovely face

Well, my little cabbage, I think this is the last of my literary tributes to you since you will be home in 2 more days and I think I can remember to tell you the rest. I think of you almost every moment and miss your warm kisses & sweet caresses. I wonder what you're doing and how you're feeling at all moments of night and day. Today was the first day of school and I was thouroughly (sp?) depressed and discouraged. Gone were the days of tension free pressureless, noncompetitive classes w/Gay and Liz over vacation. After the first plié in Flynn's class, I could feel the tension and rigidity flowing through my body. The preclass chatter and acknowledgment of tans was wearing on me and I felt worthless in every *class. Why, you ask?*

1. My tendonitis is getting worse not better

2. Everyone seems to be doing better than me as far as what one can do in a class. (I keep comparing myself to Lori F. and it's just making me sick. Teachers don't look at anyone but her. I'm ever so jealous.)

3. I realize that it's going to be even more trying and demanding of my mind and body this semester. The first day of classes, and I was in the building from 8:30 to 5:00. I keep wishing I had studied clothes design or cosmetology. I must be feeling down cause I actually and truly want to be somewhere else besides the school of Dance. YUK! I'M SO TIRED OF GOING NOWHERE. PATIENCE DEAR MAD, PATIENCE. Oh dooooo come home soon I need your fragrant, soft shoulder to cry on. You know I knew something was missing in my day at the factory and it was you and your reassuring embraces I had become so accustomed to in between classes. I love yourself

Oh my Whitley I miss you so much already — you have left bits of yourself everywhere but they make me want to be able to touch you even more — come home soon

I just received your phone call and am elated to hear from you — you don't sound far away at all — like your in the next room. Lucky for you — you've in (Cape Cod) caused to soon as I hung up — yours and my favorite — Ken called. He said he wanted to speak to you before leaving to Penn. (stop touching) Why do I love you so?

I had a dream last night that I won the ice cream scooping championship and then I became a poet and wrote beautiful poetry.

Egads Whits I had a period today! wouldn't you know all the tampax have been demolished by that nasty pipe under the sink.

Had rotten terrible nightmares — I was sweating & afraid people were trying to get me and hurt me. I was alone and scared. Couldn't sleep. had no Whitley to cry out to.

I had a dream that I stumbled on a native land while exploring w/ friends and the natives came and said they wouldn't kill anyone if they could take meds, a wife & slave to the head native. they put me in a hut but when there was a big commotion outside I escaped and my father was waiting with a car to take me away. I also dreamed that I swallowed alcohol thinking it was water and started spitting up blood everywhere.

Oh Annie Fanny — more horrid crazy dreams. Mark spent the night — we slept (slept) apart of course. We gossiped all night. Who slept with who ect. Went to dinner at Geof's with Sab — ate like a Queen (pig) I've been eating so much lately — you will mistake me for the chair when you come home and sit on me. Snuffles has been kind. Went to the B.F. to see Steve. He is prettier & nicer every time I see him. He is a musician. We danced. We are having a rendezvous tomorrow pm. Hurry home Sweet Pea!

Gee whit — since you been gone we don't get any mail at all. ▇▇▇▇▇ keeps callin and buggin bout this fuggin apardment. She says we should put another ad in the news paper. But I say if they haven't called by now they're not gonna. Besides I outgot no mood. Then she says well I'll lend it to you. Well I'm not gonna let ▮▮▮▮ manipulate me so I just told her no — besides I'm really havin second thoughts about hangin in with them. She really bugs me.

What a beeeeeeyooootiful day it was today. (Fri. 23.) Class w/ Gay was great. Mark and I drove Sab. to the airport (Mark's car). Sun was firing away, sky so blue and me so happy.

[respectfully omitted]

my sweet, warm, loving Whitley back. Come home my little cabbage head. Anyways, Steve is a musician in a band called "The Art of Swing." They play only original music. and Whitley — they are really fine. NO SHIT! Steve plays drums very well. You've got to see him some time. They performed at the "roadhouse" a bar-night club outside of LA? Steve came + picked me up w/ the rest of the band and I went out and listened to compositions that are all worth recording. They're so good and it's great to dance to. Not like monotonous disco. He came home and slept w/ me in my virginal bed. We couldn't really make love (although we both wanted to) cause I had no birth control. I really gotta get a diaphragm. But he's wonderful and soft + warm. and kisses good too. And I'm thrilled to be liking someone so much. (My first thrill was you) Well Anna goin home today. Until then MC + HO HO HO ❤️ love you

(See what I'm a real mess. It's Tues. afternoon — class is over with — Day is crazier & reinjured my leg in my hip socket. Gay says I probably have tendonitis and that I should get x-rays & anti-inflammation pills.

whoopee - I got home late last night - boy was I glad. If I had to sit around one more day doing nothing but eating Xmas cookies & listening to my little brother scream I'd go crazy. I did have a few enjoyable moments visiting old friends but for the most part it was tense & anxious. Wondering what you're doing as always. To aggravate things more - I have rent to pay in 1 day with only $50.00 to my name. Joel & Jab have left me no money. The electric bill came for $20.00 & I have no money to pay that. To top all of that off - I'm trying desperately to get a diaphragm. Health Services are closed till school opens so I called Planned Parenthood the only thing I can do is come in tomorrow night and be very very late for work at Millers (can I find a sub? no.) or wait till the next opening in the middle of January. Well Steve and I practiced celebacy until then? Not only that - but its going to cost me $35.00 and I absolutely haven't got a cent. I'm all mixed up I don't know what to do. I wish you'd call & tell me what to do. Oh Whitley I need you right now.

Oh Whitto Baby what a day - what a night so much to say - so much to write. After walking 3 miles in the blizzardy snow - feet like frozen turds, tears streaming from eyes. & 3 hours of anxious waiting. Insistant probing measuring, question at urine & blood & yes, no, yes, no, lubricating jelly I recieved a diaphragm, a bill for $35.00 and a strange feeling in my stomach as Steve came to pick me up. I had that same feeling you did before you went to the Bahamas - Jimmy expecting sexual fulfillment and alot of other things you weren't sure you could give him. A very scary feeling. I know that I had my diaphragm he could fuck all the time - I haven't an excuse not to. Do I want to fuck all the time? Boy this subject really causes me alot of anxieties. As it turns out we did sleep together and we did make love and it was much better then I thought it would be but not good enough to make me want to do it all the time like every other seemingly normal person wants to do. Not only that but Im liking Steven more & more each day. He is very good & good to me. Very sensitive and aware and intelligent & he dances good and so far there are no bad points against him. Guess who followed me home last night? ——————→ Willie

I'll explain that later. Millers is gettin to be a real bore were gettin a new manager and she's gonna be alot tighter with the previous half ass system. No more rip offs. It's colder than a witches tit and you're a lucky bitch to be where its warm. I miss the hell outa you girl. But I've got lotsa new books to read so they'll have to do till you come back. I've realized how much I've grown to depend on you for a listener advice giver & taker and generally all around most wonderful intimate friend in the whole world. I miss the hell outa you, girl! The rent's due tomorrow & I aint got it only 3/4 & your check nothin from Joe! or Seb. I don't know what to do I wish one of them jerkoffs would call. I'm generally scraping the garbage can for food & money, but that doesn't bother me one bit as long as I got popcorn. Later darlin ....

Forgive me love for neglectin my literary duties to ya. I'm also so sad & bummed after you call me, I never know quite what to say, because I feel like I really have too much to say and, besides I don't want to hear you. I want to see you and enevitably after we hang up I have found that I've forgotten to say at least a hundred different things. No matter you will be home soon. My N.Y. eve parties were incredibly exciting - think because I didn't expect much from any of them. Jeff Linke and Picked me up in his audi (borrowed) we went to ████████ (boonsville USA) stayed & danced awhile but the people there were so clearly uptight that I could've done a striptease act on the table + no one would have merely nodded their heads. Went to a very chich party (Mark's friends). There was a doorman in a tux - he took our wraps. We were led into a room with a table bursting oysters, clams, mussels, salmon, chicken, liver pate, caviar, raw vegatables, creamy rich dips & chocolate chees-cake! Oh oh oh my taste buds were abused. Next was a table laden with champagne glasses all filled to the brim with the appropriate New Years drink. The next room was large & spacious (wood floor) where we all commenced to dance in the New Year. Music was perfect for dancing. When the clock struck 12 we all poured champagne on each others head - everyone hugged & kissed - mucho fun - and oh how I danced, danced and I must say amazed & entertained quite a few people. Jeff was quite intoxicated so I took over the driving the rest of the evening we hopped from one party to the next stayin for a while eating, dancing then getting bored & leaving by this time we had acquired Mark & my sister. I remained straight (in mind) the rest of the pm.

It was quite entertaining to watch everyone get plastered. Although Willie had given me some speed earlier in the day and I don't believe it had any effect? on me. Came home at 5:00 went to sleep was awakened by Steve at 12:30 who drove me to Detroit to have dinner at his Grandma's and see Movie (Close Encounters) - I loved it. I cried at the end and if you haven't seen it. SEE IT.

[respectfully omitted]

off for now. PS. I snooped in Gay's grade book - Signing you and I both got an A- in her rep. That cunt only gave me a B+ in her modern class the only one to get an A was [redacted] I'm jealous of her. Should I be. Oh come home and make me feel secure. I LOVE YOU

Hey there most loved and missed friend that is sooooooo far away - it is the absolute coldest its ever been in H² and I do not, do not want to get out of bed. After this vacation it's gonna be hard trying to make it to a 8:00 class. Fortunately I'm not in it alone. But if I have to beg you out of bed every morning - well forget it! Anyways as usual I had only a few hours of sleep either cause I stay out late or cause Steve spends the night. Last night I went dancing at the BF w/ Linda. I've been using your ID to get in everywhere (you left it in your coat pocket) well I sure had a good time. Mark came later and Steve was working so we didn't have to worry about drinks. People were not shy in expressing either disgust or delight in the way Linda and I were dancing. We were verbally accused of Lesbianism several times. Boy it sure was fun. This little Jamaican man (rubber body) sneered and challenged me to a dance. When I we put on a show. I spent the night at Linda's and we ate popcorn all night and talked about being crazy and sleeping w/ men, and diaphragms, ect. it was lots of fun, but I always wished it was you the whole time. Well gotta go. My mind's a blowin and its time to get dressed or class. YUK! I DON'T WANT TO DO ANY MORE PLIE'S I JUST WANT TO BE NATURALLY GOOD

miss your lovely

Well my little cabbage I think this the last of my literary tributes to you since you will be home in 2 more days and I think I can remember to tell the rest. Thinking of you almost every moment and miss your warm kisses & sweet caresses. I wonder what you're doing and how you're feeling at all moments of night and day. Today was the first day of school and I was thouroughly (sp?) depressed and discouraged. Gone were the days of tension free, pressureless, non competetive, classes w/ Gay & Liz over vacation. After the first plie in Flynn's class, I could feel the tension & rigidity flowing through my body. The ~~~~ pre class chatter and acknowledgment of tans was wearing on me, and I felt worthless in every class. Why you ask?

① My tendonitis is getting worse not better.
② Everyone seems to be doing better than me as far as what one can do in a class. (I keep comparing myself to ▮▮▮▮ and it's just making me sick. Teachers don't look at anyone but her.) I'm ever so jealous.
③ I realize that it's going to be even more trying & demanding of my mind & body this semester than it was last semester. The first day of classes and I was in the building from 8:30 - 5:00. I keep wishing I had studied clothes design or cosmetology. I must be feeling down cause I actually & truly want to be somewhere else besides the school of Dance. LOVE I'M SO TIRED OF GOING NOWHERE. PATIENCE DEAR MAD, PATIENCE. Oh agooooo come home soon I need your fragrant, soft shoulder to cry on. You know I knew something was missing in my day at the pitory and it was you, and your reassuring embraces I had become so accustomed to ~~~~ in between classes. I love yourself

Boppers

By the middle of January, the novelty has officially worn off. The apartment seems to have shrunk. I'm not exactly sure why, but Maddie and I are sometimes tense with each other. I can't put my finger on it. When I'm not at peak exhaustion after dancing six hours-plus a day, plus rehearsals and regular class work, I scribble in my journal trying to figure out what's going on. Topping it all is that blasted attention thing of hers. It's fine when we're alone. Then, she's my buddy, my confidante, and seems to truly care for me. She listens and gives sage advice when I weep dramatically about Jimmy or the department or any little thing—and I cry a lot these days. Sometimes I even amaze myself—the sheer volume of the moisture. She bolsters me and reminds me of basic truths. So this, I say to myself, an only child, is what having a sister is like.

But in a group, any group at all, that pesky switch is thrown and her need to be front, center, and universally adored and commented upon sucks the air from any room. It is annoying. It is deeply tiring. I am no longer amused.

And Madonna isn't the only one having crazy dreams. One night I'm jolted awake at 4:00-something, breathing heavily. I grab my notebook and a pencil and write this in the dark:

Madonna-and-me dream: the end of the world. Everyone thought Madonna was sick and weird—a slut and a threat to the middle-class community (which was really the Holiday Inn hotel.) Me and M would walk around with combs in our mouths and make people think we were vampires. It scared the kids. Madonna and her boyfriend (who? I don't know!) went right into the middle of a fancy residential area and started making love out in plain view. Neighbors called the cops and locked their doors. Then this lady—kind of a responsible PTA type—was sent to talk to her, to give her some kind of therapy. The lady asked Madonna to describe a certain tree, but M couldn't, though she tried. Madonna started screaming, "I can't express myself without moving!" Then there were a bunch of big explosions—kind of the end of the world—and everyone was killed. Except for Madonna, whose hand just fell off, but she didn't seem to mind and made me go get it.

So yeah, there's a little bit of tension.

When I pull away, even slightly, I can feel her change. The affection, the protestations of love and undying friendship, the caresses and nuzzling grow rampant, then turn off, abruptly. We're like spinning magnets, drawing together, pushing apart. We develop other friendships. She becomes very chummy with Linda, a dancer in the department who is also a terrific photographer. In Madonna, Linda finds a most willing subject. She takes rolls and rolls of pictures: Madonna in pointe shoes, Madonna in a big fancy hat, Madonna nekkid as a jaybird. While I'm somewhat relieved at not having to be the Only Friend, I spin into jealousy when they go off on a weekend trip. I spend a lot of time with Patty and Hallie, other dancers with whom friendship is less work. And then there's Colin, whom I continue to see casually. I suspect this bothers her more than she admits.

And so I do an unexpected thing.

I have made friends with a man who owns a leather store across the street from our apartment. No, not that kind of leather store. Cowboy boots, hats, belts. Leather, alright? Chatting in the store one day, I see a sign he has in his window: studio apartment for rent, $75/month.

Whoa.

It's a bit of a hike—clear over on the other side of Packard—but I don't care. It's $75/month that I don't have, but I don't care. It's hardly an apartment—a converted garage attached to the leather guy's house, but to me it's heaven. Tiny, but with a cozy loft for sleeping, and a great, fully tiled bathroom with a tub. It is cute, private, quiet, and far from the Dance Department. But what I love most about it is that it is part of the world. It is in a neighborhood with children and dogs and people who are not dancers. People I don't know. Old people. For some reason, this has become extremely important to me. I tell Madonna. I put a positive spin on it:

"And I'll only be there on weekends, for the most part. You gotta come see it. You'll love it. It's very peaceful and we can have sleepovers and—"

She narrows her eyes. "Whitley, we already have sleepovers. We have a sleepover every night. We're roommates."

"I know, but this is different."

"How is it different? All I know is you're sort of moving out for no reason."

"I'm NOT moving out. I would never do that. I just ... you know I hate that apartment. It hurts my soul. I need this. Come see. You'll understand."

And she does come see the little room, and I think she does eventually understand. My mom sends a big box of antique quilts from home. I put foam pads up in the loft and pile on the blankets. We have sleepovers. We take hot, luxurious baths in the quaintly tiled bathroom, then clamber up the rickety ladder and snuggle together and talk. On Valentine's Day she hands me a little kid-style card that has a bear on it. "Happy Valentine's Day!" it reads. And then scribbled in black pen: "I love you more and more and more ..." and so on—too many "mores" to count.

One thing's for sure, through good times and bad, Maddie and I do have some very interesting discussions and the new room facilitates these. We talk about boys. We talk about sex. We talk about Colin and actually compare notes. We talk about dance and the department and who's getting fat and who's kidding themselves about ever dancing professionally, and why this or that faculty member did whatever bonehead thing. We do not talk about pop music or yoga, or a rabid, clawing quest for cultural iconhood, at least not that I can remember. But we do talk about sex. For all our promiscuous and liberal tendencies, for all our big talk and freewheeling behavior, there is much we do not know. We both know that we do not know. It is the blind leading the blind. It's really pretty sad.

On a snowy evening, I'm alone in the bad apartment studying in the living room. For no reason I can recall, I suddenly get up and go into the bedroom, turn out the lights, and discover something about my body and myself that has somehow escaped my attention until this moment—a peculiar and highly personal trick with blessedly tangible rewards. I am amazed by the success of my newfound technique and can't wait to tell M. The second she gets in the door, I grab her and sit her down and share this valuable tidbit. It's slightly embarrassing, but simply too important to keep to myself. Her green eyes go wide as she takes in what I say. A day or two later, Maddie announces her own little victory.

We dub it "the nightly ritual." And enough of that.

Each spring is made more stressful by the advent of repertory auditions. Each faculty member is responsible for creating a new piece of choreography for the big Power Center concert at the end of the semester. I must, I *must* get chosen for the concert. Preferably for Susannah's piece, as she is the current guest artist and, in my eyes at least, the choreographer by whose hand and aesthetic the sun rises and sets.

The day of the audition, we gather in Studio A. Maddie and I are already familiar with some of the movement as Susannah's been teaching lengthy segments in class for a week or two. It's hard: big, wild, slashing legs that I really have trouble with as my hip joints have always been relatively inflexible. But on the plus side, it's funny movement, to be done tongue-in-cheek, with dancers dressed in karate suits and brightly colored kids' boxing gloves. The piece is called called *Boppers*. Funny dancing is my favorite.

But there's another problem. The dance calls for some wild and energetic partnering. One section involves the woman flying horizontally at the man who catches her gracefully midair and swings her around two or three times. I can handle the swing-around part, but the flying horizontal headfirst toward a man of any stature is going to be a problem. I have my qualities as a dancer—good jumps and leaps, subtlety, OK emotional depth, and of course my almost freakishly pointy feet—but I am not, nor have I ever been, particularly brave and fearless. I do not like to be upside down. And I do not like to be horizontal, unless I'm on a bed or a sofa. Or perhaps grass.

Worse still, I'm paired in the audition with Mick, who hates me 'cause ... well, maybe 'cause I get to be M's roommate and he doesn't. I'm sure he knows I got the full report on their quickly aborted tryst of a few months back. Or maybe he doesn't hate me at all, but the Department is so proficient at breeding paranoia in its sweaty denizens that by this time I have begun to sense disapproval in even inanimate objects.

At any rate, after throwing my massive self at him about eighty times, he has every reason to hate me, or at least dread my approach. The other women, practicing with their partners around the room, take off with light-footed abandon. They are like sprites, like sails, flying wingless toward friendly waiting arms, backs arched artfully, smiling even. And the men catch them and they swing round and round. "It's fun!" they say. I hurtle toward Mick like a bus. I try, I really, really try, but never quite get it. He's pissed, I'm mortified. I spy Maddie across the room yukking it up with Joel, who is her very capable partner. She flies into his arms grinning. They look great.

Miraculously, I make the first cut and so does my roomie.

That night I write:

I want to be in the Bopper piece so bad I can hardly see straight but at least three women have to go. There are not enough men to go around and besides it's only a small-cast piece. We all know who's in for sure: grad students (one of whom is the most boring dancer I've ever seen). What it comes down to is that Madonna and I are among the "maybes." How awful it will be if we both aren't in it. If she makes it and I don't—I don't know if I'll be able to stand it. But I'm going to lose weight to further my chances. I've got to do it.

Well, miracles abound because Maddie and I both make the final cast, though Susannah takes me aside for some stern counseling about "the lift" and how I simply have to get past my fears. The entire population of Apartment 10A comes together in my support. In the basement of our hideous building is a large, dark room where junk is stored. One night all four of us go down there. Joel lays old mattresses on the floor, and I practice flying into his arms while Madonna and Tony cheer me on from the sidelines. I get a little better, a little more reckless, and if not horizontal then at least somewhat diagonal, but eventually Susannah just figures out a way I only have to do the damn thing once. Sheesh.

My mom comes to visit. She wants to watch a day of classes, to see how I live, who my friends are. She drops her bags at my beloved garage, then we call a cab and go over to U Towers to pick up Madonna. This is their first meeting and I'm worried about it. Is she going to do the attention thing with my mom? Will my mom respond? How will I feel about this? But in fact, Madonna is very ... normal. Gives my mom a friendly hug, is dressed more or less innocuously (for her), and doesn't belch loudly or dance on the table when we go out to Seva, Ann Arbor's famed vegetarian restaurant, for dinner.

My mother is the picture of the open, friendly, liberal parent in her usual khaki couture. Her finely boned hands are weighed down with silver and turquoise jewelry. She is beautiful, but in an artfully unconcerned way. The conversation flows. And though I have occasional flare-ups of proprietary feelings about my mother, I keep them in check. I am very aware of Madonna watching us, studying our interaction. I understand and feel for her. It's so terribly unfair, but I can't think of anything to do about it.

We all walk back up Liberty Street towards State, then cut over to North U and past the Bell Tower and Hill Auditorium. There are people everywhere, Christmas lights are still up, and scattered snowflakes swirl in the air. We're heading back to the Dance Department for a grad student's thesis concert and it's pretty good. Then we drop Madonna at U Towers. For some reason, I feel bad about leaving her there and hug her extra hard. She smiles gamely and heads for the elevators. Two days later, my mom goes home and I'm flung into depression.

"I'm so lucky to have her," I sniffle into my journal. "She is my best friend." In fact, I tell my mother almost everything about me, and what I don't tell I suspect she figures out. There can be no secrets. Over the years, a remote section of my brain has grown large, complex, and overdeveloped in response to my need to love my mother at all cost. In fact, she is very far from perfect.

At this point, though, I am immersed in the good stuff—like the recollections of worldwide travel: just the two of us taking off for Greece, Paris, London, Russia, Jamaica. I focus only on her oh-so-contemporary takes on childrearing: the long, involved conversations about sexuality, about the "charmed life" we led, and how the two of us were somehow special, different, above the masses. I remember and cling to the heady boundarylessness of this bond, how when she was depressed, or drunk, or both, I would feel what she felt but gilded with guilt and shame (for surely I was the cause of her pain). But it was a welcome misery, even for a child, because it pointed once again to our "specialness," the uniqueness of our love. It was fate, it was timeless, it was a love story without end.

Yes, I'm depressed when she leaves, but at least I can get something done.

Excellent news: Tony and Joel and I are planning a trip back to Brockport to visit all our buddies there. Tony's got the loan of a good car and we're gonna drive through Canada—takes about six hours to get there, very doable. I have an ex-boyfriend there, Donny, who I'm still good friends with and would love to see, plus lots of dear friends. We can take class and show off our vastly improved technique to the faculty. We're discussing the details when Maddie walks in and announces that she wants to go too. She's already talked on the phone to all our Brockport friends and feels like she knows them already. She can help with gas and driving. She needs to get out of town. She wants to take class too, you know, try something different. Sounds like a done deal, and conveniently the guys think it's a terrific idea. I suddenly remember someplace I have to be right at that moment and tell them I will talk about this later.

That night in my journal:

If she goes to Brockport I'm not going. She's not going to usurp anything there that's mine. Donny will instantly fall in love with her and all the teachers will too, and I won't have anything to do with it. Right now she's on the phone with (name of random Brockport friend) *making plans ... and he didn't even ask to speak to me.*

The trip falls through, to my great relief. I spend more weekends at the other apartment, and this allows me to continue and even enjoy the times that my roomie and I spend together.

The weeks and months of rehearsal are coming to an end. The big concert at Power Center opens tonight. I guess we're ready. I'm in Susannah's *Boppers* piece, which has turned out to be pretty fun, as well as Vera's African piece, which is fun except for one extremely strange and embarrassing element: the white students are required to wear body paint in order to look African. There has been some grumbling about this, but Vera's the grande dame of the department and a very good soul and no one, including me, wants to bother her. Still ... orange-brown body paint? In about seven years, the term "politically correct" (now hackneyed and mocked) will be fresh, new, and "cutting-edge" (equally passé), and painting reluctant white people orange to make them appear black (or rather, African-American) will be politely frowned upon. But for now, we're on the wrong slope of the cusp and there's nothing to do but slather on the goo.

The Power Center show is always exciting. In preparation, we stay late into the night at the theater, setting light and sound cues, practicing on the massive space, making sure we can function in the bright lights and not fall into the orchestra pit. When we're not needed, we lounge about the cavernous house, or hang out in the dressing rooms gossiping and eating junk food. The Dance Department faculty takes dress rehearsal very seriously. We must wear full makeup and remove all our jewelry. Even hair barrettes must be covered with black tape to eliminate their potential glare. We run through the show without the benefit of an audience, then go home to rest up. Our teachers are kind to us the next day, giving us classes that are easy and relaxing. There are no negative comments. We are as thin as we are going to get. Everyone goes home for a quick meal then gathers backstage at 6 for an 8 o'clock hit. I am very excited. Since my mother has been here recently, she will not see this show, but I don't care. I have friends in the audience, plus I'm feeling a bit blue that, due to my innate fear of hurtling, my part in *Boppers* isn't particularly cool.

It's the first piece in the concert and most of the cast (excluding me and one other girl) is stationed out in the house as the audience comes in. Clad in their karate suits, they walk barefoot over the seats and in the aisles, improvising and chatting noisily to each other. From backstage I can hear Madonna whining, "C'mon you guys!" in an improvisational way, then something I can't make out. Slowly, as the seats are filled, the dancers make their way to the stage where hundreds of Boppers in all colors are hung from the grid. I amble onstage and grab a blue one and a red one and take my place for the start of the original percussive score. Suddenly, the stage explodes into a blur of Susannah's signature punchy, whimsical movement. It's way fun and by the end we're all grinning and dripping. The audience loves it.

Madonna and I are in a dressing room with about ten other women. She's all done, but I have to stick around to do Vera's piece at the end of the show, so we sit around gabbing with our feet up on long, white tables, which are littered with makeup, tampons, sweat socks, brushes, and barrettes, and the occasional book of Hesse. Bottled water, of course, has not yet appeared on the scene; we just drink out of the water fountains. Over the next hour we watch as costumes are peeled on dry and peeled off drenched, as feet are bandaged and the tape daubed beige with Revlon Cover Stick, as hair is braided, clipped, and sprayed. Dancers come and go, running silently on bare feet. Almost everyone is in Vera's piece, however, and the room is suddenly filled with white girls turning black and black girls coaching us. I get out my pancake cans and a bunch of damp sponges and get to work transforming myself. When I come up for air, I stare at myself in the mirror and bear witness: a WASP-Armenian, too long in the tanning booth, and sporting a beige leotard and fake batik. I run upstairs and get down with the drummers as best I can, all sticky like that.

After, we all scrape the orange off each other and take long showers before reporting on the stage for strike—taking down the lights, wrapping up cables, putting delicate, colored gels in their proper folders. We have work to do, but we're as happy as we are tired.

But ya know, just when things are going so good ... there's this silly exchange, recorded in feverish red ink a couple of hours later:

Madonna: (already wearing my favorite scarf): Whitley, can I wear your scarf?

Me: I need it for strike.

Madonna: Can't you wear something else? I just washed my hair and I don't want to put any barrettes in it. Do you have another scarf?

Me: No. Oh, I don't care. Go on and wear it.

Fuck! She manipulated me! I didn't want to continue the conversation so I gave in ..."

... and more blah-blah journal analysis of this nonevent. So, this is what having a sister is like.

Now that the pressure's off, I feel like choreographing. Back at Brockport, I was 100 percent sure that I was not a choreographer, that my career (such as it might be) would consist of me dancing other people's visions. That seemed fine to me. But Susannah has seen something in me. She is a magnificent teacher, capable of presenting ideas in such a gentle, nondidactic way, that one suddenly finds oneself sailing foreign waters and embarking on strange lands, and liking it very much. Under her careful tutelage last semester, I made my first real meaty solo, and suddenly fears and limits have fallen away. With the tools she has given me, I come to suspect that making dances might be no more mysterious than making a beautiful pot on a whirring potter's wheel. What a hoot—all those dances I've seen in my head all these years, all these ideas that seemed so impossible, can interact with flesh and bone and sinew and music and the wood of a stage and make *something*. Just takes a little trust. And some scheduling skills.

The Bach Sinfonia record that our entire apartment is obsessed with is the perfect testing ground. I choose a short piece—about four minutes of lush 6/8 time allegro and spend about three hours lying on the black Naugahyde sofa with my eyes closed, getting up every four minutes to put the needle back, much to the dismay of the Saudi engineering students one floor above me. I get some good ideas and write them down on a legal pad.

Madonna and Joel both agree to be in my piece. I also ask Patty. She's from Westchester County, New York, and has a side extension that I can only—and actually do—dream about. (When I'm not dreaming about Madonna sparking the end of civilization, I continue my series of dreams about effortless extensions.) Patty's also nutty and irreverent and up for what I have in mind.

All year long, Joel has amazed us with his pratfalls. He doesn't just fall, he cascades. Somehow, my fellow New Yorker can tumble from one side of the room to the other, as if the floor has suddenly been turned vertical. It is ruthless and painful and thrillingly funny to all of us who seek, every day, to *control* ourselves.

The Young Choreographers Concert, a showcase for student work, is in three weeks. On a Saturday morning, Joel, Mad, and I walk the two blocks to the Department, feeling the warmth of the sun for the first time in many months. Patty meets us in Studio B and we warm up quietly. Then Joel starts teaching us pratfalls.

We face the mirror, in a grim line.

"It's like this," Joel says, as if it can be explained, "You just take one leg out like this, then kick the other one out from under you and—"

Whump. He's down.

He stares up at us. "OK, now you go."

We all try, one at a time.

Me: Whoomp.

Patty: Whamp.

Madonna: Ka-whoomp.

"Ow!" she whines, smiling, sort of. She has less padding than the rest of us and I think fleetingly of her tailbone. Oh well. We lie in pretzeled heaps, looking unsure. It sure looked better when Joel did it.

"Get up, and try it again," urges Joel, and we do. Pretty soon we're staggering, flailing, and dropping like leg-warmered safes. It is SO fun.

I start teaching the basic phrases: a pretty, pseudoballetic leggy bit that ends in physical chaos. The idea is to turn grace on its ear, to make the audience suspect one thing then deliver another.

"OK," I say. "Now Joel, after the Flail-Leap you end up here, downstage right, then Madonna, you just run at him, like a bat outta hell and leap—that's right, he'll catch you—good. Now, Joel, just carry her all the way to the other side of the room—cling, Maddie, cling!!!—that's good, and put her on the barre. Yeah, Mad, just get stuck to it like you can't touch the floor. Yeah, oh, that looks great. Now Patty, you jump on him and get carried over to the other side and—"

"Whitleee!"

"What? No, just stay there. That's perfect."

Madonna is sideways, attached to the barre, her skinny arms and legs hugging the wood. She twists her head around and looks at me.

"But if I'm over here on the barres, there won't be any light on me. No one will see me."

"Oh, shut up. Yes they will."

And so on.

Young Choreographers, May 17, 1978

The second dance I ever choreograph comes out really good.

The lights come up, dim and blue, on three dancers, postmodern and minimalist. I have hired a music student to play Cage-ish prepared piano while they improvise badly-on-purpose and the audience prepares to get bored, then really does get bored. Of course, many years later I grow to love postmodern, gesture-based minimalism and do a fair bit of it myself (or so say my reviewers), but at this blastocystic stage of my aesthetic maturity, it's just something to mock.

Up in the sound booth, some student getting a tech credit sits with her finger on the pause button. Madonna is front and center (where else would she be?) and slowly points her finger at the audience and ponderously wags it up and down. What can it signify?

It's the cue to crank up the Bach and pump up the lights. But the dancers are stunned.

"NO!" Madonna screams up at the booth, waving her arms. "This isn't the right music! CUT THE TAPE! CUT THE TA—"

Then she's caught up in a tsunami-sized swell of Baroque inspiration and carried off into that leggy, pseudoballetic phrase, and on into the rest of the dance. It's a big success.

Saturday is the last show and I decide to watch from backstage, just for fun. I peek out at the audience and see them laughing—I love when audiences laugh—but from my angle, I can't see much of what's happening center stage. The music swells to a finish and the audience claps as the dancers bow and run off. They hurtle past, not seeing me there in the dim light of the wings. Joel runs for the stairs, but Madonna whirls around and faces Patty.

"You *fucked it up*, Patty! You *totally fucked the whole thing up!*"

Patty looks as if she has been slapped. The euphoria of a minute before falls from her and cracks on the floor. She stares at Madonna and doesn't say a thing.

"I can't believe it. The whole circle section. It was totally ruined."

Patty finds her tongue, finally. I know Patty well enough to know that you don't talk to her like that. She gets right up in Madonna's face.

"Madonna, I made a *mistake*, OK? I'm sorry. It didn't *ruin* the whole dance. People *loved* it. Couldn't you tell that?"

And like a switch is thrown, Madonna lets it drop.

"Oh, never mind. Forget it. Yeah, it was fine."

I stay in my corner as they leave for the dressing room. I feel very strange.

Later Liz, the department head, finds me and congratulates me, says that Madonna had "just the right comic touch," and I share this with her later, just outside the dressing room. I don't tell her about the other stuff. The stuff I saw.

"Really? Liz said that? Shit …" Madonna smiles. Then she's off down the hall, humming Bach.

Little Slugger

Journal, March something, 1978, very late

Went to the Rubaiyat with M. I felt pretty good but the floor was crowded, and M accidentally smacked me in the face while we were dancing and I felt "out of sorts" afterwards. It was alright tho.

If I hadn't had to blow out my candle, here's what I might have written:

Everybody's asleep but I have to get this down before I forget it. I won't remember this on my own 'cause tonight's the night I lost about 600,000 brain cells that I'll never get back. So, we're at the Rube—me and M and a few others from the department. We're having fun, I guess, and we're in the middle of the dance floor, lots of sweaty bodies, the whole thing. And we're really getting down to it.

Then, Madonna starts using her arms in a BIG way and I swear, she punches me in the nose. I have never been punched in the nose before. I've seen it in movies and cartoons, and it looks painful, and let me tell you, it IS painful. And the part in the cartoons when the punchee sees stars? Stars. Yes. Every fucking mirrored tile on the disco light was a star. I wanted to just lie down on the ground and nap, but there was this instantaneous clarity at the same time, this voice saying "keep dancing! Whatever you do, keep dancing!" and so, miraculously, I did keep dancing, although to a lesser extent and not as creatively as before. And then I start thinking, If I punched someone in the nose, wouldn't I notice and ask them if they were OK?

I look at Madonna. She's got her eyes closed, ecstatic little Sufi thing. Then she opens her eyes and looks at me and kinda smiles and looks away. Dance, dancity, dance. The bridge of my nose is on fire. I stumble off the floor and go up to the bathroom and splash cold water on my face. I blow my nose but all I get is sweat and snot and a little blob of blood. I'm OK. I go back downstairs and pick up where I left off. I don't even think she noticed I was gone. And so I keep dancing—all the way through the percussion solo in "Turn the Beat Around." I dance and dance. Falling down would spoil everything.

Mississippi/Al Pacino

Early morning, Mississippi summer, and the cool is just a trick. Later, the skin knows, heat will grip and press and go right through to the bone—a shift most folks take no notice of, hidden in their homes and churches, walking the mall. The heat will come and only the very poor will know. There are people who eat the kudzu here, make tea out of it, and some kind of jelly. This hungry vine makes weird sculptures out of telephone poles, abandoned shacks, billboards. These monsters fly past the window of my grandfather's blue Valiant, the perfect old-guy car. I have my head sticking out, escaping the smell of his pipe, sniffing the morning, willing cheerfulness and confidence to be my lot.

My mother sits beside him in the front seat. She takes her sunglasses off for a moment then puts them back on and smoothes her hair, which has been whipping around her face. We have all just narrowly escaped death—at the crest of a hill a massive truck appeared, coming at us, in our lane. My grandfather veered onto the shoulder and we closed our eyes in fury and hope. But no death. He was quite angry but didn't cuss, though he should have. Just pulled back onto Highway 12. We pass a farm where horses walk intently toward a barn. We pass a trout farm, a tiny cemetery, and fields of late summer crops.

"Daddy, that was amazing," says my mother. "You handled that beautifully." Each word is crisp and toned, very proper and clean. She has trained her native lingual kudzu into some sort of careful topiary. Years ago, in another southern car ride, my little cousin Susan turned to her and said, "Aunt Jean, you talk so *straight* ..."

My grandfather says, "Hmph. Law, Law, Law ..." and speaks volumes with these words. When he was a young man, a high fever stole his eloquence from him and for half a century he has spoken simply—no abstractions, no flights of fancy. But those who love him see it all in his eyes, hear it in his tone, weep for his bristling, anxious, trapped intelligence. Back in the '20s, there were no "special services" for young men with aphasia, just gentle nudges into a life of farming, maybe, or milk delivery. His leathery face fools you; he could be an English lord, or an old, Native American hunter, watching the ponies come in. Long, thin, aquiline nose, high cheekbones, bright blue eyes. And a baseball cap bearing the insignia of the Columbus Dairy, where he worked for years after the railroads turned him down.

We drive on. The sun is not yet up, but there is a golden light through the shadows and I do feel sad about leaving. We pull into a motel parking lot and stop the car. My grandfather opens the trunk and hauls out my green backpack, props it up beside the car. He stands in the fresh sun and relights his pipe. My mother goes off to hunt for a ladies' room.

I am here to meet my ride, an architectural student who is driving back to New York this morning. I see him at the other end of the parking lot and wave. He drives his white Celica up to our car and opens the hatch, which is filled with his stuff. Dan is thin, dark-haired, with an angry face. I have never met him before. He looks like what he is: a New Yorker who has just spent two months in Columbus, Mississippi, documenting the thousands of poor people's houses which will soon be under water. The massive Tennessee-Tombigbee Waterway will be completed within the year, crafting a river which will flow over villages, roads, homes, places that have been baked dry in the summer; places that have heard the calls of scrappy children dazzled by an occasional dusting of January snow. Places now doomed to dark wetness. I've thought of this plenty over the past week—of bass and croppie swimming from room to room, or down the central hallways of the shotgun houses. Progress. Fascinating, horrible.

I've been traveling much of the summer. The spring session at U-M was spent learning the "carillon piece" from Susannah and Liz, and performing it outdoors, beneath the Bell Tower, during a rainstorm. My plans—to spend the rest of the summer waiting tables at Seva, saving money, taking class, and doing the Ann Arbor-in-summer thing—suddenly seemed hollow and lifeless. Found myself crying a lot and confused.

"Get out of town," Liz told me. "You need to get away from dancing. Don't dance, don't take class. You need to get hungry for it again."

The ride board at the Michigan Union yielded a caravan of Chevy vans headed for the Rainbow Gathering. This yearly coming-together of thousands of hippies and seekers like me was slated for the Cascade Mountains of Oregon. It would surely be an adventure but I was almost paralyzed with indecision. Many hysterical, probably infuriating conversations with friends ensued as I toyed with the idea of doing something unexpected.

We are taking a break from rehearsal, eating cream cheese-raisin bread sandwiches and drinking Drakes' signature limeade: crunchy sugar at the bottom, ice water and a half a lime crammed into a glass. Later, if we have the inclination, we will steal fudge—we are professionals—and hoard for later.

"Mad, why should I be so afraid of this? Going seems impossible, but staying seems just as awful. I mean, I don't even know these people I'm supposed to travel with, not one of them. They could be sociopaths or something—they probably are, in fact. And this Gathering—do I want to hang around with the long-hair element? Am I like that? I'm ... a dancer, right, Madonna? I mean, I smoke a little pot, but I'm a dancer, an artist. What am I going to talk to these people about? Besides, I'll miss you. I was really looking forward to all those days at the river and baking and maybe camping like we said ..."

Madonna looks out the window as she says this next bit: "Well, you'll miss me either way."

"What? What do you mean?"

"I'm leaving too. I was gonna wait to tell you but I might as well do it now. I've got almost enough for a ticket to New York and I think I can get someone to loan me the rest. So I'm gonna go and take all the classes I can take."

A moment to take this in.

"Are you coming back?" And I somehow don't know how I want her to answer.

"I dunno. I don't think so, but I just don't know. My dad's gonna shit a brick if I don't. Oh, Whit, while I'm thinking of it, your dad knows lots of interesting people doesn't he? Maybe he knows someone I could stay with? Can I have his number?"

"Well, that settles it. You go to New York and I go ... panning for gold in some stream. West. The Rainbow Gathering. It'll be cool. It's time I widened my horizons."

"Yeah, and you have that nice India print skirt and that—"

"Which reminds me, I can't find that skirt anywhere. Do you have it?"

"Yeah, but I'll get it back to you. Now, will you stop interrupting me?—and you also have that pretty stone pipe with which you've contributed to my moral corruption on numerous occasions. You'll do fine, Whitley. I wish I could go with you."

"Why don't you? We'd blow a few minds, I guess. I can just see us in the middle of a drum circle."

We don't say anything. We both know that she won't be coming, that we need to go in the most opposite directions possible. I know pretty well that I don't want or need Madonna Ciccone standing beside me on some western highway with her thumb sticking out into the setting sun. I don't want to watch the snaking line of pretty boys being reeled in like so many quivering bass. I need to clear my palate, and a continent should do the trick. Is this abandonment? She's my best friend, isn't she? She needs me.

Madonna takes a deep breath, picks up her glass, and softly bites the rim, gazing out at the teeming Diag.

Two weeks later, I'm standing in a circle with about a thousand other people, in a mist-shrouded valley, being served the evening meal. A bare-chested man with a long, scraggly beard and bright eyes nears me, carrying a bucket of steaming lentil-something. He wields a ladle and deposits a gray, wholesome splotch of it into the bowl I hold out to him.

"Thank you, brother," I murmur. This is what you say at Gatherings and I am determined to get used to it. I eat by myself. I haven't made any friends. Three days ago, as the van neared the entrance to the park, we saw a double rainbow, certainly a good omen, but just a bit closer were ambulances bringing out a girl who'd dropped acid, jumped off a waterfall and died.

But omens and bad decisions aside, it feels good to be in the wilderness, to see the beautiful circle of teepees and smell the near-constant pine smoke, to walk barefoot, half-naked, with my hair hanging free, and feel mostly safe, except for one weird stalker guy who was in my van and won't get all spiritual about this experience. My thoughts keep hopping the red-eye to where my thin friend is tackling New York. I feel frightened for her, jealous of her, and somewhat protective of New York, my home. I picture her walking the streets, getting someone to buy her an Orange Julius, sitting on a stoop, dancing in a dark, dark club, not knowing where she is, not caring. I see her in a Graham class, legs opened wide in second position, contracting deep into her abdomen, her hands bending, feet flexing away from the floor. I see her taking ballet downtown at Maggie Black's if she can talk her way in, her bony, scabbed-up feet gloved by old slippers, grabbing the floor, soaring into a leap. I see her pulling in a lover, a father, a mother, a sister, when she needs one. And I feel her missing me (I know she does) while waiting to cross a choked, hot, howling street, walking thirty blocks to the next class, wondering what train is the right train. I feel as if I've cast off a fierce child.

After a couple more days of stumbling stoned about the Gathering, I finally realize that it's just true: I don't belong and there isn't any forcing it. Early one morning, I get dressed, pack up my stuff, and start walking down the mountain. No one knows where I am and this is very, very good. A white pickup truck slows for me and I climb in the back with my stuff. In the front: a mother, Terra or Land or something, and her child, Willow—a future Republican, but today just a hippie child. They're both dressed in soft deerskin. The people I've met recently are passionate about the concept of "roadkill"— they want to know all about it, if anyone's seen any, how fresh it is. And in this way, they can "harvest" their skins without killing. I lie on my pack in the back, freezing in the gray, mountain rain, thinking of all the deer waiting for just the right moment to dart across the road, in front of this truck. I pull an oily tarp over me and try not to shake. I am not dancing. I am having an adventure, goddammit.

They drop me in some little town where I get out and look for a cheap motel and a hot shower. I lock eyes with a dark-eyed, spiritual-seeker-looking man and we fall into step. The next morning, as we part, he hands me a rice paper card which reads, "May your heart blossom on this journey of adventure. I am happy to share a portion of it with you. May new blessings come in the light of each new day. Love, Alehu." That's nice. I see from a sticker on his duffel bag that his real name is Steve.

I spend the next month hitchhiking, doing dangerous things with strangers, meditating, and getting sentimental about the human qualities of rocks and rivers. I become obsessed with "signs" and let serendipity direct my path. In Eugene, I drop anchor for a few days to nurse a sore throat. I hear on the college radio station that there's a room for rent by the week in a little house next to Skinner's Butte. The people are kind, the basement room is cozy. It is peaceful there.

I call my friend Linda back in Ann Arbor to tell her where I am, as she's heading out to Eugene soon. She used to live here. We'll get together and she can show me around. I give her the address of the house where I'm staying and she grows quiet. She asks me to repeat it, and it turns out that I'm staying in the room where Linda used to live. That's what I mean by signs. I bump into the weird stalker guy on the street. That's what I mean by signs. I get a ride down to San Francisco and, on the way, camping by the side of the road, I ask God to send me a shooting star and God obliges with a huge arc of firmament. Wandering the throngs of Fisherman's Wharf, I hear someone call my name. A friend? No, it's just the weird stalker guy. I sometimes wish the signs would get their act together, but they're signs nonetheless, and I revel in the excitement of it all.

By mid-August I'm starting to get tired of San Francisco. I stay one night with the Krishnas. They're very nice and normal when they stop chanting for a second. I spend my days on the Wharf, trying to perfect a lost and bereft countenance. The ultimate adventure, it seems, is to be picked up by the Moonies and taken to their retreat and I'm so ready to go. They never approach me, however, and I eventually receive word that my grandmother is ill, her spine crumbling. I am on the next plane out.

Which puts us in Mississippi. My mother, of the sunglasses and blowing tendrils, is there when I arrive, so grateful that I've come, but within hours I regret it; the situation is not critical and there's nothing to do. I stay a week, living in the city library. Leafing through a *Time* magazine, I come face to face with … Jimmy. A double-page spread of him painting on the dunes. Jimmy.

School starts soon and my adventures seem a distant dream. Mom offers a plane ticket home, but I think of Madonna struggling alone and motherless in the cruel city and decide instead to save money and find a ride. After all, this is my Summer of Adventure and twenty hours in a Celica with snarling Dan will surely make me hungry for dance.

Somewhere outside of Knoxville, I'm discovering that I hate all adventure. I'm sitting alone in the car, sweating noisily, with Dan's cat Ruthie crawling back and forth across my thighs, panting. We've blown a tire and Dan's gone for "help," though I'm not sure what this means. I can't open the windows or Ruthie'll ditch and pizza-fy herself. The diesel trucks seem to have all been alerted to the presence of a lone woman and cat sitting timidly in a white Celica on the shoulder. How close can they come and not actually accordion me? The challenge! Cool pond. Cat dope. NOW.

Dan gets angrier and angrier as we drive; I'm not sure why. Like other men I've known, he expresses himself by going 90 MPH whenever his cop-detector thingie says he can. I am irritated, frightened, I smell bad, and I want to be home. Any home, anywhere. At dawn, we're heading north, along the Hudson. The tunnel across is just ahead and the city, my city, stands like a maiden in the mist. Dan's really booking now. Ruthie's nested in the back somewhere so I roll down the window and rest my chin on my arm. I've always loved seeing it like this. From a distance, you remember the water.

(In my hardest NYC moments, stranded in the subway, or locked out of my apartment, or enduring the hisses of the construction workers, I've always told myself, "I live on an island. I live on an island surrounded by two great rivers tumbling to the sea." And then I imagine the lay of the land as it once was: the springs, the pines, the tiny, rocky bays where you could swim. I love my poor city, gleaming quietly in the early sun.)

I watch the city, so massive and stolid, like one big graceful thing. You can take it all in like this, from a distance—see it all, contain it. And somewhere in the middle of it is Madonna Ciccone, worn out, asleep.

Dan drops me off at my apartment, shoots me a quick grin, and speeds off into the morning. I stand on a sidewalk and breathe in the smell of my block. The city is waking up. First Avenue is pretty busy, but the street is clear for the moment. My neighbor Pete and his two fat pugs, Tessa and Timothy, walk by, but Pete doesn't recognize me. Ten years ago, I was the little girl from up the street who loved to pet his puppies. And now, well, I'm not sure who I am. Still it's good to be home. I dig out my keys and go up the stairs.

The apartment is tiny and, after two weeks empty, stuffy and hot. I go around and open all the windows. I was brought home from Mount Sinai to this one-bedroom-with-eat-in-kitchen and I know everything about it. I expect a certain peace from my home at times like this and I get it. I welcome the music of the street, take a shower, then fall into my bed.

"Hello." I have been yanked from the ultimate REM experience by the ringing of the phone. I stumble to the foyer to pick it up.

"Whitley? Is Whitley there?"

"It's me, Madonna," I say, kneeling on the old green carpet. "Doesn't it sound like me? You, of all people, should know what I sound like when you wake me up."

"OK, what the fuck are you doing sleeping at this hour? I've already been to class and I'm on my way to work, but I just had to call. You know, I've been calling you every day for a week 'cause I knew you'd be back home sometime, but did you call me and let me know when? No. So I've been forced to risk life and limb in these horrid phone booth/urinals trying to catch up with you. How are you?"

"I'm good. I'm really sleepy—just got in from the deepest South. And the farthest West. But I'm home for now, and talking to you. My Little Bowl of Farina. In New York. I can't believe it. Are you OK?"

"Oh, yeah, you know, I'm fine. Just taking class and modeling and thanking God that I'm here and not growing stiff and cold in Ann Arbor. I'm through with that crap. My dad still thinks I'm coming home, but I'm not, no way, lady."

"Oh. Well, where are you? When can I see you? Madonna?"

But Madonna's talking to someone else for a moment. She's not alone. I hear her laughing, squealing, "Shit! Shit, oh shit!" Maybe someone has spilled something on her or is tickling her neck with an old pigeon feather.

"Madonna, talk to me, please. Who's with you?"

"No one. Just a friend. Oh, shit, I'm late. I've got to get to work.

And yes, I have to see you. Immediately, OK? Tonight? Whaddaya think?"

"I think yes. Can you come to dinner at my mom's? She's not here. Maybe I can get Joel to come too."

"I get off a little before five. Can I come after that?" I say sure. I don't ask her where she's working. We hang up. And suddenly I'm crying so hard, gripping the phone cord, twisting it into tight kinks, wondering why I said it was alright for her to come. Now I've got to face her, this person who's come into my city and is busy learning how to own it. Emotions that have been stirring around, building up for a year are taking a break from subtlety, are hitting me over the head with a tire iron. Why isn't she afraid when she has every reason to be? Why is she never afraid? Where the hell are her inhibitors? Did she slip me hers? One night, when we lay head to head, did they seep out her little ears, osmose through the Formica headboard and seep into me via my tear ducts?

Crying harder, I switch gears, stick in the righteous grown-up tape. She needs an education. She's just turning her back on the very thing she needs. What will she learn here besides physical technique? She's already got that. What she doesn't have is not so simply seen. I breathe easier, get up, and go to the window.

The city's really moving now, with an energy I know well. The bedroom looks out on the corner of First Avenue and a midtown street. Manholes with escaping steam, trucks that pitch and crash as they turn sharply, fat women watching their poodles crap by the gray gingko trees. And the white brick apartment building opposite me—floor upon floor of windows through which I have observed my numerous, nameless neighbors in their most private moments. What should I have done, turn away? Now that was an education.

As a child, I used to sit in this window on sunny days late in spring, when I got home from school. I would think and think, until I could make myself believe I was unbelievably lucky, the luckiest little girl in the world, to live alone with my mother. My mother, more a sister, really, or a best friend, yes. That she'd hit me for no reason, fly into fearsome rages, and sit in dim light for hours at a time, saying nothing, always seemed incidental. "We live a charmed life, my daughter, a charmed life," she'd say, her husky sotto voce steeped in mystery. And I'd believe her, nodding, my hand reaching for hers.

It was charmed in that our rent-controlled apartment was under $100 per month, allowing her to buy me anything I wanted: summer camp, trips, lots of evenings at the ballet. It was charmed in that she was a "different" kind of mother, a creative renegade who encouraged me to stay home from school and write if I felt like it. And it was charmed in other ways too. Fairy-dusted by some ancient, Southern-Gothic secret I could never quite grasp. This tragedy, whatever it was, stalked our two rooms wraithlike and persistent.

And on those sunny afternoons, I'd write notes on sheets of white paper, fold them up tiny, and drop them to the sidewalk below. "To whoever finds this note: I just want you to know how happy I am. This is such a beautiful world and I want you to remember that. I am 11 years old and I am very happy and this is my message to you." I'd launch seven or eight inspirational missiles onto the sidewalk and watch the passersby from my perch. No one ever picked them up. Later on, I'd go downstairs and gather them up, throw them in the garbage cans by the front door, feeling silly.

Madonna would have dumped water on those people, or worse.

I sit on the cool, bumpy radiator and lean my head against the windowsill. I'm just not done being young with her. She's taught me how to play, play dirty and hard, and I can't imagine her growing up and leaving. I'm afraid for her—afraid that the city will stomp all the life out of her. That the glimpses of brilliance I've seen, in class, in rich conversation, in the way she reads an Anne Sexton poem, will soon be drowned in games and city-cool. She needs time to think, doesn't she? To be young?

I have never, *never* had a friend who can pull from me such powerful emotions: delight, confidence, jealousy, courage, rage, and sweet safety. She scares me, then enchants. This woman, the closest thing I have to a sister, treasure box for my most private thoughts and tender trust, is pushing ahead of me, out of the bay and into the breakers. I should be there, not to guide her, but because the breakers should be mine, my challenge too. And I'm just not ready. She's fearless and I'm not and this, of course, is the thing that's making me cry. I'm probably also just really tired.

Late in the afternoon, I have everything looking just right. My mother's antiques shine so hard you can almost hear it. On the floor is a veritable mattress of oriental rugs, three thick (you have to layer them when your living room measures 10-by-12, if that). The big mirror is gilded gold, dulled with a comfortable layer of dust. The little wooden table in front of the sofa is the one my dad would turn upside down and swing me around in, back when he lived here too.

The windows are old and ripply and recently cleaned. If Edward Hopper and Salvador Dali got married and had a baby and that baby painted the buildings across First Avenue from me—that's the view. I've put out a summery array of fruit salad and fancy French cheeses, a loaf of crusty bread and a slab of Land o' Lakes sweet creamery butter. My mother's collection of antique coin silver flatware has come in handy and graces the table, catching the light. I decide it all looks too studied; I pick up the forks and knives and toss them onto the table, willy-nilly. There. Better.

Joel's the first to arrive. He was glad to get my call this afternoon, glad for a chance to visit and talk about his summer, to plan events—maybe a party?—for when we're back in Ann Arbor. He's found a house in Burns Park, only a few blocks from where I'll be living with Hallie on South Forest.

Because yeah, I'm going back to school.

Joel's in fine form. Takes one look at my spread and falls flat on the floor, setting the paintings askew. In a minute, he's got me laughing hard, reciting the speed version of *Gone With the Wind* he's been working on for a while. Then the buzzer rings again and Mad's here. I could say that immediately the focus is on her, but that's not the case. We're good friends, the three of us, and Joel's no longer in her thrall, which is always refreshing. It's an easy time. She hugs me hard and teases me about my tan, chatters on about classes, with Marcus Schulkind, with Pearl Lang, at the Ailey School, at some yoga center. I've never seen her so happy and sure. Her hair is longer now and flops about her face. She's got on a loose, white T-shirt, no holes at all, which looks like she just got it off some man who's walking around down on Avenue A, trying to remember where his shirt went. And men's Bermuda shorts, ugly ones, cinched in at the waist with a black belt. And those same Adidas, really scruffy now. And sunglasses. She looks great. When we hug, I feel her body, skinny but strong in my arms, and at this moment, I simply love her again. Where did those silly tears come from earlier? What fears did I have? She can do this work, here in this city. She's fine. I'm fine, heading back to school. It's just my way.

We eat and laugh and gossip. We are drinking wine out of juice glasses when the phone rings; it's my dad, who wants to see me tonight. He's in a boisterous mood, which I know can be both fun and irritating. He invites Madonna and Joel to come along.

"Let's meet at Joe Allen's at nine, OK? Is nine-thirty better? What ever YOU want, Pookums. I'm open," he says. Seems strange that he's so excited about including the others; usually he's shy and daddish around my peers, but for some reason, he's being fun and expansive. The roomies are up to the challenge. Everybody likes my artsy, youthful dad. And Joe's is a good hangout, a good place to see a famous face or two. Madonna and I send Joel out for Häagen-Dazs. As the door slams, we sit back on the sofa and look at each other smiling.

"Are you having fun, Whitley? Sometimes you seem kind of far away."

Instead of answering, I ask her what she's been doing.

"Well, you know I got a scholarship to ADF, don't you? Flynn got a hold of me and practically insisted that I go. Pearl Lang was teaching, and I thought it might be a good way to get to know her." She sips her water. "It was that. Durham's the most boring place on earth, but the Festival's great. I did nothing but dance all day and see performances at night. Pearl's classes were intense, and there was this terrific African class too."

"So, like, are you the next Pearl Lang dancer? I don't like that stuff. No pratfalls."

"No, no pratfalls, but I like it. We're working on a kind of Holocaust piece. And I'm gonna take at Ailey for the next few months, apprenticing sort of. It's kind of intimidating, but I just keep to myself and work as hard as I can and try to get the teachers to notice me."

"And do they?"

"Sometimes. Yeah, sometimes they do.."

I tell Madonna about my high school years dancing at the Ailey School, mostly taking jazz with Pepsi Bethel, which was like drinking club soda from a mountain stream. I learned so much from him, though I don't think he ever even knew my name. I tell her not to miss his class, and it feels good to give her a bit of advice. Joel comes back and we eat ice cream and strawberries, and an hour later we're getting off the E train at 42nd Street and heading for the stairs. I stop.

"Smell that, you guys?"

We all sniff. Here is one of the most vivid odors of my childhood: urine, ozone, and cake. This is my dad's subway stop; I've been walking these underground passageways for years, or rolling through them on my skateboard. To get to the 44th Street exit, one must pass, of all things, a bakery—a Sisyphean patisserie churning out wafts of cloying sweetness into the rank and heavy air. Along the walkway are the window displays of grimy, yellowed, cracked-icing cakes: "Happy Graduation," "Happy Birthday," "Baby is 2." We stop before each one and stare in ghoulish fascination. Joel bounds on to the next window. Madonna turns to me. She's suddenly serious. Are her eyes filling? I've never seen her cry. Why is she crying about old cakes?

"I can't believe you grew up here, Whitley. I just can't believe it."

"Oh, it wasn't so bad. I loved it, actually. I didn't miss the trees and stuff, plus I got to go away in the summer and—"

"Whitley, I'm being jealous of you, OK? Is that alright?" she asks tightly. "What I can't believe is that you grew up here and I didn't. I fucking belong here."

"And I don't?" I ask, looking hard into her eyes.

"Yes, you do, but maybe you don't know it right now. Every day I'm here in this city I can't stop thinking of all the days I haven't been here. I feel like I'm running a race and everyone's had a head start. It's like one of those dreams when you can't run fast enough to get away from what's chasing you or to get where you want to go. Do you understand what I mean?"

"Where do you want to go, Madonna?" I ask.

She's silent for a long while. She looks unsure. "I want to be in a company," she says softly. "And—"

A train screams into the station. I see her lips moving but I can't hear her.

"What? Say it again?"

She looks away, then back at me, her eyes like great, green cat's-eye marbles. Then sprints off after Joel who's miming outraged impatience in the distance.

Something happens to Madonna after five minutes in Joe Allen's. Perhaps it just happens to me. We sit in a sticky booth with my dad and talk about movies, the theater. Suddenly, my little friend is quite the coquette, calling my father "Ed," making spitballs out of her napkin, sipping a fizzy water with lemon out of her tiny black straw, looking out over her lashes. What's the deal with the lashes of a coquette? They just get longer and longer in social situations. And I don't want Madonna to call my dad "Ed." When I met her dad I called him "Mr. Ciccone."

I feel myself slipping further from the gaiety of the moment and into a vaguely trippy world where all has the glint of cheap gold plate. Madonna, Joel, and my dad gab like old buddies, unaware that I'm hovering somewhere near the ceiling watching it all. What's up? What's up is that it suddenly feels like a plan is hatching, that an ulterior motive lurks behind each grinning mouth, mine included maybe. Now there's a scary thought.

My dad keeps glancing over his shoulder to the front door and all of a sudden I know what's going on. He's invited Somebody to Join Us. This is a routine my dad has been known to pull, something I've yelled at him about and something I know he'll do as long as he lives and breathes. My dad, a respected New York actor who works steadily but never quite hit the big one, is a crony to the rich and famous. When I was a little girl, he took me to Faye Dunaway's penthouse; she taught me to make key lime pie. She had a hanging wicker chair. And even today, he likes to spring the stars on his only daughter and her unsuspecting, easily impressed friends. His goal in most any situation is to create drama, onstage and off. The world is his personal performance-art device. Just put all the pieces in the correct proximity, add the right comment or two, then sit back to see what happens.

Sure enough, a moment later Al Pacino is nearing the table and I'm staring daggers at my dad, through a smile of fake excitement.

"What's wrong, Pookums?" he says, fake-concerned, stifling a laugh, and knowing just what's wrong.

"Nothing, Pater, nothing at all," I mutter.

Al is nice enough, but really, there's no reason for him to be here. We do the polite cheek-kiss thing, the great-to-see-you, etc., and then I introduce him to my friends. Joel shakes his hand and effects the perfect blend of interest, friendliness, and boredom that puts people like Al at ease. Madonna stops messing with her drink and looks Al deep in his big browns.

"Hello, Al," she says, carefully enunciating each *"L,"* taking care to remove all midwesternisms from the *"A"* in his name. She even sounds vaguely British for a second. Then she dives into her pocket and pulls out gum. As the conversation revs up again (mostly Dad and Mr. P. talking about last night's poker game), I watch Madonna daintily unwrap the gum and stick it, bite by tiny bite, into her mouth. Soon she's chewing with abandon. I think the idea here is to call attention to her mouth. I want to go home.

We leave Joe's and head over to Jimmy Ray's, another gritty actors-are-real-people bar, but not much is happening there so it's back to Joe's. Out on the street, I try to talk to Maddie about my summer, but she's acting funny and distracted. A man walks by with a raging boom box and immediately she's dancing on the sidewalk. A lot of hip movements, as if I need to tell you that. She asks Al if he likes that song, and he says he hasn't heard it before, then gives my dad a strange, blank look. Back at Joe's it all continues. I feel like I'm watching some kind of Chaucerian morality play set in the sparkling, hypercontemporary '70s. We have our same table back and a new round of beverages. Then Madonna's reaching down into her dance bag and pulling out a container of bubbles. You know, pink plastic jar, little yellow wand thing. I sigh. Okay, it's gonna be bubbles in Joe Allen's. Why not?

Soon she's blowing bubbles in every direction, interjecting a word or two into the increasingly disjointed conversation. One particularly large bub lands on the top of Al's head where it rests for a moment before popping, leaving a slight sheen to his hair. I go to the bathroom and by the time I get back, Madonna's talking excitedly about having a party at Le Club on Tuesday.

"OK, you guys, so I'll meet you there about 11. That's when things get going good. Oh, come on Whitley, you have to come or I'll kill you, OK? OK? Al's gonna come and bring some friends, right Al? OK, you guys? Fuck, it'll be great."

Dad has his Toyota, a beat-up green Toyota with slumpy bucket seats, and says he'll drive us all home. We climb in, Dad and Al Pacino in the front, Joel, Madonna, and I squished together in the back. We rumble past my old high school, where, 33 years later, Joel's daughter, Madonna's daughter and my little brother (yes, I know—long story) will all be schoolmates. We head uptown. Madonna won't quite say what her living arrangements are, but it has something to do with a friend of a friend who's out of town and may or may not know that she's house sitting. Pretty nice building, prewar, a few blocks from Columbia.

Madonna kisses me and Joel good-bye, then climbs out and gives my dad a hug. Then she pokes her head in the window and grins at Al.

"Goodbye, Al. I really enjoyed meeting you." The enunciation is really something. We watch as she sprints up the steps and disappears into the vestibule. A sudden, awkward peace falls over the car.

"Provocative young thing, isn't she," quips Al. Dad and Joel snicker, and I stare out the window. So tired.

An hour later, my phone rings and it's my dad, laughing so hard he can hardly get the words out.

"I can't believe it, Pook ... that friend of yours ... after we dropped you and Joel off, Al looks at me—the expression on his face!—and he says 'That friend of your daughter's stuck her tongue in my ear! When we were driving home, she leaned over and stuck her tongue in my ear!' She's kind of forward, Pook, isn't she? Damn, I've been laughing ever since he told me. I just can't stop laughing ..."

Diploma

True to her word, Madonna doesn't come back to school. I mean, why should she? By the end of the summer the atoms that comprise her body have formed powerful bonds with the atoms of New York City. To break them would be unthinkable, catastrophic. It is meant to be.

I don't allow myself to fully recognize or appreciate my relief at her absence. In many ways I miss her and that salves any guilt for being glad she's at a distance. Besides, I'm busy moving ahead. This is my senior year and I plan on wringing every drop of parent-subsidized pleasure out of it. I have friends, my teachers seem to like me, I am rested and invigorated, having hitchhiked and had dangerous adventures. Best of all is the housing situation: 1133 South Forest Avenue.

I can finally have the old house experience that has heretofore been cruelly denied me. On a quiet, tree-lined street, with a dark-red stucco porch, old creaky floors and nooks and crannies, with a slant-ceilinged room of my own, with windows looking out onto a leafy backyard—it is everything I have ever wanted in habitation. I am living with Hallie (tiny fellow dancer, great extensions, huge smile, massive heart, and just-right sarcastic edge) and Freda, a quiet lawyer who pretty much keeps to herself. Freda has been in the house the longest and has the biggest bedroom, at the front of the house, but I don't mind a bit 'cause I have slanted ceilings. Also, Freda has an old gray cat named "The Lady Murasaki." I love cats and even though this one wants nothing to do with me, her simple presence makes me even happier.

Hal and I ride bikes to the co-op and the farmers market and stock our kitchen with soy products and fresh Michigan vegetables. We make stir-fries, soups, and fresh bread. I misunderstand about the usage of miso paste, fashion it into a burger, and fry it up. After one bite, I run gagging from the kitchen while Freda sighs deeply and rescues the mess from the skillet.

Classes are great. Susannah's year as guest artist has come to a close and things aren't quite the same without her, but there are new special faculty to be afraid of, get used to, then love. And the regular teachers feel like friends now, friends I have to impress every single day but still really like. I think back to a year ago and can't believe how different I feel. The first day of class Christopher grabs me and gives me a big, fat kiss on the cheek in front of a bunch of freshmen and tells me how relaxed I look.

Fall in Ann Arbor is all cider and donuts and yard sales and long walks in the Arb. And football. I've made it through my first year at Michigan without going to a single football game and I'm not about to break my record. I have less than no interest in football. I mean, I don't know those people, I just go to the same school as they do, so why should I care how handily they pummel people from another school? Maybe it's growing up in New York and going to the High School for Performing Arts, where our phys ed requirements were satisfied by having to go up and down so many stairs. Maybe it's too much dance, but I just don't get sports and neither do Linda and Hallie, so we sell our university-issued football tickets and make enough to go out for a few bean sprout-and-cheese omelettes at Steve's Lunch on South University. Deal.

Madonna and I talk on the phone from time to time. She is flourishing, dancing with Pearl Lang and taking class with Marcus Schulkind, whom she met at ADF, and modeling all over the place for money.

Here's what she says: "You've got to come to class with me, Whit. You'll love it. When are you coming home? Marcus is SO funny and such an amazing teacher. Each class, I don't know, it's like a performance or something. The other day he did this whole class on the Goldberg Variations, you know, by Bach? He had this fucking amazing pianist and first he taught the basic phrase—it was very simple and beautiful and I think I did it good—then he taught all these kick-ass hard variations on it, you know, jumping or turning, just like the music. I'm not shittin' you, it was so cool ..." Pause. "I'm kind of going out with him a little too. I know I shouldn't, but he is ever so much fun to play around with ..."

I tell her I will go to Marcus's class when I come home for break. I tell her about my classes, about Gay and Liz and Christopher, the new students, who's good, who's not, but I don't think she's listening. My present is her past and it just doesn't matter anymore. I sure do feel small-town. I kind of like it: we've traded.

Hallie reveals herself to me as a friend of a lifelong nature. In future years, she will be with me for the birth of my babies, help the midwife, and bring me my first post-birth meal. Years after that, I will cuddle her newborn daughter and dance in the new millennium with her sharkskin-suited young son. When e-mail comes, we will interrupt our future workdays with sudden reminiscences of our youth, our treasured vintage dresses, and fall in Ann Arbor.

I agonize, occasionally, about my seemingly fickle allegiances. How could I have been so close to Madonna just a few months ago? Now, it seems, days can go by without my even thinking about her. Ah well, I say, we're still close, in our way. And isn't this just the way of college friendships? It's okay. Just let it be.

One nice perk of the new year: my friend Billy has, at the last minute, been accepted by the department. (Boy dancers can pretty much show up unannounced, get accepted, and get a scholarship all on the first day.) But I forgive Billy this inequity. He was one of my best buddies at Brockport—a gorgeous, natural dancer—and the first person I've ever choreographed with. Remember how Maddie and I used to "bop and leap" together, making up phrases and stringing them together? Well, Billy coined the phrase; we spent hours playing, dancing, sweating. I'm so thrilled that he's here.

You see, I have the biggest, baddest, most virulent crush on him. He doesn't know it. He will know.

Billy's from working-class Long Island, complete with accent. Funny and irreverent, he certainly appears to be straight, talking about his ex-girlfriend and fashioning girly genitalia out of half-eaten Hostess cherry pies. Or maybe those aren't clues after all?

Billy has long, hyperextended legs, and feet more pointy than mine. Billy can jump in the air and hover a second before deciding to land on his deep, juicy plié. Billy can penchée to a 180-degree split, turn three times in relevé with the ease of breathing. Billy can dance, all the while smoking a Marlboro, cussing like a longshoreman, and smiling his crooked-teeth grin. He's perfect in every way.

We start hanging out—nothing serious. Class every day, then he's over to my house to eat some healthful concoction with me and Hal. We ride out to the swimming hole and spend one of the last warm days cavorting naked in the rapids and startling families in canoes. We go dancing at the Rubaiyat. With Madonna gone, I feel like I own the place, and Billy and I easily clear a space for ourselves on the sticky parquet dance floor. When we break for wine, the conversation is as easy as ever: no holds barred, exploratory, and deeply salacious. Except for one subject: us. Even as he plays Fred to my Ginger, Tristan to my Isolde, Billy's holding me at arm's length. One night, after weeks of this game, I wipe a bit of sweat from his face and tell him "Happy Birthday"—'cause it's his birthday and I have to give him something, right? One kiss and everything falls away.

And from that day on we sleep together—just sleep—and kiss. Which somehow is enough. But alas, a few weeks later, Billy's offered a place in a ballet company in New York. I try and try to get him to stay but he hates it here. We say our good-byes up in Zeet Lounge. Then we get in the elevator, he gets out on the ground floor and leaves, and I continue down into Studio D where I'm working on a new piece.

Journal Entry (undated, but from shortly thereafter):

Something's chewing at me. Just had a long talk with Madonna. I'm so sure I don't want what she has. My paths lead to greener, more fertile pastures. Well, I keep telling myself that anyway. Yet part of me still wishes for that "accepted" success of the big city, "professional cards" getting stamped, class by class ... Can she be happy? Then, get this: She told me something that she heard about Billy. Which makes me cold inside. She said she hadn't seen him, just ... heard. What does she know? I don't believe it, and I don't know how to live with that kind of idea rolling around in my head, for it creates doubt, wonder, etc. I miss him a lot, and I want him to be here telling me angrily what nonsense that is.

Today, I really don't remember what it was that Madonna told me on the phone that day, though I have my suspicions. God, lighten up, Whit. She was watching out for you. She was worried, in her way.

About a thousand grande battements later, it's Christmas break and I'm on the Second Avenue bus heading down to meet Madonna for one of Marcus Schulkind's legendary classes. Maddie meets me at the appointed time. She hugs me hard. She is skinny still, but not in a scary way, and seeing her is, in fact, like drinking an exotic soda you'd forgotten you liked. She pulls me through a nondescript Bleecker Street entryway and up three flights of rickety stairs.

Class is held in a small loft studio. Someone appears to live behind some curtains at the far end of the room. There are portable barres along one brick wall. There are about twelve other dancers there, mostly women. Madonna seems to know some of them and sidles up to a spot at the barre. The girl in front of her smiles and makes a space for her. The girl behind her tries to smile, but really just shows her teeth. What's that about? I find a place way at the end, near the door, just in case.

Indeed, Marcus is a trip. Small and quick and strong, he has a mind for music that I immediately connect with. He has branched out from his Martha Graham training and developed a technique that breeds precision and crafty intelligence in movement. Each two-hour class is a journey from one's center to the farthest reaches of endurance, then back again to exhausted understanding. As Maddie has made so patently clear, Marcus and music interact like intelligent lovers conversing over dinner.

His class starts at the barre, like ballet, but this is unlike any U-M barre I've ever done. It follows the usual order of things—pliés, tendus, degagés, ronde de jambes—but everything's skewered and wacky. He actually has us standing parallel, even turning our legs in, dropping our weight down, down … Abomination! Sacrilege! Yum, I love it.

The frappé exercise, for instance. I like frappés: striking the floor with the ball of the foot, then quick extension to a full point, then just as fast back to the starting flex-foot shape. You do this to the front, side, back, and side positions (or "en croix" if you're spouting the jargon). I like the decisiveness of it, the sound of all those feet whacking the floorboards. In ballet class, you gotta lift out of it, as if you weigh 90 pounds, which I haven't since sixth grade. Here, after we toss off a few rounds of frappés, we suddenly get to flop our weight toward the barre, flop our weight away from the barre, then toward again, in these delicious rag-doll, turned-in releases, then out of the blue, swivel the working leg on the ball of the foot: Out! In! Out! STOMP! Then fly away from the barre, turning into the center of the room, throwing weight and energy—and all that pent-up, eighteenth-century, "Will-they-chop-my-head-off-because-I'm-royalty?" ballet tension—then circle back, grab the barre, lift the weight, resume our prim-and-ditzy fifth position, then a few more gratuitous frappés before flipping around and tackling the other side.

And Marcus's teaching style is a combination of anatomy lecture, Lenny Bruce, Steve Martin, and squirmingly obvious conceptual leotard-removal of every woman in the room. Which I kind of like, actually. See, as a straight male dancer, Marcus lives in a world governed by a peculiar double-edged sword. On one blade: proximity to thousands of bright, nubile nymphs wearing little more than nothing, getting to pick them up—literally—and carry them off into the sidelights, to massage their weary muscles, to share the ineffable magic of performance, to … desire them. It's a wolf in the henhouse kind of thing. But on the other blade: worldwide assumption that one is not remotely interested in the hens. So Marcus and his small cadre of straight-dancer compatriots have a job to do and an image to uphold. They attempt to accomplish this by a brand of nuclear flirting that in another ten years will be renamed sexual harassment. But for now, I don't mind. I think he's cute and enjoy his attentions. And Madonna was right: I love the class.

Later, doing center work, we are in separate groups, and I get a chance to see how she's dancing. And she's dancing pretty damn well. She's still strikingly bony, but she's developed a strength and punch that go with it nicely. Before, she just looked like she'd blow away in a stiff breeze, but now … there's a substance to her movements, more thrust and attack. When it's my turn to dance, I see her watching from the corner, but I have no idea what she thinks. Probably not much, 'cause it is, after all, my first class with this guy and I'm flailing around like a dog on ice much of the time.

You think this is neurosis and paranoia? This constant caring about what other people think? Well, this is what dance is at this point in my career. I don't think I'm spilling any great terpsichorean secrets. It is all-consuming, it defines day and night and dreams and wakefulness. This constant caring is a damp hand on the joystick that controls bliss and misery. One "Good!" from a teacher and you can live off it—

like actual calories—for days. One casual criticism—"Hey, don't jut your chin out like that!"—can metastasize from sleepless nights into a lifelong obsession with chins and jutting. Hey, at least I don't have an eating disorder. Actually, an eating disorder seems very appealing at times. I could really stand to lose a few pounds.

After class, Madonna and Marcus and I walk east along Bleecker to the bus. It's about 15 degrees and Maddie's got several scarves wrapped around her head and neck. Her jacket's too thin, I notice. She and Marcus jabber on about her rehearsals with Pearl Lang. I cannot even begin to deal with my jealousy about this. An apprenticeship! So I just don't think about it.

"So, Whitley, you gotta boyfriend?" Marcus asks, piercingly friendly but self-mockingly too. "Are you single? Wanna have an affair with me? It'll be fun, I promise."

Ooh, I bet.

I laugh and tell him that I do have a boyfriend back in Ann Arbor. And I actually do. I've been going out with, of all things, a brilliant Lebanese-Belgian Catholic engineering student who is also a world-class long jumper. He takes me to I Musici concerts and fancy restaurants in Detroit where we speak French and he tries to teach me about the importance of wine. I tell M & M about this and we all laugh at the absurdity of it. I like the guy, but there's a little too much money floating around. My chosen career goes hand in hand with poverty and I'm damn proud of it. In about ten years, when I'm raising kids on my own and dancing in near-constant pain, poverty will not seem as glamorous, but for now … mock the wealth, by all means.

We split up at the bus stop. Madonna has to go model somewhere. She's always vague about where she's staying and I don't push it. Somewhere downtown. With a friend. She waits with me until I get on the bus and we wave through the grimy window. Then she's surrounded by people and lost to view. I don't see her again for almost one year.

After Christmas, I have my work cut out for me. At the end of April, I will present my Senior Concert with three other graduates-to-be. Our requirements: one five-minute solo work and a longer group piece with at least five dancers. There was a time that this would seem a daunting task, but I am so in love with choreographing that I think I would be doing this anyway, regardless of credits or requirements. I don't even have to write a paper. What a scam.

Still, I approach these pieces with great seriousness. I have thought for a long time about my solo. It will be an exploration of my mother's family. I will do it to honor her and them. I will use old-time fiddle music and the strange, dissonant, and nasal songs of the Sacred Harp. It will be powerful, disturbing, and life affirming. I don't care particularly about the group piece, a truly dreadful (but structurally sound) examination of vulnerability—something I should have quite a lot to say about. But the dancers like it.

My friend Geoff—the one Madonna spent New Year's with—spends a lot of time helping me through the process. He's a bit of a misfit in the department: not a great dancer in the conventional ways, but so clever and wry. He's from Detroit, gay, Jewish, with thick, red hair and freckles that cover him like a joking tan. The teachers don't quite know what to do with him. He's so bad—tight and somehow ungraceful—but he's so terrific at the same time. Everything he does is so refreshingly different, precisely because he doesn't (won't? can't?) play by the rules. In fact, I think the teachers are learning a lot from him.

He's in the senior show, too, and we're all helping each other, critiquing each other, designing the poster, learning how to produce a concert. The first time I show him my solo, up in Studio A, late at night, I pour my heart into it. I relive the agony of my mother picking cotton in the fields, enduring the humiliation of raggedy clothes, the undercurrent of racism that blew through the tiny, hot town like an evil wind. By the end I'm a panting mess. I hold the final pose then get up to turn off the tape.

Geoff stares off into space.

"Well, my goodness," he says. "That was heartfelt and intense."

My heart sinks. He is not moved.

"But ... but ... it is heartfelt. What's wrong with that? I'm just being honest."

"Look, it's beautiful, and you dance it fine and everything, but it's not enough that you're feeling a lot while you dance. You know that part where you do the gestures of your grandmother? Well—how do I put this?—*I didn't know her*. I wish I did, OK, but I didn't. I don't know why those gestures are special. I can tell by the expression on your face that they mean a lot to you. But you can't expect us ninnies out here to know why it's important. You have to show us. You know, draw us in. What you've given is … too personal. I felt a little … embarrassed."

And all at once, even through my blurring tears, my perception turns on its axis and I see he's utterly, totally right, and I'm ever so grateful to him for having the courage to tell me. It's back to the drawing board. My work is not wasted, exactly. I just have to go back and look, really see, what I've made.

Fast-forward twelve years: Geoff will come to a party at my dad's apartment. I see him almost every time I come to the city. He works as an editor for *Penthouse*. No longer dances. We will stand in the kitchen and talk. He is terribly thin.

"How is Christopher? I haven't talked to him in a couple of weeks," he will say.

Christopher Flynn has died the week before, in Los Angeles. I have written his obituary for the *Ann Arbor News*.

"He's gone?" Geoff will ask. "Christopher … We've been talking a lot, you know, keeping track of each other …"

He will go into the living room and pick up a friend's baby, hold her close. She will arch away from him, squirming.

"Don't fight it," he will say, "it's bigger than both of us."

And he will be gone about two weeks later.

In February, everyone in Michigan is mostly resigned to endless cycles of snow and rain and thankless, mean-spirited cold. I'm dancing hard, working hard: classes, late-night rehearsals, papers crafted on my sleek little IBM Selectric. But I'm also feeling pretty broke and pick up an extra job as a cashier at a medical and law bookstore over on South University. It's in a little, old yellow house that's been added onto sporadically through the decades. I love this job. When it's not too busy, I cruise the rickety shelves and read up on exotic diseases, cleft palate repair, venereal diseases, and various surgeries, effectively paving the way for an obsession with trauma, surgery, and other medical TV shows that await me twenty years in my future. I can't believe the things they have pictures of...

One night, just before I close, I spot a book I've never seen before, in the Ob/Gyn section. Its spine, covered in intricate blue and white patterns, stands out from the plain blacks and reds that surround it. I pull it out, then go lock the door from the inside, turn the OPEN sign around, turn out most of the lights, and squat down on the floor behind the cash register. And as the students trudge by through snowy darkness, I turn pages and feel my axis turn once again, tonight, when I least expect it.

How did this book come to be here? Are there really instructors at the University of Michigan Medical School who have this on their syllabus sheet? If so, then there's hope for us all. It is a book about birth. It is a book filled with stories and pictures of beautiful, aware, painful, ecstatic, emotional, wondrous births of tiny, wondrous babies. It is a book about God and spirit and the unexplained and the unexplainable, and yet so clear and practical. The book is *Spiritual Midwifery* by Ina May Gaskin. I take it home with me for the night and stay up 'til four in the morning reading birth after birth.

Ina May is married to Stephen Gaskin, a hippie-activist-teacher guy who spellbound legions of longhairs in Haight-Ashbury about ten years back. Then, with several hundred gentle, young followers, he led a school bus caravan across America, going town to town, giving talks and lectures. The group bought land in Tennessee and formed The Farm, a renowned vegetarian commune. Pretty soon, it became obvious that someone had better learn how to deliver babies and Ina May, a no-nonsense woman with long, brown braids, jumped in and figured it out. I read that The Farm's statistics rival those of the best hospitals in the world, but their attitude about the whole thing ... I have never heard words ring so true.

"Your sense of humor is a priceless jewel during labor."

And …

"If you're living together, you're engaged; if you're pregnant, you're married."

I'm particularly intrigued by her invitation to women who are dealing with an unplanned pregnancy: "Come have your baby at The Farm. You can leave it here if you want to, and if you ever want it back, then you can have it."

Ina May renames the female anatomy to make it more friendly. The perineum becomes the "taint" ("taint what's above and taint what's below …"). The urethra becomes the "pee-hole." I love it. I love how mad it must make doctors. I love that it's taking birth back from a bunch of guys who somehow got hold of it. Who knew I was interested in this?

Until this night I have given no thought whatsoever to the honor of womanhood. I've given plenty of thought to the "rights" of womanhood, the "freedom" and the "choice," but I have never thought that I might one day be a mother, and the process that transformation would involve. But suddenly, I'm thinking about it a great deal.

What happens when you have an innate fascination for something that you never encounter? What if no one had put Mozart in front of a piano? What if Bill Gates had been born a cowboy? Ina May's book fits a need and a yearning I have not even been aware of. Childbirth? Homebirth? Midwives? Mom's really not gonna like this at all.

I read by the light of three candles, but when I'm too tired to read anymore, I find I cannot sleep. Word is there might be northern lights tonight, so I bundle up and crunch through the snow to the playground of the Burns Park Elementary School and lay down in the snow, looking up. I see nothing but stars, but my axis spins and spins and turns them to a blur of circles in the sky.

I graduate. Well, I get a diploma. I've never been much of a "graduation" type of girl. The prospect of dressing up in a strange gown like hundreds of other people, waiting on long lines in hot sun, and listening to inspiring speeches while wondering how your divorced parents are going to behave at an overpriced meal is not appealing to me at all. My diploma eventually comes in the mail; I put it in a file cabinet.

At the end of May, I pack up and move to Dexter, five miles into farmland, where it has suddenly become of vital importance that I "live with" someone. Is anyone surprised that by now I have a new boyfriend that I am extremely serious about? He is seven years older than I. He is blond, chiseled, and muscular. He is a Vietnam veteran with a huge, jagged scar in his leg where a bullet whizzed in one side and out the other, missing the bone and major arteries, and supplying a valuable ticket home. He is a talented carpenter who has built an eccentric home for himself on a verdant hillside. He is also a dancer. Let's just say that at the time, it all seems like a stellar idea. I'll call him Rex.

That summer I get a scholarship to the American Dance Festival, in Durham, North Carolina. Madonna was there last summer and has regaled me with accounts of its coolness. Linda's going too; we're gonna drive down together and figure out a way to live in a house instead of a dorm.

But what to do about Rex and Dexter, Michigan? Picking strawberries and wandering barefoot in the tall grasses surrounding my new "home?" My relationship with my boyfriend is tempestuous. He is—how shall we say?—moody. But gee, that's a familiar drama. Now that I'm not living with my mom, he'll fill the drama bill quite nicely. Besides, I'm positive my vast, churning, bottomless vats of butter-flavored love can cure him, bring out the cheerful, creative, and sensitive man I sometimes catch glimpses of and would dearly like to spend more time with.

We talk and talk—endless, circuitous, frustrating conversations that lead, mazelike, right back to where we started. It always ends with him recounting his experiences in 'Nam and I'm reduced to sympathetic tears. How can I abandon him, after what he's gone through? I work and work to make him happy. I cook eggplant casseroles and clean his house and teach him about dance and how to make spaghetti sauce. Sometimes it helps a little.

Strangely, we both find ourselves talking about having a baby.

A baby. Now there's an idea. Later, much later, my string of expensive therapists will at least concur on one thing: why would I consider having a baby with a man I've just met and with whom I fight almost constantly? To break from mommy, of course, in the most "fuck you" way conceivable.

There are other options. I might go to visit my mother in our creaky apartment and sit opposite her on the moss green couch and say, "Mommy, I am planning on being a little less dependent on you. I'm planning on not being one person in two bodies anymore, OK? Bye." But that would be so … tidy. Instead, I set about to effect simple maternal separation via the most elaborate Jackson Pollack-style life experiences I can manage to create. You'll see.

But at this point, the plan is for me to go off to the Festival with Linda the dancer/photographer, then move to New York, and see if Rex and I feel like doing the long-distance thing. He's heading off on a camping trip with his friend Chris, so it doesn't feel so much like I'm ditching. The morning I'm to leave, the phone rings. He's on the phone five minutes, looking intent, then hangs up.

"Chris's mom died last night. A stroke or something."

We absorb this.

"So I'm not going camping."

Time, a thousand thoughts.

"Well, do you want to come to Durham?" I ask uncertainly. My axis slows to a stop and awaits instruction.

An hour later, it's me and Rex and Linda, southbound in a Datsun, singing *Suite: Judy Blue Eyes* at the top of our lungs. It's summer, the last blast of the '70s. What else are we gonna do?

True to Maddie's word, the Festival is pure candy-store for the likes of me. Modern, ballet, improv, repertory, and a host of movement-related disciplines that I have only a hazy understanding of: Feldendkreis technique, Alexander technique, deep tissue work. All of this, every day, plus performances by the best companies in the world every night. All of this on a gracious southern campus filled with old, history-drenched un-air-conditioned buildings, vast branching magnolia trees, and the ever-present sound of some kind of shrieking locusts. We find a gorgeous apartment in a 20s-era bungalow that we can sublet for next to nothing. We find the local co-op, buy soy products, and settle in.

Despite an abysmal performance in the placement auditions, I'm assigned to Marcus's technique *and* repertory class—both—quite the coup for clumsy me. I am starting to figure out that a lot of this business is who you know and whether they like you or not. Marcus remembers me from New York, immediately starts good-naturedly hitting on me again (and the girl standing next to me, and the girl standing next to her), so I guess that means I rate on some scale.

Perhaps I sound self-deprecating. I'm really not. In all truthfulness, I'm sort of midscale on the dance-o-meter. At this point in the American dance history timeline, thin is everything. It'll be a few more years until different body types begin—just begin—to be welcomed into the hallowed halls of acceptance. My body is borderline different. My proportions are okay—torso just a tad on the long side, compared to my legs. Legs are pretty good—muscular, just a tad bowed, but with just the right amount of hyperextension when I straighten my knees. My stomach is not flat enough, but I can fake it sometimes. Buttwise, as I have already said, I am very compromised, as thin, flat and nonexistent is all the rage and mine is very definitely there. I hate it and wear long, flowing T-shirts to hide what I see as a dangerous threat to any future career in the field I love.

Thank you, God, for my pointy feet. Without them I wouldn't stand a chance. Well, nor would I stand. My back and hip joints are tight and unforgiving. I have never been able to achieve a full front-back split stretch on the floor, though I can sit in second position—legs open to about 150 degrees—and lie my chest on the floor. My arabesque line is problematic as well. When a standing dancer extends her leg behind her, say, at a 90-degree angle to the standing leg, her body really should remain almost upright, showing off the exquisite curve in the lower back. It's weird, but I can do this with my left leg extended: it goes right up there and I barely pitch forward at all. But on the right, no go. If my leg goes up, my back dives forward, like a goddamn tippy bird on someone's dashboard. After about twenty years of misery fighting this—willing, cajoling, pounding, and pleading my right leg and back to comply with classic line, an X-ray will reveal a huge malformed vertebrae, L5, on the right, which curves down and actually connects to my pelvis. This explains a lot.

My hair is long and dark. I have the kind of face that can be pretty or utterly ordinary, depending on my mood, and I think of this as one of my greatest assets. I am clearly "ethnic" and people are always asking me "what I am." Of course, I never know quite how to answer this, so I say "a woman" or "an American" or some other unnecessary cheekiness.

My journal writing at the Festival goes into overdrive. I am so blissed-out by the dancing, the heat, the southern Gothic ambience, the wondrous performances, a dramatic and wounded boyfriend, and the daily availability of ace-quality marijuana that I must fill hundreds of pages with my observations on life, God, art, dreams, and me. Oh Lord, is it boring to read.

Rex is increasingly miserable. He has nothing to do in Durham but wait for me to come back to the apartment, all charged up and ecstatic. So one day he packs up and finds a ride home. But we are still "together," whatever that means.

What's a repertory class? It's where you learn a dance from a choreographer. Sometimes it's a dance that already exists, and you might learn it from another dancer who knows the piece, or from a video tape. A long time ago (and still in some remote corners of the world) you could learn a dance from a complex system called Labanotation—which looks on paper kind of like Navaho blanket designs. I can read enough Labanotation to walk across the floor in a straight line and that's about it. But in the case of Marcus's vaunted repertory class, to which I have been so happily assigned, he is (hushed voice) "creating a new work." How cool to be able to watch him in process! I show up for the first classes terribly excited, but manifesting only blasé unconcern.

I may as well be unconcerned, because Marcus seems to have virtually no use for me in his aesthetic decision-making. It's a complex piece, with lots of interesting duets that I get to learn from the sidelines but never really dance. It's never said out loud, but I know it's because I weigh probably five pounds more than the other girls who are having a blast getting flung about by their manly Siegfrieds in stirrup-tights. I and one other nonemaciated girl spend a lot of time stretching on the sides, affecting a supportive and interested demeanor. When my attitude is at exactly the right calibration, I find myself learning a bit of something about choreography, but mostly, I'm just bored and pissed off. Why did he ask me to grace his *oeuvre* in the first place? I just don't get it, but practice humility.

He comes to the first rehearsal with loads of movement material (much of which is familiar to us from technique class) set to lush music by Prokofieff. Everybody learns and perfects these long phrases of movement, then Marcus starts "manipulating" them in various ways to see how it all looks, to find connections and through lines that might not be readily apparent. I discover over the coming years that if you step back, watch, and be open, *the dance will reveal itself to you*. But I don't know this now. This is what Marcus making a dance sounds like:

"OK, Cynthia and Mark, you do the duet—but just the first 32 bars—over here, stage right, and then do the leap phrase together across to where Diana is holding that shape on the floor. Don't worry, she'll be out of the way by the time you get there. Then repeat the duet, but face upstage and do it way slower, yeah, like halftime. Then Mark, just pick Cyn up in your arms, spin her off stage as fast as you can. Good. Now, Sarah … where's Sarah? Oh, you're right in front of me. Excuuuuse me! OK. While Cynth and Mark are doing the duet, I want you to be doing that waltzing thing, but do it in a circle, around them while they're, you know, duet-ing. You'll probably be able to get around them about three times before they burst out into the leaping thing, so be careful and don't be in their way. Right. And after they leave, take their place, and Andrew … ANDREW??? Yes, jump right in here and start the duet with Sarah. Riiiiight. Good."

After about three weeks of manipulating phrases, though, things hit a standstill and it seems clear that here is a dance with no force of its own, no raison d'etre beyond the fact that Marcus is being paid to be here and make it up. We're all bored with it, and each other, and particularly with Prokofieff. And so Marcus does a very clever thing: with much of the dance sketched in, he changes the music. Not only does he change the music, he changes it from Prokofieff to *Randy*

Newman. And then, though the dance is still troubled, it suddenly has a freshness and newness that invigorates us all. Another week and the piece, which he calls "Magnolia," is finished and seems to be vaguely about Louisiana, mainly because that's what Randy is singing about.

My part? At the start of the dance, the other well-nourished girl and I stand on either side of the stage, then walk slowly backwards across the stage until we bump into each other's back. Then we slide, back-to-back, to the floor and sit there, knees up, kind of blocking the audience's view of the dance. I suppose I do other stuff, too, but I'll be damned if I can remember one other thing. I don't understand it, but I'm a dancer and I do what I'm told. I myself go on to a career where I tell people to do incomprehensible things onstage. Sometimes they make sense and sometimes, assuredly, they do not. But none of it's about sense, is it? This is art….

On a hot afternoon, I witness something that stays with me for the rest of my life. I make pieces about it, I dream about it, I talk about it. It is simply this:

I've never had an idol really. Well, I'll admit to a little Donny Osmond and Bobby Sherman fascination in junior high. But if I had to write an essay on the person who has been my greatest influence, my muse, my own personal Beatles, without the screaming, that person would be Paul Taylor.

I have been going to see Paul Taylor's dances since childhood. Score a point for my nutty mama—she did get me to the theater about twice a week for a long time. What he does, the way he crafts movement, is a direct line to some part of my brain that makes me feel the richest, most complex feelings. Erotic, weird, disturbing, joyous, primitive, and true. I could write in my journal for a week and never figure it out. I know. I've tried.

And so when the big PT comes to the Festival with his company, I'm all aflutter. And when classes are canceled for the afternoon so we can all gather in the biggest studio on campus and hear him speak, I can hardly believe my luck. And when the Festival director walks him in the door and leads him to a simple folding chair at the front of the room, well, "Mah salts! Fetch me mah smellin' salts!" is all I can think.

The room is airless and ripe, filled with maybe 400 students crammed tightly together on the floor, hanging from the balconies, bare feet dangling from the window wells. Sun streams in like an affirmation. In beige pants and a blue sports shirt, PT talks for maybe forty-five minutes, taking questions from the audience. Answering some, going off on tangents …

"Well, of course, there's no democracy in dance or theater …"

"I'm not interested at all if a dancer is a good composer …"

"You should be obscure, clearly." (That's beautiful, no?)

"Ballet is a branch of modern dance …"

Marcus pipes up, "Why did you leave the Graham company?"

"Well, I won't say anything against our living ancestors. I just needed to leave. I found no company to be my second skin …"

Then, some luckless student asks about "going to New York" or "What are our chances?" or some such. And the big man takes a deep breath and lets us have it.

"Look," he drawls disdainfully. "Look around you. There are too many of you. Can't you see that? If you have any doubts about being a dancer—any doubts at all—just do us all a favor, will you, and get out now. Don't come to New York. Please. If you can think of anything you'd rather do, even something you think you might find vaguely interesting, then you're not a dancer. Just get out. Now."

Whoa, I think, as my adoration axis turns on a dime.

Looking back, I see what he meant. But it sure pissed me off then.

How could he say such a thing? I spout madly into my notebook that night, through my four hundredth dance-induced blur of tears.

I have doubts. Everyone has doubts. And not go to New York because I have doubts? Fuck that! I'm from New York! He's from what … Iowa? But here's the thing: if you go to New York to dance and do only that, then what kind of person are you, ultimately? I don't just want to dance, I want to be a person, a woman, a mother, and so much more, and have those experiences, those feelings, tactile and emotional, enrich me as an artist. I'm not going to be any fucking hot-house flower!"

Fair enough. But what am I gonna be?

PART TWO

Soho

The Broome Street Bar resides in an ancient brick building at the corner of Broome and West Broadway, down in Soho. And nuzzling around it, like a protective L-shaped fortress, is the building where Rex and I decide to set up housekeeping. One enters on Broome Street. The foyer is dim, gray, and scented with a combination of odors that I never come to fully recognize. There's got to be some urine in there, and vomit. But mostly, I think, it is the smell of many little dead furry animals under the stairs. I don't know. I get used to the smell after a few days, actually grow to like it in a way.

Our loft is on the fifth floor, so that's ten flights of stairs total, a winding and angular bit of ascension several times a day, punctuated by grimy views out of the landing windows, if one ever looks. When the landlord, a thin businessman named Mr. Moskowitz with an office on Canal Street, brings us up to see the place, it takes us about five minutes to know it's just about perfect. L-shaped, like the building, it has plenty of space for living, dancing, carpentering—hell, you could race dirt bikes in there. It's 3,000 square feet. You enter at one end of the L, next to a bank of windows (yep, ripply panes), then travel about 40 feet through raw space: wood floors, more windows, vast views of sky, rooftops, the World Trade Center, water towers. Not much in the way of actual rooms, which is fine with me. Turn a corner at the kitchen (fridge, stove, some nasty cabinets), then 40 more feet to the end looking out over West Broadway. There's one flimsily drywalled bedroom in this wing. There's also a tiny bathroom with a pull-chain toilet, and a freight elevator that works.

Rex has sold his house in Michigan. I feel mixed about this. Not only because our relationship is as erratic as Morse code, but because he built that house with his own hands, with the money he inherited when his beloved dad died, years before. It seems kind of a final act, but he says he's sure, up for adventure, ready for a change. Besides, we love each other, I think. And besides, who ever said love was easy? This is my mantra. He returns to Michigan, picks up all his belongings. I add my few to the pot, and we settle in. It costs a $4,000 fixture fee, paid to the previous tenants who made it livable (by doing what? Sweeping it once?), and $1000 a month, which we'll split with a couple of to-be-determined roommates. It's all very exciting. I'm now a dancer, living in New York. With a boyfriend. In Soho.

My parents, in an unusual show of unity (or arrival time coincidence), visit to inspect what I've done. Rex and I take them on a tour of the premises. I am busting with pride and make sure to correctly use the word "joist," which has the desired effect.

"Well, Pook, I'm impressed," says my dad. "I was worried about this move, but you guys seem to know what you're doing." I bet he's jealous 'cause I get to live here and he's still in that dingy Hell's Kitchen one-bedroom. This, of course, years before Hell's Kitchen gets all ooh-lah, designer-marble, rehab-ghetto chic.

"Anne, what a truly wonderful space this is," enunciates my mother. "Are you planning on dancing in here? You could teach, perform—and all this light! You'll need some plants …" I tell my mom that I will indeed be dancing in here, but for now we have lots of fix-up to do. Rex is champing at the bit to get started. Within days we are putting up walls for a new master bedroom suite, really a loft bed in a tiny room, just off the main studio space. We get along best when there's a project going, so things are relatively peaceful.

Marky moves in—haircutter Mark with the best red hair in Michigan—friend to Madonna and me, friend to all, sunny-natured and funny. And Joanie moves in, a dancer from Michigan who likes Bach as much as I do and responds to her first view of the loft by running and leaping across the floor, falling in a heap, and rolling like a puppy in the sun. She gets the bedroom on the far side. Marky creates a bedroom out of screens and pillows over by the freight elevator. It's all very *Boheme*.

We find an old piano on the street and get some guys to help drag it to the freight entrance. Up it comes. Then we find the guts of another piano on the street—just the sounding board of an ancient upright—and drag that in too. It goes up against the brick wall in the studio, where it makes both a sculpture and a source for eerie, thrumming music. But street finds often come in threes, and the best is yet to come: a genuine turn-of-the-century Detroit Jewel white enamel gas stove, up on graceful little legs. We drag it home and hook it up. Works like new. I bake and bake and bake. This is going great.

Dancewise, I'm experimenting: Marcus is teaching in the West

20s and I go there every chance I get. Both Rex and I go up to take class with Laura Glenn and Gary Lund, who we both know from their recent U-M residencies. One day I see an ad in the *Voice* about classes with Dan Waggoner, up on 17th Street. Somebody, I forget who, has told me I'd like the place so I take a chance on it. On a gorgeous fall day, I head north on West Broadway and cut through Washington Square Park, the monument blazing white against a Brillo-blue sky, and on up Fifth Avenue. "Damn," I mutter to myself, echoing what my daddy says at least once a day, "I love New York!"

As I turn east onto 17th, a man approaches me, gets real close, and hurls hatred at me, right in my face. Says he's gonna cut me up real bad, but I put up my Teflon deflector shield and keep going. Don't worry, this is a pretty rare occurrence, and I still somewhat love New York. Half a block later, my heart has slowed to normal and I find the entrance: yet another nondescript commercial building sheltering the complicated, scrappy universes of artists, dancers, musicians. The elevator opens right into a swirl of dancers signing in, paying their $4, other dancers sprinting to the miniscule dressing room. The place has a goofy energy that I really like. And Dan's classes are terrific: so, so hard, but doable, and infused with an irreverent physicality. I feel my insecurities fall away like last winter's coat. I find myself dancing with an abandon I've been abandoning for some time. Waggoner's becomes my studio of choice, in part for the dancing, in part because the people are so nice. Sort of like greeters at a Wal-Mart in Alabama, but all cool and arty at the same time. You know, Wal-Mart greeters who take off skipping, turning, and leaping down the sportswear aisle.

You know there are so many things about a dancer's life that the average American just knows absolutely nothing about. I'm not talking about ballet. Enough people know about ballet that it's not a complete affront. But modern? The average American does not know that the thing I have devoted most of my life to even exists. Pathetic. So guess what? You are about to learn the highly guarded trade secrets.

Modern dance.

I have to say, I've got some issues with the name. It's just bad. It's a bad, self-serious name and makes me cringe inwardly whenever I'm called upon to tell someone what kind of dance I do.

And what kind of dance do you do?

Uh (attempting to gauge asker's aesthetic sophistication), I'm a modern dancer ...

Oh! I don't think I'm familiar with that. Is that like on TV? You know, like on *So You Think You Can Dance*? *Living Color*? (or Ed Sullivan? or Lawrence Welk? depending on the age of the asker).

Well, yes, sort of. It's ... It's ... Well, modern dance is a uniquely American art form that has some shared roots with ballet and jazz, but it's very different. For one thing, we mostly dance barefoot (asker begins to glaze over) and, um, well, it's a way of making art using movement as the medium.

Oh, that's fascinating. (Pause.) Modern dance. You're a modern dancer. OK. That's cool ... So it's like J-Lo?

Modern dance.

Whoever thought to call it that? Is it intrinsically modern just by calling it so? And then we get into "postmodern" and all that labeling crap, which is of no interest to me even though I skulk around wearing various modern-dance subcategory labels for the next twenty years. Problem is, modern is so many things. It's high drama and satire and abstract expressionism and nudity and people expressing their feelings about the environment and poetry and violence and athleticism and bad poetry and let's not forget beauty ... moments of unutterable beauty. There just aren't a lot of limits in "modern." You call it modern, it's modern. And the through line is a small, highly specific culture that embraces its citizens with a warm sense of belonging. Here are some little known facts about a modern dancer's life:

FEET: As I said, we dance barefoot, most of the time. When I was young and still nurturing some starry illusions about my talent for ballet, I went "en pointe" (i.e., I put on pointe shoes for the first time) and realized that I could no longer feel the floor. Wearing pointe shoes is like having your feet encased in metal, leather, and plaster of Paris. In fact, that's what your feet are encased in. Kind of like a Doc Martens boot, but all graceful looking and pink with salmony ribbons. Looking back, I think it was the pink satin and the ribbons that were the lure. But that feeling ... no, uh-uh. I lost one matching set of big toenails and that was enough for me.

The barefoot business means that modern dancers get big honking calluses all over the bottoms of their feet. These calluses are a mark of pride. We compare them. We soak and trim and peel them. They identify us, give us good turning surfaces, and protect us from splinters. Sometimes, though, they crack open. We call the resulting bloody, painful fissures "splits," and they, too, are a mark of pride, and are compared and discussed, but they can make you pretty miserable. My treatment for splits? Clean your split out with tons of hot water. Disinfect with peroxide or something, then open it as wide as you can and fill it up with Vaseline. Don't be stingy. Then wrap your favorite adhesive tape around your foot over and over. Never enough tape. Tape is very important to us. Repeat daily until split heals, if it ever does.

CLASS: The heart and soul of a dancer's life is class. (Note the jargon: you don't "take a class" or "attend a class" or "go to a class"—you "take class.") *Class* regulates the day, the week, the life. *Class* makes you strong. *Class* makes you flexible. If you want to dance for a choreographer, you *"take class"* with him or her. You probably stand in the back for a good, long time, then inch your way to the front, where you might be noticed or not. Dancers take at least a class a day, preferably more. It's the only way to get good.

After *class*, modern dancers will very often find that the bottoms of their feet are covered by a strange gray substance. I guess it is dust and dirt and skin cells and fibers. You can rub the soles of your feet together to get rid of it. Or rub hard on a piece of carpeting; that'll do it too. The name of this substance changes from state to state, from studio to studio. Many call it *schmutz*.

Ballet classes pretty much follow a set routine: pliés, tendus, degagés, rondes de jambes, adage, and so forth. Modern classes pretty much follow the whim of the teacher, the experiences of the teacher, the injuries of the teacher. Many classes start lying on the floor, with a "floor barre"—a series of exercises that slowly warm the back, the abdomen, hips, and legs without the added insult of gravity. From there we might work sitting on the ground, rounding our backs over, reaching to the side, circling the head in ever-increasing arcs. When we stand, we abduct much of the ballet vocabulary, the turned-out positions of the feet: first, second, fourth, and fifth (hardly anyone ever uses third). But we modern folks have the secret bliss of another position: the magnificent, rich, mysterious, beautiful and ultrahuman *parallel*. That's right. We stand with our feet right under our hips, like people do, weight balanced, toes pointing straight ahead. Looking down on parallel feet, one sees cool neutrality, endless potential, symmetry, sculpture, the Twin Towers, the number 11. With *parallel*, metaphors abound. We modern folks turn out when we choose to, but lovely parallel is where it's at, as far as I'm concerned.

So when we stand, in parallel or not, we do exercises that warm up the back, the legs, the feet. We begin to move out from our centers, to step in intricate patterns on the floor, patterns that have exquisite logic and bring the dancer back around to the beginning with the other foot free so that you can do it again on the other side. See, when you dance, everything's done twice, to the right and to the left. Sometimes right, left, right, left, sometimes lots more than that, but almost always even. If you leave out a side it'll bother you all day and you'll have to get up in the middle of the night to make it right.

SWEAT: Did you know that when we turn, we fling sweat in gorgeous, salty circles that spatter the floor around us and create mystical force fields?

FLOORS: We like to dance on wood, but often dance on a surface called "marley" which has nothing to do with Bob and comes in long rolls of black, white, gray, or occasionally beige, which are taped together in strips to cover imperfect surfaces. Many people hate marley. I love it. For one thing, you can clean the hell out of it, and after about three hundred people have danced on a floor barefoot and rolled their sweat on it, and their snot, and sometimes their blood, it's nice to give it an occasional swipe with a mop. Also, wood floors, as natural and lovely as they are, can splinter in unpleasant ways. I recall rehearsing with a friend back at Michigan who ran across the floor to get momentum, then jumped and slid head first onto the floor in a very dramatic fashion, made all the more dramatic by her sudden screams and the four-inch dagger of wood that sliced into her tender abdomen. So. I do like marley.

COMBINATIONS: We dance in "combinations"—movements strung together to make chains of dance that can be done, usually, on the right and left. Combinations can be tiny—just eight counts long, for instance—or lengthy masterworks that could stand alone as a solo or group unison work. The big, fancy combinations usually come at the middle or end of a class, after you are really warmed up.

The methods of teaching a combination vary widely from teacher to teacher. Some show the work once and expect the class to have it memorized, and on both sides. Some take it apart, bit by bit, analyzing and talking about dynamics, motivation, musculature. But often, once the basic teaching is done, the class can get a chance to "mark it"—to do a kind of half-assed version all together to make sure we're all on the same page. Not knowing a combination can be dangerous, especially when a lot of multidirectional running and leaping around are involved. If the class is big (or the studio is small) we do our combinations in groups. Dancers waiting their turn on the sidelines often "mark" the combination in miniature, or even with their hands, as they watch the others dance.

After everyone's properly warmed up, and after the first major combination has been taught, the teacher may decide to break the class into groups. The choosing of groups can be casual and easy, or a process rife with tension, competition, and paranoia. When I teach, I simply trace a path down the center of the room. Those to my right are Group One, the rest, Two. Well, if Group One has a preponderance of people who have no idea what's going on, I'll scramble them up to achieve a better mix of abilities, so the at-sea folks have someone to copy. We do a lot of copying in class. Back in the early '70s, before I had discovered the distinct pleasures of and my own personal affinity for modern dance, I strove mightily in hundreds of ballet classes. I'd leave Junior High School 104, in the East 20s, take the First Avenue bus home, eat toast, do homework, then head out again to take class. I'd take the F train down to 4th Street, then walk up to 10th and pull open the downstairs door of the Joffrey School. Elevator up, scuzzy dressing-room experience, then into a massive gray studio for the 6:30 intermediate class with Francoise Martinet.

Now, I didn't really belong at the Joffrey School, but damn, I tried. I wore the perfect bun, I wore broken down pointe shoes instead of the soft leather ones, I wore leg warmers made out of the arms of old sweaters. And I showed up at that class and gave it everything I had, time after time after time. And every night, after we left the barre and came to the center of the room, Miss Martinet—thin and French and so utterly cool—placed me in the back row, at the very end of the line. Truthfully, I didn't care too much where I stood. In fact there was a certain privacy there in the far corner, looking out onto Sixth Avenue. But the process of being placed there was a nightly misery.

"Alright, let us have … yes, Marie, you … Hee-aire. Yes. And now, Paula, hee-aire, next to Marie. And—where ees Jennifer? Ah, you go, next to Paula …"

And so on, through the thirty-something hopefuls in that gray, fluorescent-lit room. Until the very last student remained, unplaced, without a home. And it was always me.

I'm not sure she ever learned my name. She was not unkind, she just didn't want to look at me as I danced her lovely combinations. But I forgave her every time because I had a massive adolescent crush on her that defied explanation. It was more a fascination with her and her black leather-jacketed boyfriend, the young actor Michael Moriarty, who would show up at the end of class and adore her with his eyes. And on the train going home, I would taste the sweat on my upper lip as I imagined and imagined where they were going tonight, what they were doing right this very minute.

COUNTS: "Four for nothing …" That's what the teacher says to count off a combination. You say, "Four for nothing!" then shout out, "five, six, seven, eight" (or whatever counts you are working with), and the pianist knows when to come in, the dancers know when to start. The combination begins its brief and vigorous life.

WEIGHT: In ballet, everybody's all lifted way up and lighter than air and stretched up and out of the hip sockets and 100 percent graceful and well-behaved. And we modern folks throw our bodies on the ground and make nasty weird shapes and improvise, and the girls pick up the boys and talk onstage and make general nuisances of themselves. It's a great way to make art. It's a great way to get strong. And it's apparently one hell of a launching pad for shape-shifting, iconic pop stars in the firmament.

Speaking of which …

Madonna and I keep in touch via phone. I have about eight different numbers for her, but persistence pays off. She's still dancing but keeps squawking about all this music stuff she's getting into. Band this, boyfriend that, club here, party there. I listen, but I'm not remotely interested in hanging out in this kind of scene. I have choreography, baking and relationship wrangling to do. I ask her to do a piece with me, though, and she says she will.

Dance Theater Workshop, on West 19th, sponsors a choreographer's showcase once a year and the audition is coming up. About 80 million unknown choreographers will audition for about ten slots. I will try out a trio that I made back at Michigan. Dancing will be me, Maddie, and Patty—who has just moved to the city. The piece is about three figures from Buddhist mythology, which I actually know very little about, but the piece is really beautiful and serene. The music is by Samuel Barber—you know, what they played when Roosevelt died? The judges' eyes will mist over with complex emotions that only my choreography can liberate. They will motion me over after the audition and shake my hand. They will call me that night and offer me a slot in the showcase. How else could it go?

Madonna and Patty come over to the loft one morning to rehearse. It's the first time that I have used my new studio for more than casual stretching. I supply coffee and English muffins and we chat about the department, jobs, friends, and scandals. I teach the dance pretty quickly. Madonna looks bored; it's not her kind of movement really—restrained and peaceful—but she tries. Patty leaves for another rehearsal, and Mad and I lie on the floor, just like old times.

"So, Whit."

"Yeah, what? Did you have fun? Do you think we'll get in the showcase? It's pretty ... serene. I don't know what goes these days. I'm always so pitifully unaware of trends."

"I like it, Whit. I do. It's different though. I bet we get it. I hope so."

Broome Street is a surface artery for big rumbly trucks bound for Jersey, and a large herd tears past drowning out conversation for a moment.

"So, Whit. What would you think about ... I mean ... do you need another roommate? Here?"

Oh.

Oh.

"Wow, Madonna. I never thought about it," I say. "Do you need a place?"

"Well, no ... but I will. Soon, I think. I hate it where I am. I can't sleep. People fucking buggin' me all the time."

I tell her that we already have four people in the loft, that all the sleeping areas are full. She tells me that she could just make a space, like Marky did, out of screens and stuff. I tell her that it's an interesting idea and I'll talk it over with everyone.

It is an interesting idea, if you're interested in sudden, heart-pounding, irrational conflict.

We give each other quick massages, then she checks to be sure I have her number and heads back out into the city.

Well, Rex says he doesn't mind. Joanie and Marky think it's a great idea: anything for cheaper rent, right? Plus it'll be fun. And it will be fun, won't it? Long talks and late-night popcorn and dancing and new, cool friends, and a party every night. We'll get all close and sisterly again. We'll fight and make up. She will be my best friend again.

I just don't want this.

You think I'm worried that she'll sleep with my boyfriend? I am not worried about this at all. You think I'm worried that she'll cause conflict in the loft? I'm not worried about this—not much anyway. Since moving to New York, Maddie seems way more comfortable in her skin, and less frantic about the attention thing. But it's still there and I don't feel up to dealing with it.

In fact, everyone in New York seems to have the attention thing. I feel like I'm supposed to have it too, but it's not working. What's wrong with me? I've been back in town all of three months and I'm already plotting my escape. New York is my home. I was born here, but I just don't feel I belong here any more. It seems as if I grew up secure in the knowledge that this city was my home, that no one could ever change that. Then I traipsed off to college, braids flapping in the breeze, and returned to find … a whole lot of people who moved here in my absence and changed my city in some fundamental way. Can it be true? It just seems way more crowded. That, plus the fact that my collegiate peregrinations have yielded a thirst for something that is not found in a dance company, in the rote behaviors of an automatic relationship. I don't know what it is exactly, but it has something to do with—yikes—God.

Now no one has really ever talked to me about God, not since my sweet grandmother sang me old Sunday school songs when I went to Mississippi for Christmas—and my mother wasn't looking. I've never quite been able to figure it out, but religion to my mother is somehow horrifying. Silly, backward, restrictive—in a word, ridiculous. She has done her very best to raise me up right, into a smart, savvy, sexually aggressive, liberal, atheistic American girl. My mother's instructions regarding sex: "Go out and get your needs met!"

My needs. Okay.

I really have tried, but things keep getting in the way, things like emotional immaturity, logistics, common sense … and so the prescribed behavior really never has made me very happy. But I soldier on, with my diaphragm and contraceptive cream keeping things tidy, and with boys, hearts, memories, and one-night-stands churning idly in my widening wake. I'm only 21 and I already have detritus. Is this the way it's supposed to be?

Problem is, I really would have made an excellent Christian, or something—anything. Since my earliest, dappled days of childhood, I've been aware that people have souls, that there's life before birth and after death. Life is like water—it's everywhere, and in so many forms, even the ones you can't see. All my life I've had memories of people and feelings and textures that I know have not been part of my life. It hasn't really bothered me. There have been times when I've wanted to talk about it, but when I've tested these waters, my mother just looks at me strangely and I suddenly know better.

And in school—blessed, distant, independence-inducing school—every hint and suspicion has been validated ten times over. Bizarre coincidences, moments of total psychic wonder, and, most important, the sense that there's a current that one can plug into if one's mind and heart are open enough. It can pull you along in the most delicious way, if you let it. During those four years I have discovered Ram Dass, the Bible, Hesse, and, of course Stephen and Ina May. I don't have strong opinions about Jesus, except that he's hired himself some pretty strange PR firms. Rather, I think that holy people are around us everywhere. Back when I was hitchhiking out west, I had several convincing encounters including a person on a bus in San Francisco who looked me in the eye with enough power to run a factory.

So yeah, I'm hardwired for God and have spent a lifetime trying to reconcile these warring factions: liberated New York modern dancer versus prayerful, meditating, journal-writing seeker. And I'm getting tired. I want to live on a farm and have babies. Oh yeah, and make dances. Right?

One night I'm in the loft talking on the phone with my mom and somehow the conversation turns to prayer, and people who pray.

"Well, I pray," I say, trying to sound casual, like it's obvious and natural. My mother is silent for a moment. I can hear her breathing so I keep going.

"I do. I feel God around me. If I'm open and aware, I can feel God in my life, directing me. My whole trip out West? I was following God's lead, everywhere. It was like magic, so cool, and I ..."

Click.

My mom hangs up on me. I talk about prayer, I talk about God, and my mom hangs up on me. To her credit, she calls me back about ten minutes later and apologizes. She's been reading some novel about a mother and daughter, and it's been intense for her. Religion, God ... she just doesn't understand these things, never has. I tell her it's okay, no problem, and we move on. But of course, this is a pretty serious divide.

Anyway, one day after we rehearse the trio again, Madonna says, "Hey, tomorrow after class why don't you come over to where I'm staying?" So I do. The building's a tenement beast in the West 40s. She buzzes me in and I climb a lot of stairs trying not to touch the walls or the banister. At the end of the hall, there she is, leaning out of her door to flag me down with a grin. We hug tightly and go inside. Where she's living makes my heart hurt: a grimy couple of rooms, broke-down furniture. It's not her apartment, but she's tried to make her "area" pretty with some hanging beads and a candle. The whole issue of living with me in the loft hasn't been mentioned in a while and I feel renewed surges of guilt.

We sit on the floor and catch up. I tell her about Rex, whom she's never met, how my dad's doing. She asks about Al Pacino, but I don't know anything at all about that. Then I ask her how the music's coming. She blithely tells me what happened to her over the summer while I was prancing around at ADF. Something I guess she forgot to mention before.

"Well, there was these guys that saw me play downtown, and they asked me to go to Paris with them, to do backup for this French singer. So, of course, I went. But it was stupid, really. I mean I liked seeing it all, and I met lots of cool people, but once I got there, they didn't really *do* anything. We went to the beach and hung out and I got plenty to eat for once. Oh, God, Whit, the food was sooo good. But nothing ever really *happened*. So a few weeks ago I just said, 'Sorry jerkoffs, I'm going home.' And so they got me a ticket home."

I can't remember if my mouth hangs open, but it probably does.

"Yeah, they sent me home on the Concorde."

The Concorde! Well.

I push for more details, 'cause this is a really good story. Something about motorcycles and cute Vietnamese boys and lots of flirting. She says a few things in French and we laugh.

We turn to gossip about friends, sex, Christopher back in Ann Arbor, dancing, what parts of our bodies hurt. We check up on each other's "nightly ritual" and crack up, rolling around on the futon. Then, after a pause, and in soft, but matter-of-fact words, she tells me something that has happened to her. Right here in the city. After a fencing class. On an ordinary day. It's a secret I keep for decades, until it's no longer a secret—she tells the world—and even then I keep it.

I can't remember what I say to her. Do I hold her? Do I tell her to get help? Do I tell her to take it very seriously? See a doctor? Contact the authorities? Whatever I say, whatever I do, it's not enough. At any rate, she seems to be okay, or at least I tell myself that.

Fall turns cold quick, and Rex and I persevere in our efforts to be in love. After all, he likes to remind me, no one ever said it would be easy. My money has run out, so I hit the pavement and get the first job I apply for, at a cute little Greek-inspired clothing store on Bleecker Street. I think the boss likes the fact that I look moderately Greek. In fact, despite my inherent swarthiness, I turn out to be a terrible salesperson, but he is too nice to fire me and I work many, many hours until the boredom becomes something alive and palpable, like a mole you keep picking at, and then I work some more. I start playing piano at Dan Wagonner's studio, and at Mary Anthony's on the east side of the Village. I can't read a note of music, but I can sort of fake improvising, which is what improvising is anyway. I discover that if you only play the white keys, or you only play the black keys, and you keep a steady rhythm *and* look very intense and confident, then you can pretty much play piano for modern dance classes. It pays well, plus I get free classes.

Rex is coasting for a bit; he's made quite a nice profit on the sale of his house and isn't quite ready to start building cabinets for the snooty New York types who are sure to give him a hard time. He experiments with spending money, something quite foreign to him. One day, on a whim, he walks into the most expensive men's store in Soho and buys a suit. It's good for him. It makes him happy, and that makes me happy.

Distracting projects abound. We both take dance classes. We learn how to do stained glass. We take the subway uptown to some building near Columbia and meditate with Sri Chinmoy. Ohmmm, the whole thing. I get very enthusiastic about this for quite some time. The meditation is otherworldly, but there's a disturbing side effect to it: whenever I reach a certain level, I feel my being slip dangerously sideways inside my body. It's not unpleasant, just unnerving. As if I'm all calm and serene and everything, but *tilted* at the same time. But this is not the reason I stop going. I mostly stop going because I can tell Rex isn't really that into it. It seems the more you want someone to join you on a spiritual quest, the less likely that person is to want to come along.

We do manage to find one thing we like to do together: we take singing lessons from Bob Murdock in a tiny studio in Carnegie Hall. What I like about this more than anything else is going in the Seventh Avenue entrance of Carnegie Hall and wandering the dark, cavernous hallways to his door, passing dancers, actors, singers, all on their deep, little quests. I like belonging in these halls. I mean, I have my check in my hand, and I'm going there to sing, to work on my craft. I have every right to be here.

I don't think there's any question that Bob actually lives in his studio. It's one small room, filled with a beat-up grand piano, a couch, a couple of chairs, and piles and piles of the stuff of Bob's life. Boxes, books, clothes, magazines, half-empty take-out containers, ashtrays, musical scores, *New York Post* sports sections from four months back—it's a scramble of color and cheerful decay.

One must listen at the door. If someone's singing, you just wait in the hall, leaning against the wall or squatting down on the brown linoleum, shuffling through your music books, getting the right one out. Then the heavy door opens, spits out someone who has just finished singing an Italian art song, or Cole Porter or Gershwin, and admits the next postulant.

Rex and I never quite learn Bob's story—he's a friend of my dad's, that's all we know—but we don't care. He's a story in himself. Bald and baleful, Bob sags on his tall frame like a February Christmas tree. It's clear that he takes no real delight in teaching people to sing, but in spite of himself, he's pretty good at it. Rex and I take separate lessons, once a week, then come back together on Wednesday nights for Group.

Group is Bob's way of getting certain of his students to come back for another lesson every week. But it's really a good idea. There are usually about seven or eight of us crammed into the room, perched on stools and radiator covers and a couple of shaky folding chairs. We start with scales and arpeggios (the singer's pliés and tendues), then sit back down to start singing for each other. We have assignments: songs we're working on, songs we've perfected, and, of course, the horror of sight-reading. Now I have never had a problem getting up in front of people in little more than my skivvies and cavorting around, Isadora-like, or Martha-like, or Merce-like, or even like myself. I like it. It doesn't bother me. I don't get scared. Any adrenaline your glands squirt out into the stream only helps you to jump higher, run faster, dive more enthusiastically onto the floor. But singing solo in front of an audience—worse still, a small audience—now that's nudity for you.

I have sung all my life. I love to sing. I have a capable voice, perhaps a bit better than capable as the years have progressed. But put me in any solo singing situation and my throat closes up like a worried clam. It's very annoying. Bob's Group definitely helps, mostly because we're all in the same boat. The other participants are probably C-list New York actor/actress wannabes, who regard me and Rex—a dancer and a carpenter/Vietnam vet—with some wariness. But after a week or two, we're all yukking it up, urging each other on as Bob mournfully calls out the name of the next victim chosen for performance duties.

Our actor groupmates are living on hope and dreams and the peculiar smell of the air in the Carnegie Hall studios. Before we start scales, they talk about their other classes, the scenes they're working on, who auditioned for what, and who's hiring waitstaff where. There's Heidi, friendly and brash, perhaps a bit too ungainly for the ingenue roles she craves. And Jim, who is very farmer-boy sweet, but truly cannot carry a tune or hear a rhythm. One night, out of the blue, he amazes us all with a heartfelt rendition of "O Del Mio Dolce Ardor," his cornflower eyes shut tight with feeling. Even Bob is moved, peering out from behind the piano. About once a month or so the lovely Alexis drops by to share her vocal magnificence with Group and make everyone else feel like quitting. Everyone but me and Rex, 'cause we're just in it for kicks and self-improvement. Over the months, Rex and I learn "Amarilli," "Caro Mio Ben," "I'm a Gigolo," "All in Fun," and "Summertime." Weekly enforced singing: it's really quite a nice way to patch together a relationship.

One cold, dirty Saturday, I meet Patty and Madonna at Dance Theater Workshop on West 19th Street, to audition for the Young

Choreographers Showcase. There are about fifty other folks there, in the dressing room and lobby, lounging around in various stages of warm-up, eyeing the competition. I've brought white costumes for everybody. White works with Buddhist, right? No one argues. Patty is just happy to be dancing anywhere, and Mad's busy chomping on a piece of gum and seems distracted. She's just gotten out of a job modeling for this painter guy she knows and has to get over to some other guy's studio for another session by three, so she doesn't have a lot of time. This piece isn't really *her*. She doesn't say this—she'd never—but it's pretty obvious. Still, it's good to see her. They call my name, I grab my bag in one hand and my cassette tape in the other, and we go into the theater.

I have no memory of the audition itself. I only remember that it was a quiet, emotive work, filled with sculptural gesture. It could be that this particular performance of *Deva Duta*, a mercifully short-lived blip on the radar screen of my choreographic oeuvre, was so exquisitely transforming, illusory, and enlightening—hey, like Buddhism, right?!—that memory cannot adequately serve as its incarnation to the present day. It could be that we screwed up so magnificently—slamming into each other to the strains of Barber's sad, sad, music, forgetting an entrance, messing up obvious unison—that I have blocked the memory in defense. But it's probably that it was neither a memorable dance, nor a memorable performance of it. At any rate, the panel of judges did not favor us with selection. Onward.

After less than a year, my long-anticipated career as a dancer and choreographer in New York City is winding down. I want desperately to make dances, think about it all the time, but I simply do not want to play the game. At auditions, I'm one of hundreds and hundreds of sleeker, thinner, faster, tougher girls than I. At auditions, we're often asked just to "walk across the floor," which I think I'm pretty good at. I walk, oh, I walk, but God, how do you walk to make a good impression? I have no idea what these people want. Meek walking? Powerhouse walking? Neutral walking? Do they want someone who will refuse to participate in the walking, thereby demonstrating a brave and gutsy attitude that is just right for the choreographer's next project? I don't have the remotest clue, and perhaps more troubling,

I just don't care.

So in the early summer of 1980 I produce my own concert at a loft space called Eden's Expressway on Broadway, just north of Canal. I've never done this before but I just plunge in. Rex has gone down to the Festival in Durham, so I'm on my own, hanging the lights by myself until three in the morning, printing all the programs, making the calls. And we have two good shows, with lots of people. I don't know who half of them are, which is always gratifying. I show a bunch of old pieces, don't even do anything new for the occasion. It's not great, but at least it's a start—or, as I'm starting to suspect—a nice way to finish.

There's one disturbing element though: my mom. On opening night, I arrange an impromptu party on Broome Street. All the dancers come, and their friends. My mom and dad come. My godparents, Tom and Margaret. People I don't know. And for some reason, there's champagne. My mother shushes everyone and proposes a toast, something about exciting new beginnings, my immense talent, a star in the firmament. That sort of thing. And everyone clinks and cheers and smiles. I find this troublesome. You see, I have no illusions about the work I've just done. I know it's weak and sophomoric and derivative. There are some nice moments hither and yon, but please. … I'm only twenty-one years old. Ten years ago I was eleven. I have absolutely nothing to say. And I'm actually able to grasp this about myself. So, though I appreciate the support, my mom seems a tad, shall we say, *overinvested* in my success. Little do I know… .

I look at everyone at the party and get a sudden jolt. Did I invite Madonna to the show? I flush—and I never flush—then run find my guest list and search for her name. It's there, yikes, third from last. Did I call her? Did she get a flyer? Do I even have her address? I can't be sure. Shit, I'm a bad friend. Oh well, she won't care. We're not that close anymore. She's not interested in dance anymore, right? It's been, what, seven months since I've seen her … since the trip to Queens …

Back in January, Linda calls me up. She and Loi, another dancer from Michigan, have gone to see Maddie at a club where she's performing. Maddie has asked them to come out to Queens to watch a rehearsal. Do I wanna come? I do. I think. Yes, I guess I do.

I've lived in some cold places in my life, but there's no cold like New York in January. There's really no explaining it, I mean a temperature is a temperature. It's as cold as it is. But somehow combined with the wind streaking in off the Hudson and whirling through those sharp-edged canyons, the cold gets magnified. Anyway, it's one of those days, the day we go to see Madonna sing.

I've lived in New York my whole life and been to Queens maybe three times. We get on a train in midtown and ride and ride and ride. When the train comes out of the tunnel and becomes elevated, it feels like we're in a whole other country. Linda and Loi sit in the molded plastic seats and catch up while I stand by the door and look out the window at Queens. Apartment buildings, vacant lots, factories, the shell of the old Unisphere from the '64 World's Fair. We are going to see Madonna in Flushing Meadows, Queens. I don't know how I feel about this. We get off the train and walk about 100 blocks through ravaged, ugly streets.

Madonna is living and working in an old, abandoned synagogue. We pound on the door but there's no answer, only the shrieks of an occasional guitar, a sudden clatter of drum. We pound again, then hear her screaming, "Come iiiiinnn!" We come in. There's a dusty vestibule. We stand awkwardly wondering where our hostess is. And then she appears. The usual: thin, cut-up clothes, funky boots, but more eyeliner than I'm used to seeing on her. She looks great. She hugs us each in turn, but I can see from the git that things are definitely not the same. She is appropriately jokey-friendly, but not warm in any way. Whole new ball game, folks. This isn't about hanging out with old friends and sharing with them some cool new thing you're doing. This is, in some inexplicable way, part of the plan. She is going to perform for us. Is she trying to prove something to us? Why? Oh shit, why did we ever come?

She ushers us into the sanctuary. We meet some people. A couple of guys. Where the altar used to be, where the Torah used to stand, where the cantor used to intone his sad and mysterious words, there's a full gear setup.

"OK, you guys," she nasals. "Come on. We gotta run this again. That last one was shit." The guys take their places. Madonna sits behind the drums and the band starts pounding away.

Now this is not my kind of music, at this point in my life. Later, maybe a little, but not now. So I can share absolutely no opinion on what Linda and Loi and I witness that day, sitting primly in our synagogue folding chairs. I just know that I am supremely uncomfortable by the dynamics of this little show-and-tell. What is this feeling, I wonder. What is it? Why do I feel like running, flying from the room?

Oh, looking back, there's no doubt about what I was feeling: pure, 100-proof, moonshine-quality jealousy. In the face of her power, her willingness to fail in the service of the larger goal, of her stark beauty and fuck-you drive, I feel like a pigeon, a gray, ordinary pigeon, scared to flapping by the sound of a distant backfire. But I sit there and sit there, song after song. We applaud politely after each one, sending flat claps ringing throughout the once-holy room, place of marriages, funerals, and sermons in ancient Hebrew, now home to my skinny ex-roomie, now gyrating with a microphone in front of the band singing, "Whipping ... Whipping ... the wind is whipping me ..."

That was the last time I saw her.

But that's not what I really wanted to talk about.

Cape Cod

Cape Cod, April 1981

Face down, lying in the sand.

The winter has been mild, but for one deep and magnificent snow. Today is the first day I can feel the warmth of the sun. I stuff a blanket into my basket and ride my bike to the beach along South Street, the beach of my youthful summers. I trudge along the narrow path, through pine scrub and beach grass, and past not one single remnant of last summer's litter. The ocean opens out in front of me like a palm. It's the middle of the afternoon on a Wednesday, and there's no one about. The few hotels are shuttered against the season, the fake-quaint beach condos also tight and drawn. I stand at the top of a small dune and survey sand and a gray Atlantic with noncommittal waves. Gulls. Wind. The whole bit. All my life, this view has lived in my summers and my dreams. Endless, nightly dreams of coastlines, familiar and strange. Deep, sudden drop-offs, or long slow shallows, riddled with sandbars and life. Evil waves or calm, flatness all the way out to the horizon line.

I make my way down the steep sand and collapse to my knees in a more or less protected spot. With mittened hands, I dig a hole about one foot 'round, and maybe eight inches deep. It has to be perfect. Then I shake out the blanket and lay it across the hole. I pat the blanket down into the little hollow then, carefully, I fit my stomach into the hole and lie face down in the sand. I'm out of the wind, mostly, but still cold, so I pull the edge of the Army-issue green wool over me as best I can. I pull it over my face and look through a small hole out across the water. I am eight months pregnant. In just a few more weeks I will have a baby.

Rex and I have moved to Cape Cod. We'd been thinking about it for a long time, had decided to take the money from the sale of his house and buy the South Yarmouth Playhouse on Old Main Street in South Yarmouth, a small town about five miles from Hyannis. Rumor has it the building was built in Nantucket in the 1800s and was floated to the mainland around the turn of the century on some kind of raft. When my parents were young actors, doing summer stock in the late '50s, they worked in that theater, performed there. After I was born, we returned, our brief family, for a summer or two. I played in the sandy dirt in the parking lot. I paddled about in a tiny blow-up pool, or down in the inlet near the old windmill, where the Bass River flowed past to the sea. I watched rehearsals, uncomprehending. I swallowed a penny. I had babysitters. I ate ice cream sandwiches at Mrs. Henschel's house next door. I took my naps in the rickety actor's shacks behind the theater. And I breathed in the dusty, passionate smell of the theater. It was like a reverse inoculation, that wondrous attar, instilling in me a desire to smell theaters, to live in theaters for the rest of my life.

My mother moved north from the apparent shame of Mississippi sometime in the mid-1950s. She'd somehow obtained a job doing summer stock on the Cape. I sometimes imagine that when she met my father there, a swarthy Armenian from the West Virginia coal mines, reciting Tennessee Williams, that she immediately pegged him for the perfect antidote to her pasty WASPness. I mean, he wasn't black, but he could get pretty dark, and thereby provide the desired shock to her nice, southern parents. With his combination leading-man/sultan looks and Middle Eastern/hillbilly-moonshine cultural blend, he had the necessary complexity. He ate red-eye gravy and cooked with garlic. He was educated and eccentric and brilliant like her. One glance and it was a done deal.

I don't know. I wasn't there. I was merely hovering, a curious miasma awaiting a toehold on the planet and particularly eager to get involved with two such interesting people.

Their first summer on the Cape, my parents met Tom and Margaret Knight, native Texans, 40-something and childless, who had lived in the same one-bedroom walk-up apartment in the East 50s since 1935. Tom was a director that year at the Playhouse; Maggie ran the box office. Soon, they became fast friends with my parents, driving to the beach in the Knights' beat-up VW Beetle, eating endless bowls of chowder, and drinking gin and talking theater late into the night. When the apartment across the hall from them in New York opened up, my parents got married and moved into it. The year was 1955.

For three years, my parents were fashionable, young, New York, arty, theater types, working day jobs—my dad at *Time* magazine and my mother as an English teacher—before they conceived their first and only child. No one, even my dad—who lived through all this—knows quite what happened after that. Pregnancy seems to have changed my mother in some unalterable and terribly sad way. She became distant and depressed. At one point, she threatened to throw herself down the grimy apartment stairs. And then there was the thing about her weight. In later years, she told me that her doctor had ordered her to stop eating—some new obstetrical vogue—and so she did. At term, she weighed about 90 pounds. But I'm not at all sure I believe this version of events anyway.

The night I was born, my mother and father had tickets to see *My Fair Lady* on Broadway. Within minutes of arriving back home, my mother's body began the efficient process of my expulsion. This was, of course, way before the days of prenatal classes, Dr. Lamaze, Dr. Leboyer, and people watching ladies have babies over the Internet, so I'm not sure what, if anything, my mother knew about the process. As she bounced moaning about the living room, my dad summoned Tom and Margaret from their apartment across the hall, and they all stood around watching her solemnly until she bellowed at them and they snapped out of it and grabbed her suitcase. Somehow, the story goes, they got downstairs and hailed a cab for the trip from the East Side over to Mount Sinai Hospital on Fifth Avenue, across from the Park. I'd like very much to say that I was born in a New York City cab on Fifth Avenue, but it was only my amniotic fluid that burst forth in dramatic manner therein. While nurses hurried my poor mom inside, my dad was left with the disgruntled cabbie to mop up the puddles with paper towels.

Sometimes, to torture myself, I watch those awful birth shows on TV, where women are sweetly encouraged to accept an epidural and lie around watching reruns until they open up enough to push their babies out. Then, often because the moms can barely feel what's going on, the docs use forceps or resort to a C-section, "just to be on the safe side." And the husbands are right there weeping, and somebody's cousin has the video camera, and everything's quiet and civilized and sanitary and nice. Plus the doc can get to his golf game in plenty of time. Well, it's a good thing my mom gave birth to me in 1958 because my mother would never have stood for all that chintz-festooned birthing room business. As it was, she received the cutting-edge treatment: gas, stirrups, flat-on-your-back, shave, slice, and complete, total lack of consciousness.

When I was a little, little girl, I was fascinated with the story of my birth and asked to hear it over and over. Once I told my mother a secret: "Mom, do you know when it was that I first saw the world? Well, when the doctors gave you a shot in your arm, I snuck up there and peeked out the needle hole." I remember that she really liked that story. There were some things about me that I think she liked a great deal.

Mom's prenatal dietary quirks aside, I arrived healthy and with all my parts. I was taken home to the third-floor walk-up and lived there until I left for college. In between: three years of a Jamaican nanny named Alma Codrington. Alma, if you're reading this, could you give me a call? I'd like to thank you for raising me in what I think must have been an environment of kindness and laughter, though of course I have no memory of you. Well, that's not entirely true. I have in my mind three snapshots of you. In one, you sit on a bench in a line of black nannies in white uniforms at the United Nations playground while I play in the sandbox. You are looking over your left shoulder, out to the East River. In another, you are talking to someone on the corner of First Avenue and 51st Street, next to Smiler's grocery, while I rub the heel of my shoe on the metal curb of the sidewalk. You tell me not to do that. And finally, I remember skipping down the street holding your hand. When I turned three, you disappeared. There's one photo of you, laughing, but you do not look pretty in the photo. My mother always said how pretty you were. Anyway, thank you for the thousand or so days we spent together. I hope I did not keep you from your own children.

At three, I go off to Prescott House Nursery School in an old mansion on 53rd Street, where on hot summer days we run up to the roof and get hosed down in our underwear. Sounds barbaric, but really, it was fun. At five, my parents divorce. My dad moves half a block away. It's a blessed relief because by this time things are pretty twisted, and I'm getting tired of hiding under the bed every time they fight. I spend every Friday night with my dad and lots of vacations. He calls me every single day on the phone, to the point of irritation. He takes me to great restaurants. He takes me to "happenings" in the Village. He casts me in his plays. We watch *Star Trek* and *Zorro* and eat Chinese food from the Asian Pearl on Second Avenue. He is handsome, cool, and an actor. He drives a bright red Triumph Spitfire. He is the best dad in the world.

Summers with Tom and Margaret on Cape Cod. Trips to Mississippi and West Virginia. Friends: Donna, Marianne, Sarah, Hani.

First grade to sixth grade at P.S. 59 on 57th Street. At Junior High School 104, I "major" in choral music and sing all over the city. A scout from the New York City Opera Children's Chorus picks me to audition for a production of Gian-Carlo Menotti's *Help! Help! The Globolinks!*, a children's opera about alien invaders to be performed at City Center, where I have long seen my favorite ballet companies. We rehearse at Lincoln Center, and later, upstairs at City Center. Mr. Menotti needs one of us to be the first child to scream when the Globolinks appear. So there is a screaming audition and I win. I get to scream first. I am very excited. Right before dress rehearsal, we're waiting in the wings for our fake little school bus to be rolled onstage when suddenly everyone starts whispering madly and turning around. Jacqueline Kennedy Onassis is there, in the faint, yellow backstage light, with Caroline and John-John. They are getting a tour. Am I wowed by their fame? Do I wish I were the daughter of the fallen president, part of history, pursued by the paparazzi? No. I feel sorry for them, because I'm in *Help! Help! The Globolinks!* and they can't be.

My last year in junior high, I play Emily in *Our Town* and get *way* too into it. But when I audition for a coveted spot in the drama program at the High School for the Performing Arts, I ace it with the "Goodbye world" speech. They even videotape me with their Neanderthal video machines. Three years at PA (as it is called) fly by. I learn Method Acting, and even though I have not experienced any interesting emotions or life experiences that I might possibly call upon in creating some fascinating character or other, I do my best. I play everything from Eleanor of Aquitaine, to Hermia, to a little old lady selling hard lemonade on the side of the road.

Horse camp. French camp. Trips with my mom: Paris, London, Athens, Russia.

Despite my adoration of anything remotely connected with the stage, I am almost paralyzingly shy and ill at ease around people my own age. Except for Ben (the Stage Manager in *Our Town*.) Ben becomes my best friend in 8th grade then comes with me to PA and we are stuck like glue. Ben lives in Stuyvesant Town and is sarcastic and funny and has very shiny brown hair. We tease each other mercilessly and view our world through a deeply critical lens. Occasionally we let someone new have lunch with us, but this invariably creates stress. I have a stock explanation of our friendship: "He's-not-my-boyfriend-he's-my-best-friend." Our two sets of parents are mystified, then worried, but try to be understanding of our leechlike need for each other. To their credit, they even let us sleep over at each other's houses. Ben gets me into John Denver and Elton John. We go to concerts. We go to movies. The city is our big, fancy playground. And though I think I desperately want a boyfriend, I have absolutely no idea how to go about this. Certainly no one at school seems a likely candidate. And besides, any kind of relationship would really cut into my time with Ben.

In my senior year, my mother thinks up a big surprise. She sends patches of cloth to everyone who has been important to me throughout my childhood. They are instructed to create a quilt square for me, via embroidery, appliqué, Magic Marker, or ballpoint pen. When it's done, it's a massive work of something that, at the time, I take to be love. At my high school graduation party, a picnic at Carl Schurz Park next to the mayor's mansion, the quilt is presented to me. My friends and family see it. My mother is beaming and takes home movies. It is very beautiful. It is filled with heartfelt words and pictures and funny memories: my childhood, in cloth, stitches, images. I keep it, to this day, folded up in a cedar chest; I never, ever look at it.

I turn away from the hole in the Army blanket and cover my head tighter. The wind is really blowing now and it's starting to get dark. How long can a girl like me lie face down in the sand with her stomach in a hole?

※

In August of 1980, Rex and I are on the verge of splitting up forever. There's only one problem: my period is late. We climb the rank stairs of the Broome Street building and sit down on the roof. We decide that if I'm not pregnant, we'll split up, and if I am pregnant, we'll get married, move to Cape Cod, and have a baby. Deep down, I know that a baby will be just the thing to make him/us happy. This could work. We walk down West Broadway in the fading light of a late summer evening looking for a drug store. There's not much to say. I feel that fate is surrounding me like Plath's bell jar. It protects me from the thudding thunder of the passing trucks. The fancy Soho stores are seen through a haze of a thousand furiously gesticulating ancestors. What are they trying to tell me?

I keep walking, tears pooling then evaporating, block by block. I glance at Rex, but his eyes are straight ahead, his face set and angular. He seems angry. He always seems angry. But I know him well enough to know that he is very deeply frightened. Is he frightened that there might be a baby, or that there might not be? How simple it would be to ask him, but it never occurs to me. And what difference would it make anyway? We've had our conversation. We've made our decision. We are big, big people, with educations and good intentions. How hard could life be? And besides, no one ever said it would be easy.

The next morning, I unwrap the pregnancy test and head off to the bathroom where I manage to pee into a tiny plastic cup then insert the small white test strip. I leave it sitting on the sink and go curl up in one of the windowsills and watch the tops of the trucks and the people walking around all unpregnant and normal. I wait ten minutes to be good and sure and go back to the bathroom. Rex is rummaging around somewhere—I don't know where. And of course the strip is a deep, dark, ravishing blue. I think for a moment how considerate it is that the pregnancy test people thought to make the "positive" sign such a pretty color, then I go off yelling for Rex.

§2

This, I can tell, is going to be one of those evenings where the sky simply melts into the sea, with no break, no line. I sit up and hug the blanket to me and look out over the water. If I make my sandy hands into blinders at the side of my face, all I can see is water and sky, and if I make a certain adjustment with my eyes, I can pretend that there's nothing before me but water. Perhaps I'm flying over it. Or lying in the cold deep, looking up. Perspective: a cheap and heady plaything. I get up and brush off my ungainly self, go and stand by the water. I squat down and reach a hand out to the soft little waves. I touch it. Yep, it's cold. I taste it. Yep, salty.

It takes about twenty minutes to ride the old black three-speed home. Down South Street past the hotels: the Deco-pink Riviera, the '60s-era Blue Water, the Surf and Sand, and Smuggler's Cove, the last in the line and next to the public beach, where the Bass River meets the sea. When I was three or four, there was no Smuggler's. There was an old beach house on that spot, amid some dunes. A man in a wheelchair had built it long ago, was the word on our lane. Ramps snaked up and down the exterior walls. We would pass this house in the mornings, my mother and I, on our way to a full day at the beach with baloney sandwiches, apple slices, and grapes in a paper bag that I got to hold because I was the helper. She wore sunglasses—always sunglasses—and a scarf around her blond curls. Pedal pushers, sandals. We'd hold hands and she would sing: "Got a little, brown hand, a-holding mine, a little, brown hand, like a clinging vine..." (Once, as we passed the old house, I ran up to a window and peeked inside. A table, with a dusty glass on it—that's all I remember.) And so I pedal past Smuggler's Cove, now a massive brick headache, its parking lots stomping down my old dunes.

I pass no cars, not a one. Across Run Pond, through the trees, I can see Tom and Margaret's simple little cottage, shut up for the summer. I turn right and go one block to the ambitiously named Bass River Parkway, really just a tiny bit of crumbly blacktop that runs along the water. Past Windmill Beach, right on Pleasant Street, all the way to the end.

We are living in a 150-year-old house where the pine floorboards gleam in the candlelight, when we light candles. It is quaint and snug. Sometimes, probably more times than I should, I shut my eyes tight and try to feel the presence of the people who used to live here. I leave my bike unlocked on the back steps and go into the home I've made. I'm a real grownup of some kind, I guess. Rex isn't home from his carpentry job yet, so I sit by the kitchen window with a cup of tea, stroke my belly, and watch the streetlights come on. A block away, someone's boat is swaying gently in the river's current, metal hitting the mast with a sweet, rhythmic ding.

The days following the bright-blue test strip are a blur of doctors and clinics and sullen girls in waiting rooms, anguished "talks" with Rex in which I sob until my voice becomes a dry, coarse, swollen thing. He does all he can do. He gets down on his knees and proposes. He holds me until, inconsolable, I make him angry and he storms off. He brings me tea and marijuana. He reminds me that it could be worse: I could be wet and in 'Nam. I make an appointment for abortion information, because for about five minutes I think I'm supposed to, but never go near the building, never even call to cancel. Someone tells us the name of a doctor in a nice building on Fifth Avenue who examines me—cold jelly and crackly paper—scooch down, down, that's right, right to the edge of the table. He tells me that yes, you are pregnant; no, you'd have to be a crazy sadist/masochist to have a baby at home; no, you can eat whatever you want 'cause the baby's a parasite; it'll take from you whatever it needs.

A youth? A career? A mother?

I sit with my secret for weeks, as the New York summer rolls into a dusty, hot fall. One day I go with my mother to a yoga class somewhere on Second Avenue, up in the 70s. I have no memory of how or why we do this. This is the last thing she'd ever agree to do. But we go. We stretch. We chant. After, she giggles giddily on the sidewalk, "Did you see me? I did it! I did yoga and I even went 'ooooohmmmmm!' " She is convulsed with the ridiculousness of such behavior, delighted to have let down her guard so handily, at least for an hour. A woman we both know walks past us and we hug and catch up. This woman takes one look at me and knows everything. She has two young children.

"Oh," she says, startled, looking at me. "You look so ... different. Are you OK? I ... you ... something's different about you. Did you change your hair?"

I tell her that yes I have changed my hair. We lock eyes, this woman and I. Kindness and truth pour from her, warming me, for I am suddenly cold there on Second Avenue. My mother flutters about in the periphery.

A couple of days later, I go to my mother's apartment.

"I am pregnant."

Traffic. It is rush hour. All the trucks and cabs and buses in New York cannot drown out what I say, or protect me in any way. Through the clattering, pounding din slices a silence that terrifies me. She gets up and stumbles into the kitchen, then stumbles out. She is breathing heavily, holding on to the highly polished table by the radiator. Her words grind out like old, ill-used machinery.

"Get it taken care of."

"Mom, I can't. I want to do this. We're going to get married. We're moving to Cape Cod. It's going to be OK." I am crying, collapsing onto the arm of the moss-green sofa. I do not see her face, but her rage forms a thousand daggers and points them at me. At my belly, at my heart. Daggers, knives, swords, ropes to hang me, rivers to drown me. I keep hoping. Words drop from me, ineffective pebbles in the path of the torrent.

"You're just going to end up barefoot and pregnant ... I knew it, I knew it ..." I don't know what she means. I'm already pregnant and I dance barefoot. But nothing's making any sense.

"No, Mom, no. I can do it. We're getting married. We're having a baby. Why does this have to be so bad?"

Our words, so neat on the page, are hurled and sobbed. They scratch and maim us.

For a moment we both just sit there. Outside, horns honk endlessly. People scream their anger. There must be some obstruction. Gridlock.

She gets up and goes to the window and looks out.

And this is the last thing she ever says to me:

"Then there can be nothing more between us."

You'd think I'd question. You'd think I'd run to the window and pull at her, hug her to me, beg her to love me, to forgive me, to love me. But I don't. I just get up as best I can, and leave my home. A living room, a bedroom, a kitchen, a bath. Two closets. Some cabinets. Four windows.

I still dream about it.

And that, Madonna, is how I lost my mother.

Rex and I are married in the Washington Square Methodist Church, before a kind and openly gay minister and a small cadre of family and friends, on Halloween 1980. My mother, of course, does not attend, but Tom and Margaret and my dad put a good face on it, smiling broadly and springing for lunch at an Italian restaurant. Within a month, I am living alone in South Yarmouth while Rex attends to the sale of the loft fixtures. I just want out of the city. Recent events have left me stunned, which wouldn't be so awful but for the rampant nausea. I don't know why they call it "morning sickness" because I am sick all the time, walking around gingerly, as if my own body were a stinking fishing boat on a choppy sea.

I can't remember exactly why, but Madonna does not come to my wedding. Actually, I'm pretty sure I don't ask her. We're no longer in touch. The pilgrimage to the synagogue is officially *it* for me in that regard. I miss some things about her, but I don't miss the churning internal conflict that her presence elicits in me. I have enough churning, internal conflict going on with no help from anyone at this present time.

In early May, just after my due date, Rex and I are moseying about on Route 28. We've just come from a psychic fair, of all things. I have had a hankering to see a psychic. Maybe she'll tell me who my baby is. Maybe she'll tell me my mom will like me again. Maybe it will be worth my 20 bucks. The woman is thin, with wiry blonde hair. She sits with me awhile, in the fluorescent-lit hotel banquet room which, presumably, is alive with helpful psychic energy. My baby is a boy she tells me. Then she tells me a bunch of other stuff that doesn't make any sense to me, but I nod and pretend it does. I'm tired and have a stomachache. As I'm getting ready to go, she pauses and says, "Who's Esther? Someone very close to you is named Esther."

Ummmm. No.

"Well, then you haven't met her yet, I guess. But there is—or will be—someone very close to you named Esther."

Many years later, I will learn that Madonna's Kabbalah name is Esther and I will wonder briefly if that was the Esther the psychic lady was referring to. But no. Clearly she was referring to my buddy Esther Kirshenbaum, who gives great advice and even greater parties and adopts hapless street mutts then drives them around in her convertible.

But I don't know any of that at this point, so as we drive home from the fair, we wonder about Esthers. Rex stops in at the local bike shop. There's a guy there he likes to talk to, a fellow Vietnam vet who knows something about Agent Orange. We're wondering if Rex might have been exposed. Could that explain his moodiness? A strange rash on his back? Now that I'm rotundly pregnant, it seems a little late to be wondering about the genetic ramifications of this information, but it's something to do.

After six months of winter on Cape Cod, Rex and I are often in the market for something to do. He's worked more or less steadily as a carpenter. I've taught exercise, babysat, read countless childbirth books, taken ballet class in Harwich, eaten a lot of fish, and gestated. I have also discovered Phil Donahue in the middle of the afternoon. I have written letters to my mother, sent a few, received none back. But I'm not worried. She just needs time. She'll work through this somehow, and when she does, she will see how okay it all is. She will see my baby and fall in love with it. She will see me dance again.

So we're talking to the 'Nam bike-repair guy when I feel something on my underwear. I go into a back room and pull down my sweats (all I wear now are sweat pants held up with suspenders) and take a look-see. I wait for a lull in R's intense conversation, then tell him something's going on and I want to go home. Oh, boy, are we excited…

At home, we call the midwife, who lives about forty minutes away, to put her on alert. We call our childbirth-class teacher, who's the midwife's apprentice and lives about twenty minutes away to put her on alert. Then I make a massive casserole for the midwives to eat when they get here. Rex and I go for a long, long walk down Pleasant Street and sit in a grove of giant pines, listening to the wind. I'm having some mild contractions, but I take them very seriously and do all kinds of wacky, unnecessary breathing. Wow, I think. This is not hard at all. It must be because of my excellent dance training that I am finding these contractions to be so manageable. I am so glad that I am so in touch with my body. Childbirth—what in the world is all the fuss about?

Things pick up a bit back at the house and the apprentice comes over to check me. When she pulls out her hand, there's a long silence, then she goes in the kitchen and she calls the senior midwife. They decide to send me to the hospital; the apprentice isn't sure whether the sticky goo on her glove is the normal mucous signaling a busy cervix, or the sinister meconium, which signals fetal distress. If I weren't such a drama queen, you'd think I'd ask her to please make sure of her goo-diagnosis before we go flouncing off to the hospital, but I just turn pale and get in the car. It's midnight when we get there and the nurses at Cape Cod Hospital are more than pleased to get their hands on a little home-birth hippie girl like me. Oh, they have plans for me, including shoving their hands inside me so hard that I scream for the very first time all day.

"Just checking, dear," says one nurselike moose. "I can't understand why (shove) your midwife thinks this could be mec (shove) when your water hasn't even broken yet." I don't have an answer because my entire fist is in my mouth. Our lady of mercy says we are to spend the night in the hospital until the doctor gets in at 7 AM. Then he'll check me. She turns out the light and leaves us alone.

My pathetic little labor completely stops, but there's no way I can sleep. I can't sleep in strange places, even luxury hotels. Hospitals are completely off the charts. I have not been in a hospital since peeking out my mother's needle hole some years back. I hate hospitals. They smell like metal and fluids and bad food.

At dawn, the big doc man comes in and says I'm free to go or stay, as I wish. There's absolutely nothing going on, so I sign the necessary papers, call my midwife—the real midwife—and waddle out the door. As soon as my fanny hits the car seat, I get my first real contraction. Oh. Isn't that agreeable?

At home, the novelty wears off real fast. I'm tired, cranky, and just want to go to sleep, but some crazy maniac sadist has taken over my body and every time I start to drift off, my insides decide to murder themselves in some unspeakable way. I just want to put my head between my legs and yell up into myself and say, "Would you please cut that the *fuck* out so I can get some sleep?" It's funny, because this isn't quite going the way I thought it would go. The way I thought it would go involved candlelight and soft breathing, gentle massages and positive affirmations. And a sensation of ... *intense pressure*. Well, pressure I can handle. This is an entirely different story.

The only—and I mean only—thing good about it all is that Rex and I seem to have entered another dimension in which time speeds way up. All of a sudden it's noon. Then it's three. Then, all of a sudden, we have company. I have almost forgotten that I have invited dear Hallie to attend the birth and take pictures. She has been on a train from Michigan all night, then driven in from the station in Boston. But I am very busy now and in a supremely bad mood and I won't let her in the house. So she stands out by the car for about an hour. Then I tell her she can come in but she has to stay in the kitchen.

By about six in the evening, I am one miserable human. I labor on the toilet. I squat on the floor and pee wildly all over a blue pad. I walk around. I do every fucking thing they suggest, but the contractions just keep coming, mean-spirited little entities that I have absolutely no control over. By eight, I have to push, Oh Lord, I have to push, but I'm stuck at about 8 centimeters and so tired I just want to give up. The not-pushing idea is really uncalled for. It's like ... it's like ... oh, screw the metaphors. There's not one thing in the world that it's remotely similar to and all you nonlaboring people reading this can be damn thankful for that.

"Look," I weep to my midwife. "I can't do this. I had no idea. This is not pressure."

"Whitley, I told you that labor would hurt, hurt bad probably. You can do this," she says kindly.

"Yes, but I can't do it. I want to go to the hospital. If I go to the hospital can I sleep?"

"You are doing it. You're doing great. You can go to the hospital if you want to, but they will probably give you Pitocin to make your contractions come on stronger."

Bless her for that lie. I opt for more fun at home. She breaks my water, which brings on about ninety thousand more evil contractions that I try unsuccessfully to be thankful for. Believe me, I am way beyond gratitude at this point. About an hour later, something feels terribly different. There is no way I am not pushing. The nice lady checks me and gives me the go ahead.

All of a sudden, everything changes. Pushing is action. Pushing is power. Pushing is glory and strength and using my well-toned abdominal muscles. I am a DANCER. They get me all propped up on pillows and turn the lights on—hey, when did it get dark?—and I call Hal in from the kitchen. The whole thing takes just thirty minutes.

"Reach down," says the midwife. "You can feel the head. Go on." Well it certainly doesn't feel like a head, at least not any head I'd want on a child of mine. It feels like a warm prune. But it is the most beautiful warm prune I have ever felt and the feeling of it immediately brings on another contraction. I make noises I did not know people could make. But it feels so splendid to do this work. I, apparently, am made to push babies out. And vowing never again to make disparaging comments about the width of my hips, I pull a tiny hot baby up onto my chest.

"Oh, Rex," I whisper, amazed. "Look what we made."

They cover her with a Tweetie Bird blanket. She makes little noises, doesn't scream, but is completely there, in her body, looking around, looking into my eyes. She is beyond beauty—pure, alive and new. We name her Maya.

My dad comes up the next day, bearing gifts and kisses. Flowers arrive from Tom and Maggie. Gifts and cards from my grandmother and my beautiful aunts. A few days later, I write to my mother. I tell her about the birth, but she never answers me. Really, it's okay. I am very busy just now.

Michelle

Ann Arbor, Michigan, June 1984

My dirty brown Toyota bumps into the driveway. I stop by the side door, turn off the car, and sit for a moment, glad to be still. In the backseat, a blonde-haired cherub regards me with half-mast blue eyes. How is it possible that I have borne a matchless Aryan specimen?

The backyard is thick with green—branches, bushes, unmowed grass. The dead sweetness of last week's lilacs is everywhere. Rusty swing set, a pink Barbie Big Wheels, a broken blue hula hoop, all the set for my latest piece, being played out around me, minute by minute. Sometimes I want to stop it, to drop the curtain, dissect the performance with spiky-haired friends, and go out dancing, but it won't be stopped. There's no going back.

I unload groceries (daughter has fallen asleep, still belted in; I'll let her stay there), put them away, put on water for coffee, take an aspirin. We have a breakfast nook, my husband and I do, and I sit in it, as I should, looking out into the yard.

Somehow, I am back in Ann Arbor. I have a house. I have a car. I have a sturdy, wise toddler who sucks me dry and loves me. I have a dance company, a cool studio, and a flat stomach. I get grants. I get massages. I get good reviews in the *Ann Arbor News*. I have friends who make me laugh. And, truly, much of this makes me happy. Why not? It would make anyone happy.

I check the mail, looking for surprises. Not long ago, someone put $20 in our mailbox with a note attached, a mystery. It said, "From someone who knows the value of giving and receiving." I know the value of receiving, but haven't much to give, it seems, only my time and sweat, only my body charging through space, or tiptoeing away from a crib at night, testing each floorboard for creaks.

Since the little girl was born, I've lost count of the dances made. The company's a scrappy, dedicated bunch, each dancer lushly physical, uniquely trained. I show them what to do, they show me. I find music, or write my own, using an antiquated four-track or begging friends with music studios. The latest work, just premiered last week, is *The Ferretworks*, and features musky dancers, frenzied onstage cooking, ritual worship, and a mechanized camel. The local reviewer, a meek and pleasant woman, didn't like this one. Good thing. I also showed

Baby, which accounts for the bruises on my hips and shoulders.

It's a simple dance in which I'm thrown onstage over and over, in a glittery costume until there's just no new way to land. Upstage left, three sleek, trashy nymphs watch over the process, leave, return. I end shouting expletives, in sign language. A woman came up to me after the show and said it made her cry. Makes me cry too sometimes, but the bruises are transient, and not of the sacred, sacral, chosen-one variety. Not like hers. I don't often think about that, actually.

I check the cherub, wander into the living room with my steaming cup, despair over the clutter. I'm in the midst of working on a grant. Piles of papers on the sofa, a spreadsheet on the dining-room table, copies of reviews, videotapes needing another edit. The board of directors met last night and divvied up narratives and budgets. The week will end with a grim collating bash at Kinko's and a hysterical dash to the post office at 11:55 PM to get the application package stamped with the correct date. If we're lucky, we'll get $8,000 to see us through the year, and we'll be happy with that, grateful. I'm becoming a respected artist.

I should be in New York, I know that. But I'm determined to make it happen here. "Michigan's a good base of operations," I've said to friends. "There's loads of cheap studio space, a vital arts council (second only to New York and California!), and plenty of dancers fresh from the university." I can make it here. I can. I've got it all figured out.

I go out to the car and open the back door quietly. It's really too hot to leave her out here, even with all the windows down. And mosquitoes, too, they might be out soon, marking her damp face. She's so relaxed she seems heavy, this little one; she smells of salt and some old cookie. I crook my hands under her soft arms and hoist. Nuzzle, nuzzle, soft cheek into my neck, best time of day. Whispering comforts to someone already blissful, I manage to open the door and bring her into the cool house and up to her room, which is decorated with stenciled pink dinosaurs. On the bed, there, she's a Botticelli, or what he meant to do, anyway, and I lie down next to her for a bit. This really is a very nice afternoon.

I wonder if I should think about what I'd be doing if I'd stayed in

New York. Should I take the time to miss the unpaced fury? The neverending rivers of noisy traffic? Technique classes forever in any of a hundred grimy lofts? Choreographic showcases? Dancing at auditions with the number 447 pinned to your breast? Waitressing? Torn ligaments, tendonitis, operations your parents have to pay for?

Somehow the idea that I might have succeeded there has never entered my mind. It's much, much easier not to think about this. Succeed. Suck-seed. Succeed.

I think, instead, back to a day last week, to a moment that, once experienced, has stuck to me like a burr:

I am in a hurry, as I often am, driving out to a cut-rate clothing store seeking cheap costume stuff for the show. It has been a long day of teaching, rehearsal, mediation between two dancers who are in a snit about something, numerous calls in search of a last-minute stage manager, checking in with the babysitter, feeling miserable for abandoning my child so that I can make dances for forty people in a dank garage-theater in Michigan. I'm hungry, dripping sweat, and my back hurts. At least it will be air-conditioned in the store; at least no one will be smearing chewed-up fruit leather on my leg; at least I'm alone for a moment.

I reach down and turn on the radio. A song's just starting. And right away, I know it's the song I've been waiting to hear. Christopher Flynn, the most fun member of my board of directors, has been spouting off about this song—her song—how she's hitting it big in New York, that her song's on the radio. Here it is. Here is my college roommate crooning a sultry, driving ditty about a borderline love, getting a hold on me. The sound is very hiss-pop-synth, very sleek and shiny. Years from now, I will know that sound to be very '80s. But today, it's just right, kind of cool, and to me, pretty much from another planet.

I flash to us whamming around in the Rubaiyat, her eyelids lowering at me through the dripping hair on her brow. Flash: a good word for this memory, this music. Same person, then and now. Same person. Person close to me, far from me. A broken continuum. A fork in the road. Gone. Split. Does she remember me? From the sound of this music, I doubt it, I really do.

I pull over to the side of the road and sit, listening. I'm smiling some wacky smile and here's what I'm thinking:

1. Al*right*, Madonna! Far-fucking-out! You did it! (Who'd ya step on? Who cares!)

2. *Well*, I can see that you've really been working on your *art* Madonna …

3. Sweetie, are you OK out there? Do you want to be part of this world that you're entering? Be careful!

Now, this last thought is mighty silly. Madonna Ciccone can take care of herself. But the others are pretty strong ones, each battling for supremacy, besides the fact that I am genuinely IN SHOCK, 'CAUSE I JUST HEARD MY LITTLE BOWL OF BEAR MUSH ON THE RADIO.

I laugh at myself, at the sudden surge of closeness I feel to her, despite the fact that I haven't spoken to her in a couple of years and mostly don't think about her. Must be a pretty widespread phenomenon among long-lost friends of lottery winners and meteoric-rise movie stars. Those old friends just start coming out of the woodwork, looking for a chance—any chance—to grab a handout, to wrangle an invite, to get interviewed in a documentary. I make a decision right then and there. I'm going to steer clear of that shit. Besides, this is probably just a flash-in-the-pan kind of thing. She's not a singer, right?

I listen in close for a moment. Is she a singer? Sounds pretty good, actually, in a doctored up sort of way. I like the song. Has a good beat and you can dance to it. Did she ever sing around me? No. Not that I can remember. Wait, there's one vague memory of her walking past me humming something—Bach, maybe. That's it. One hum-memory.

The song ends. I turn the radio off and sit listening to the passing cars, gripping the steering wheel. What is this feeling? Have I any way of labeling it? It's like driving through the desert on your way to Vegas and seeing a billboard filled with the face of your sister, whom you haven't seen in sixteen years, since she stormed out of the house in a fury. It's like scuba diving in the Cayman Islands, near a reef, and seeing a large white shape and finding, upon closer investigation, the refrigerator you had when you were a child, lying on the ocean floor. It's like reaching in the cookie jar and feeling, among the cookies and crumbs, the fingers of your mother. No, there is no way to understand this. Not for me.

My daughter stirs and looks at me. Huge blue eyes, white-blonde hair, one cheek marked by the folds of the sheet. She says this to me:
"Blabla. Juk."
In the kitchen, she plays with some cardboard blocks while I cut up a banana and pour some juice. I feed the young one and sit myself down for some serious thinking.
OK, these are the facts: This woman came into my life; I lived with her for nine months. She fascinated me, irritated me, moved me, taught me, took from me. I don't think she ever bored me. Maybe once. Someone in the friendship plant programmed a planned obsolescence into the whole affair and when things broke down, I never bothered to repair them. But before that, she lived with me and made me love her a little.
I have always loved easily so this is no grand pronouncement. And I think she loved me. I think she did. She said she did in that letter, and so, so many other times. I believed her. Why would I not? But I truly don't miss her at all. It was something of a relief to have her gone, to have her replaced with safer friends, ones without that calculated look of innocence and planning. Maybe in the back of my mind, a tiny, confused part of me wanted her to get beaten back. Maybe I wanted her to be like me, like the rest of us. You know what it is? I wanted her to be nice, someday. Nice and real and kind. And now, she's chomping up the world—thousands of fascinated people sign on each day—and her way is working for her.
Hmm. Fair enough.

That acknowledged, I can get on with my day. My baby walks sagely to my chair and stands in front of me. She bends down, puts her head on my knees, and sings me a song.

A few weeks later, I'm starting to understand that something extra big is going on with Madonna. I've had a phone call from some guy at the *Detroit Free Press* and have consented to do a phone interview, which goes pretty well, no big deal. I am happy to do it. For some reason, it's important for me to tell the world that she's no slouch, that she's a hard worker, driven, brilliant in her way, and that she deserves all of this attention. The man from the paper is very friendly. Much friendlier than when I called asking for a preview for my concert. I chat for a good bit and tell the world about this woman whom I'm starting to suspect I might not have really known all that well. While I chat with him, I doodle with a pen: squares within squares within squares.

But here's the real story: about a week after that, I get another call.

"Hello?"

"Ah, yes, I'm trying to reach ..." (vague rustling of papers, stammering—this means she can't pronounce my difficult name, I've heard it all before: Whitney, Whitey ...) "uh, Madonna's roommate?"

Sigh. "Yes, speaking. This is Madonna's roommate. Who's roommate is this?"

Laugh. "Well, hello, my name is Claire Peachum and I'm with a Japanese newspaper, *Osaka Today*. Perhaps you've heard of it ...?"

"Oh my God. I *love* that paper! I read it every day."

Pause.

"You do? Oh, that's great."

"Well, actually I was kidding."

"Oh. Well, we're calling to see if you might consent to be interviewed. You see, we're doing a highly in-depth piece on Madonna's early years and—"

"Her early years? That's all she's had are early years."

Laugh. "True, quite true. Um ... anyway, we're sending one of our top writers to the Detroit area. He'll be interviewing her family, going to her schools, taking lots of pictures—don't worry, this is a really classy piece and we'd like you to be a part of it. The Japanese people are absolutely trans*fixed* by Madonna. She's absolutely *hot* over there; everyone's just *des*perate for information. You really lived with her?"

"Well, actually, she lived with me."

"Can I tell my editor that you'll meet with Tsutomu?"

"Sure." What the hell ….

"Great! That's wonderful! I think you'll enjoy the experience. By the way, do you speak Japanese?"

No, I don't speak Japanese.

Claire suggests that I go get my appointment book so we can set up a time. There is a certain novelty in this whole business, and I fleetingly wonder if there might be a living in supplying information about Madonna to a spiritually thirsty world. Nah.

"Great, Whitney! We'll see you at your house next Thursday at 7. I'll be there to translate for you."

"Claire, it's Whit*ley*—with an 'L'. "

"Ahh, I'm sorry," says Claire. "That's such an interesting name. What did Madonna call you for short?"

"Oh, a wide variety of things—everything from 'Cabbage Head' to 'Shitley'."

"Um, well, that's great. Sounds as if you'll have some interesting tales for Tsutomu. We'll see you next week!"

I hang up the phone and lean heavily against the wall, wondering if this is a good idea. I decide it is. No expectations. It'll be an adventure. An incentive to clean house. About ten hours later, my eyes fly open in the midst of a paralyzing sleep. All is quiet in the house. Just the sound of my heart beating somewhat north of my chest cavity. I roll over and grab my notebook and a pen. Here is what I write:

Obviously, this call from Japan has made this dream happen. Very strange. I feel sad right now. It started with me working alone in an envelope factory. Beautiful sunset (sunrise?) shining in the windows, making all the envelopes, in piles all over the room, glow gold and orange. I felt out of place there, but knew what I had to do: open the flap of each envelope to see if it worked. At first all the envelopes were empty, then, more and more of them began to have newspaper clippings in them. I took each clipping out and let it waft to the floor, until there was a large pile of newsprint. It seemed very important that I not read the clippings. I felt vaguely annoyed that my work had been disrupted in this way. Then, I picked up the next envelope and noticed that it felt heavier than the others. Inside was an old-fashioned calling card, with a picture of a sprig of violets in the corner and a black thumbprint in the center. I knew that the print was Madonna's and that she was somehow in trouble; that this was her way of calling for help. Then, suddenly, I was riding a small horse, galloping down one of the factory hallways. As I passed doors, I would kick them open, looking for her, but each room contained the same thing: a painting of smiling, vapid children at a suburban birthday party. I got off the horse, which promptly disappeared. At the end of the hall was a bench next to a window. I sat down and tried to still my breathing, my heartbeat, to be very, very quiet, so that I might hear her calling me, but all I could hear was the sound of the horse, walking over rocks in some other, parallel dimension.

Then I heard it, her voice, right up next to my ear: "Whitley, Whitleeeee," in that kind of sexy, whiny, wanty way she had. For a moment, I was so scared of what I might see if I turned around—something with teeth? I could feel her breath on my cheek. Ugh. But I turned around and saw her, far, far away, on a distant hill, dancing all alone, spinning and flailing her arms and laughing. She was trying to show me she was fine and strong, that she didn't need me after all. Somehow, I didn't believe her, but I turned and walked down the hall, to my work. I looked behind me one last time, but all I could see through the window was a shifting ocean, a trick by a sneaky Magritte. She was gone, painted over, perhaps, by the waves.

On Thursday, I clean the house thoroughly, then go about my business. I'm teaching at the local community college. This semester, an easy load: beginning dance technique and beginning composition. There are five students in my comp class and not one of them has any idea what modern dance is, much less choreography. Community college means "slice of America." One's students are always a varied batch, and this term yields a burly bartender, two nursing students, and a skinny girl named Verna who comes to class each day with a rotating hickey. Most problematic, or rather "challenging," is An, a fiercely determined young man who has recently arrived from Vietnam and speaks not one word of English. I try, unsuccessfully, to imagine the interchange with his guidance counselor in which it was decided that he should study modern dance choreography. Together, we struggle over his battered English-Vietnamese dictionary, but I can't seem to find the words "retrograde" or "impulse" anywhere. But An knows what to do. No matter what I assign, he runs around the room.

"OK, guys, let's take ten minutes to improvise on change of level—abrupt change, gradual change …" An runs around the room.

"Great. Now, remember the eight-count phrases we made up last week? Try doing them again, but using movement qualities of the animal of your choice!" An runs around the room. The thing is, he moves well, better than Mitch the bartender, who's only after an easy A.

After class, it's a trip to the co-op where I think about the interview and ponder the interview beverage selection. Should I serve tea? Soy products? I'm unsure of the etiquette in situations like this, so I buy a date bar and eat it in the car on the way home.

At the agreed upon time, the husband takes the daughter on an outing, and I wait in my tidy house for the Japanese journalists to arrive and ask me questions about my college roommate who has recently been seen wearing a lot of white lace. I have white lace in the form of a tablecloth.

I read that she now wears a belt that says "BoyToy" on the buckle. What does "BoyToy" mean, anyway? Are her boys her toys? Are her toys all boys, i.e., Ken dolls? That could be dull and limiting. Or is she actually reveling in the fact that she is a toy of boys? Not a chance. She's no one's toy, never was. I notice I'm feeling rather heavy-lidded, like Alice, before she abandons her sister's drab book for a trip down the rabbit hole to Wonderland, when the doorbell rings.

Claire is dressed for success in a friendly way. She's carrying a large bag, a camera, and a tape recorder.

"Hello, Hi. Yes, it's nice to meet you too. Whitley, this is Tsutomu, but he'd like you to call him Tom."

Tom is wearing a nondescript dark suit and smiles profusely as I shake his hand, welcoming him into the house. I wonder if I should bow?

"Hello, hello," he says. Tom is enthusiastic.

We settle in the living room. Claire places the tape recorder on a table in front of me and we smile awkwardly for a few moments.

Tom speaks Japanese to Claire, then she turns brightly to me.

"So, Whitley. You lived with Madonna. Can you give us a little background information? How did this all come to be? That kind of thing?"

I tell them about coming to Ann Arbor, living in University Towers, needing a roommate. The basics.

"What was she like? What were your first impressions?"

I tell them she was fun, that she initially intimidated me, but that we became friends, that she seemed determined to be my friend. I don't tell them that I hated her at first, hated her 120-degree front extension, her cocky, ripped-up clothing, her blackly red lips, her patchy haircut. I don't tell them about the time on the street when she snatched a kiss from my lips then took off running to class, and how that kiss sent confusion ricocheting through my face and out the back of my head. Not sexual delirium—it was just a plunk—but a showering of questions. Why does this person like me? What does she want? Why did she try to scare me like that? I don't tell them about watching her run from me, dance bag banging into the crowd, until she was swallowed whole by the throngs.

We go on in this way for a while. There's only so much I can say about her; the rest tells more about me and that's not who's on the block here. I give my usual persuasive speech about her attitude, her hard work, her discipline. As Claire translates, Tom nods vigorously, or looks unsure. Sometimes, he takes notes on a legal pad.

"But what about her singing? Could you tell back then that she'd go so far as a singer?"

"Well, I heard her hum once!" I say.

There is a pause, then Claire translates what I've said into Japanese. Tom looks unsure again, asks her to repeat it, which she does. They both look at me. I decide to elaborate.

"And, yeah, it sounded pretty good, I guess. I didn't feel I was witnessing a nova in the firmament or anything, but sure, I guess I *might* have felt there was something there, some grand potential … if I had really thought about it." Does that sound sarcastic? I'm trying to be helpful. I really am.

Claire smiles blankly at me, then turns to translate. I have a sense that things are deteriorating, that I'm not telling them what they want to know. How can I tell them what they want to know? That we talked about masturbation for hours, that she wrote me love letters and never was my lover, that she belched like a linebacker, that she held me when I cried?

"Tell us about her dancing," suggests Claire. "Was she talented? Be honest!"

"Oh, I'll be honest," I say. "Yes, anyone could see she was talented, but she was more than that: Very musical, very passionate, very intellectual in her way. And she could be funny, too."

I tell them about the trio for Maddie, Patty, and Joel. Millions of Japanese need to know about this.

"But the best part of it," I say, enjoying the memory, "were the pratfalls. Joel taught us some really impressive ones, kicking our legs out from under ourselves and going splat on the floor … we were bruised for days. Madonna really got into it—she'd be holding some beautiful shape, then get this desperate look on her face, then: boom! Flat on the floor."

By this time, I'm demonstrating, being Madonna doing pratfalls, looking desperate. The house shakes.

"Then Joel would come and pick her up and throw her onto the windowsill. She'd cling there for a minute, then slide down the wall into a bony puddle on the floor. All to this gorgeous Bach music. God, that was fun."

I look up from my reverie. Claire has stopped trying to translate. I think the word "pratfall" has presented a stumbling block. Both she and Tom are somewhat openmouthed, trying to be polite, trying to figure out just what isn't quite clicking with this interview. I begin to realize that I'm not providing the kind of information they seek.

"What did you do together, when you weren't in school, I mean?"

I talk about scooping ice cream at Miller's, going to shows, going dancing (leaving out certain details), talking about books, and hitting thrift stores together. They still look unimpressed. I think they seek stories of impromptu in-class karaoke sessions in which Madonna might have suddenly jumped on a desk, stripped naked, and been overtaken by the spirit of Elvis. Unfortunately, this type of thing did not happen. Well, there was the time when she was rehearsing for a dance version of the Stations of the Cross at an Ann Arbor church and got up on the altar and sang "Good Golly, Miss Molly." But I wasn't there. I only heard about it from everybody else.

"I'm sorry," I say. "I guess this isn't really all that interesting. She was a good friend and I knew her well, but a lot of our interaction was relatively ... normal."

Claire reassures me and asks a few more token questions to which I give token answers.

"What was her dancing like?"

"Well, you know, it was like, I don't know, really good. She was a good, strong dancer, very flexible."

"Did you meet her family?"

"Uh, yes, I met her father and stepmother once. We went out for ice cream. They were nice."

"Are you in touch with Madonna now?"

"No, not at all. We didn't part on bad terms or anything. We just grew apart, I guess."

They leave soon after, in their big, blue, American-made rental car, with more smiles and handshakes and promises to send me a copy of the finished article, which they never do. And I use this rare opportunity—with no one in the house, and only myself to please—to curl up on the couch and doze.

I dream, briefly, about nothing at all.

Fifteen minutes later, the doorbell. She's on the front stoop, looking serious, little Michelle Quiggle from down the street. Great kid, this one, about nine, with straight strawberry-blonde hair, a few freckles, and the voice of a dawning Bacall. Such a hoot to hear her talk. You can almost see a cig dangling from her grubby, ragged, chipped-pink fingertips.

"Michelle. What's up? Do you want to come in?"

"No."

Silence. She looks around the neighborhood.

"Well, what do you want, Sweetie? There's no one to play with here. I'm the only one home."

"Well, somebody told me something about you and I wanted to ask you if it was true."

"OK."

"Devin said his mom read in the paper that you were Madonna's best friend."

"Devin was right. But that was a long time ago. I haven't talked to her in a long, long time."

"Why? Don't you like her anymore? Hey, I have an idea, why don't you invite her to come over for dinner at your house? I could come over when she was here and I could help you clean up after …"

"That's sweet, Michelle, but I'm just not her friend anymore. I still like her, I guess, but I just don't know her anymore. And she doesn't know me."

Michelle screws her mouth into a frown and sighs.

"Oh, Okaaaaayy," she says, dejectedly.

"Did you want to tell her something? You could write her a letter, maybe."

"Naah," she says, turning away and walking down the front steps. "See ya."

"Michelle, wait a minute."

Upstairs, I rummage in my drawer, pulling out shirts and sweaters by the handful.

"Here. This is for you." I hand Michelle a tattered white shirt with a low scoop neck. It's so worn that it's almost transparent. Maddie loved that shirt, loved to dance in it. It clung to her body in the most delightful way, yet moved and swayed when she turned. It's one of the few things of hers that I have left. In a few years I may be tempted to sell it at a celebrity auction to raise money for the company. Better that little Michelle Quiggle has it.

"What is it?" she says flatly.

"It's for you. It was hers."

"Madonna's? This was Madonna's? Her shirt?" Her gravelly voice breaks in excitement.

"Yup. She wore it lots of times. It was one of her favorites, in fact."

She narrows her eyes and looks at me, grinning.

"You're puttin' me on …"

"No, no, I'm not. I really knew her. She wore it and now you can wear it."

"Do I have to give it back?"

"No way. You keep it and tell all your friends that you're wearing Madonna's shirt and if they don't believe you, you tell them to come talk to me."

She takes off down the steps and hurtles down the sidewalk, crosses the street, and runs toward her own house. Forgetting I'm watching, she stops near the big pine tree and looks at the shirt, then, tentatively pulls it over her head. She stands perfectly still under the tree for a moment, then begins to dance, just for a second—sweet, silly girl. A car nears. She whips the shirt off and runs for home. A moment later, I hear her screen door slam.

Truth or Dare

In 1989, after taking a year off from music to explore the theater, Madonna puts out "Like a Prayer." I learn this many years later from some book.

In 1989, after taking nine years to explore futility, I leave my husband.

It's really a no-brainer. We have both gotten to the point where our sanity has become endangered. And if one or both of us ends up in Mercywood, well, that wouldn't be good for the kids. There is another child now, a little boy named Sam with big brown eyes.

One night, after a particularly acidic fight, something changes in me and I know, suddenly, amid the crashing of furniture and the fists slamming against walls, that it is time. Barefoot, I run from the house and sprint through our dark and sedate neighborhood. I run until my breath tears at me like a claw. I stagger home and go up to the bedroom, our bedroom, where my son was born three years before. Rex is out back in the shed moving things around. And there, while my breathing slows and my axis spins in ancient ways, I hear a strange and terrifying sound, like a frantic, distant murmuring of something evil. It's coming from outside. I approach the window and peer out. Do you know what I see? I will tell you, if you promise to believe me. Coming up the street, in the pink glow of the street lamp, are about fifty raccoons, running at full speed. It's a goddamn river of whimpering, shrieking raccoons. Big, fat ones. Little baby ones. Mamas, grandpas with little raccoon beards. I take it as a sign. As they skitter past my house I throw myself away from the window and onto my bed, where I lie for a long time with my hands over my ears.

About two days later, when Rex is out and the children are napping, I get the paper and gingerly open to the classifieds. Apartments for rent. Tears splat onto the newsprint as I circle a couple of two-bedroom possibilities. I need something to write on. Where's a notepad? Anything. The closet's open and inside is an old box of junk I've been meaning to go through. School stuff. I grab a bunch of folded papers and copy landlord phone numbers onto a corner. Then, curious, I unfold the packet. It is Madonna's long-ago letter to me. The Christmas letter. I read a few pages. I study the words, looking for some wisdom, some message, but there is nothing there for me. Just her interesting penmanship and a bit of lively writing, old memories of someone else's winter. Hi Madonna, I say. I fold it back up and go look for another piece of paper. It occurs to me that maybe I should save it.

It doesn't matter that I know this divorce is the right thing to do. It doesn't matter that when I leave my beloved home and shut the door behind me, I never look back. It doesn't matter that I have the support of my family, friends, and therapist. Divorce is way worse than labor. It's like a long, slow flaying. One where you have to smile and make pretty for the children.

I certainly follow the economic path of the divorced mother. The bewildered children and I leave Rex in the big, nice house and move into a tiny flat where everything is beige. I give each child a bedroom and sleep in the living room on a foldout futon. Friends give or lend me furniture. I borrow a framed print of a Gauguin painting, and when the kids go to stay with their father on the weekends, I spend hours staring up at it. Naked women and rich colors in the hot sun in the beige apartment. It comes to mean quite a lot to me, that painting.

My daughter, now eight, reacts to all these changes by throwing enormous tantrums every time she has to go back to the old house. Her dad is hurt, I am alarmed, and her little brother just stands there, wide-eyed, watching the tempest. I finally discover the antidote: feeding her a hot bowl of creamed corn. As soon as she eats this, she becomes her usual reasonable self and heads off with her father. Del Monte stocks climb mysteriously.

There's no way to adequately describe the loneliness of getting a divorce when you're living in an apartment with two bewildered children. In my guilt, I do everything I can think of to cheer the kids. There's no way I can be in each of their rooms at the same time to put them to sleep, so I sit on the floor between their doors and sing endless folk songs until their breathing becomes a sweet, minimalist symphony. And then I just go in the other room and watch TV until I fall asleep. At Christmas, I buy the biggest, lushest tree I can find, and haul it up the stairs where it completely fills the tiny living room with the smell of upper Michigan and the soft color of hundreds of blinking lights. Like the Gauguin, the tree shoots me up with color, something

I didn't know I needed so badly. For the weeks that it's up, I don't have to watch any TV at all; I just look at the tree, then up to Gauguin, then back to the tree.

I'm broke, of course, but determined. The one good thing is that through all this misery, my dance company has been thriving. Through the efforts of my dear and brilliant board of directors, we get every grant we apply for, and then some. Just for teaching company class and rehearsing three times a week, I am now paid $600/month, a seemingly impossible sum. I have five magnificent dancers who take my ideas and sculpt them and send them flying. We do full concerts in Ann Arbor twice a year, standing-room only, and tour a bit too: Boston, Chicago, Detroit, Grand Rapids.

The market we can't crack is New York. Diane, my feisty board president, has put in about six months of phone calls trying to get us a booking there. It's critical, she says. It's vital to the success of the company, she says. You deserve to have your work seen, she says. She's right, of course. I guess.

Diane, by the way, is also magnificent. Every struggling Midwestern choreographer/mom of confused children needs a Diane to push her along. Mysteriously, Diane does not seem to have a job. I haven't quite figured it out and she isn't offering any details. All I know is that one day in 1984, she showed up at one of my concerts, came up to me afterward, and said that if I wanted to have a company, she'd make it happen. And she has done just that. Diane is of indeterminate age. She has the blackest hair and the whitest skin and the reddest lips and is from "outside Philly." She giggles wildly. She reminds me of a Jewish geisha. She is a good friend and, best of all, an honest, ruthless critic born of a lifetime of watching dance from all over the world.

Without thinking too much about it, I said okay to Diane's backstage suggestion and within three months of our first meeting, she had assembled a board of directors, had a lawyer drawing up the 501 C3 status forms, and was busy raising money. Today, seven years later, she is proud of all we've accomplished, but is ready to move us up to the next level, as it were.

The next level, of course, is New York. My hometown. She spends hours trying to get someone—anyone—with a good performance series in the city to take a chance on a company from the Midwest. She finally manages to snag the guy who's the head of Dance Theater Workshop, the renowned theater on West 19th Street, where I bombed so long ago with Maddie and Patty and me dancing around like Buddhists. About forty dances later, I really have come a long way since then. Here are some of the dances I have made:

The Rachel Trilogy: three dances with text in three different literary styles, about the ill-fated love between someone named Rachel and an intergalactic spaceship captain, with music by Nat King Cole. Ends in a postapocalyptic landscape in which my partner and I wear a lot of powder and move tin cans around.

Salad Days: About forty minutes from Ann Arbor, I discover a family of organic farmers who homeschool their young boys. These precocious children have made a tape of themselves singing Elvis Presley songs. They even play all the instruments. It's strange and phenomenal. So I use it to make a twenty-minute piece about childhood.

Handmaiden: A quartet about midwives set to the rhythmic chanting of the Balinese "ketchak." My ladies dance the crap out of this one, and I sell it to a company in Boston, too, and make enough to pay two months of rent.

Charlotte: Life? or Theater?: Someone loans me a book about Charlotte Salomon, a young Jewish artist who created over a thousand gouache renderings of her life in the form of "a play with music." The State of Michigan funds a full-evening work based on Charlotte's work. It's the biggest thing I've ever done, with a commissioned score and set, four actors and seven dancers. Parts of it are pretty good.

Anyway, the guy from DTW scoffingly tells Diane that "there is no dance in Michigan" and that's that. He actually snorts. She's furious but I tell her I don't mind. I didn't want to go dance for his sorry, geocentric ass anyway.

And in truth, I don't, particularly. I mean, if he—or anyone, anywhere—called up and asked us to perform, that would be great. We'd be there in a heartbeat. Oh, I love to perform, not a doubt. I live for it. When I stand backstage waiting to go on, or sit out in the house, watching my dancers' elfin selves tramping about, jumping, making interesting sense and mystery of music and language, I feel tremendously happy. But making it *happen*—in some hostile, choreographer-saturated city—that's a whole other deal. The phone calls, the letters, the forms, the follow-up calls, the friend-of-a-friend at such-and-such theater ... And the *videotapes*, let's not forget the misery of late 1980s-era "promotional video tapes" that dismember your dances and make everyone onscreen look vaguely wide and swishy. No, I don't thrive on self-promotion. In fact, it appears that I am almost completely a drive-free individual.

But that doesn't mean I don't want to succeed. When Diane corners me, as she does from time to time and insists that I tell her what exactly I do want, I always say the same thing: I want the respect of my peers and enough money to survive. At this point in my life, these seem lofty enough goals.

About this time, we are chosen as one of only a few arts organizations in Michigan to get "fast tracked" to some serious funding. By serious funding I mean $60,000 a year for three years. In return, we will make tons of dances, give tons of free performances, and be a constant presence in lots of underprivileged public schools. The application process has taken several years, with the State "grooming" us for readiness to handle such a massive fiscal responsibility. But I'm flattered and go to all the necessary meetings.

Then, just months before it's all slated to happen, the good people of Michigan elect John Engler to be their governor, and one of his first acts on the job is to dismantle our arts council. So, overnight, we're back to my board gently suggesting that I try to contact Madonna for a handout. Don't worry; I would never, ever do that.

Obviously, I'm not living on $600/month. I have what almost every artist in America has: a day job. Actually, I have many day jobs. Here are some of the day jobs I have had:

Writer: I write freelance for the *Ann Arbor News*, at $70 a pop, covering arts events. I phone up Soupy Sales from the apartment while looking severely at the children to get them to stop fighting because dammit I'm interviewing Soupy Sales. I interview talk show host Jenny Jones. I interview performance artist Karen Finley, who gets mad and hangs up on me because I ask the wrong question. I interview Pete Seeger and when I'm done, I even write a note and tell my mom about it because at one time, she would have gotten a kick out of it. She really liked Pete Seeger. She doesn't write back.

I write a daily events column called Admit One where I look at the press releases people send in and turn them into snappy little grafs with snappy little headlines. They pay me $35/column and I do six a week, so that adds up. I learn to be very snappy. I write about food for Ann Arbor's famed Zingerman's Deli. I write promo for a Detroit theater company. I write promotional one-sheets for local musicians. I write the menu for a crepe restaurant.

Teacher: Drive an hour. Take off clothes. Put on sweats. Teach movement and musicality to college students. Get all hot and stretchy. Get back in car. Get Burger King fish sandwich on way to highway. Drive home. Put ice on back. Over and over and over. This makes it sound like a grind. Actually, I love teaching.

Museum public relations coordinator: not a good fit for me, but full benefits for everybody.

Medical writer: Actually a pretty fun gig. Sometimes get to watch operations.

Music provider at school for profoundly disabled: an amazing gig.

Artist model: take off clothes, lie around, get $18. At this point in my life, this is only for when I'm really desperate.

Video choreographer #1: Sleazy guy hires me to create "aerobic/marshal arts" movement for a video series. Also involves pretending to be mugged in a dark stairwell wearing pumps and pantyhose that the sleazy guy picks out for me at TJ Maxx. Plus side: I get to beat the guy up with my pumps. When I get all famous like Madonna, this is the tape that will most embarrass me. You guys can start looking for it now. I'm not worried.

Video choreographer #2: Forward-thinking project manager in the State of Michigan court system hires me to choreograph movement for an instructional video stressing the importance of compassion. Well, that's pretty cool.

Commissions: Now this is work. Word gets out that there's this drive-free choreographer in Michigan who has tons of dances and will work for cheap. Companies (or colleges and universities) call me up and in essence "rent" a dance for a year or two. I travel to where they are, teach the dance, polish it up, work with the lighting designer, talk to the press, and collect a tidy sum. I love commissions. I get commissions all over Michigan, and two in Boston, and one in Buffalo.

Backup singer: Well, this is unexpected. I somehow fall into singing backup in a very successful folk/rock band headed by a local songwriter. We sing at huge music festivals across the country. We close the Saturday night show at the Vancouver Music Festival in front of five thousand people, we play Mountain Stage, open for Taj Mahal at the Bottom Line in New York City. The money's great, I learn a ton about arranging music, and the friendship is hugely satisfying, but after a while I realize I'm spending an awful lot of time supporting someone else's work.

Professional Madonna expert: By now, I'm starting to ask for money. I actually go on *Lifestyles of the Rich and Famous*. The editors twist my words and make it sound like Madonna and I were lesbians. They even show me standing wistfully on a bridge over the Huron River as if I am a-pinin' for my long-lost darlin'. But I'm not bitter or outraged when I see the show. I knew exactly what I was getting into. When you play in the sewer, you're gonna get slimed. Besides, I take comfort in two things: no one I know watches this show, and people who do watch it forget everything in it after five minutes, so I'm pretty safe. I take my $700 and pay some back rent.

And thus, I piece a life together for me and the kids.

After a year in the beige apartment, Rex and I are formally divorced and my dad helps me put a down payment on an old house next to a lumberyard. It's an ugly asbestos-coated thing, but I love that house. At night, freight trains shake me awake, and in the mornings it's the beeping, growling forklifts—but it's my own, my salvation, and my freedom. I patch and plaster and paint and clean. It never gets really nice, but it's filled with wood and character and has a fireplace. Upstairs, under some nasty green shag carpeting, I find some 30s-era linoleum, which I polish to a high sheen. They just don't make linoleum like that any more. I pull down all the nasty wallpaper, patch all the plaster, and paint the walls a pretty pale apricot. On Sunday afternoons, the kids and I play baseball in the lumberyard parking lot. From the upstairs bathroom window, the storage sheds of the lumberyard look like a Hopper painting in the sun. I plant a garden. We get two kittens. We do our best.

Of course, we have to have a roommate. There's no way to make the house payment on the salary of a choreographer/freelance writer/Madonna expert. The first one is Yuri, an illegal Russian with a weakness for vodka and a penchant for being mean to little boys, but before I learn this we're all sitting around the living room one Saturday afternoon. Yuri has invited some friends over to watch *Truth or Dare*, the new Madonna movie. I don't want to watch this movie, but it's TV and I tend to watch TV, so I am soon sitting on the bottom step of the stairway, chin in my hand, peering around the balustrade, sort of watching it.

It is sooooo strange. There she is, Madonna, utterly herself, but utterly different from the girl I knew. The things I see that punch me in the stomach are not the gyrations, nor the fuck-this fuck-that language, nor even the notorious bottle-slobbering scene. Of course she's gonna do that stuff. But little things pop off the screen: the way she flicks her hand, the occasionally overprecise speech, the occasionally Brooklynesque speech, that signature Earth-shoe style rolling walk across a stage during sound check: heel-toe, heel-toe, heel-toe. I recognize these things, these relics of earlier simplicity, this stray "her-ness" that flits out between the cracks in the script.

Now, I've never had any serious thoughts about contacting Madonna, much to the chagrin of my board. But there are fleeting moments when I wonder how that would go. I've dreamed about it, I think. They are meetings of an entirely ordinary nature, where we're back to being twenty, so new and guileless. Now that we're all grown up, it might be nice to just check in. You know, the occasional let's go out for a drink when you're in town kind of thing. I do that with lots of my old friends from school. I love keeping in touch with people. Linda's married a wonderful yachtbuilder. Patty teaches at NYU. Joel is married and living in Brooklyn. Loi's in Germany dancing and teaching. This contact, it's normal and fun. It's part of how we gauge the passage of our lives. But Maddie's got a bad case of Famous Person's disease. She caught it from the world, though of course she was born with a strong genetic predisposition to the condition. The result: there's simply no way to talk to her anymore. I don't want to talk to somebody if I have to go through a publicist. That would be distasteful.

Well, let's see. There are, I have to admit, a couple of celebrities in front of whom I might grovel obsequiously in some way. Number one would have been the Queen: Lucille Ball. Number two would be Dolly Parton, who appears to be beauty, brilliance, and humility all rolled into one zaftig, mountain-fresh package. Of course, Dolly, as much as I love her, is barely on the same chart as Lucille Ball. Number three? I just can't think of anyone else who truly fascinates … I mean, there are lots of celebrities I like a lot, and enjoy seeing. I will admit to having had a serious Michael York jones when I was in junior high school and he was in *Cabaret*. Oh man.

So when people ask me, breathlessly, "Are you still in touch with her?" I tell them, "No, I haven't seen her since 1980," and wonder if there's something wrong with me for not being particularly distraught about it.

These thoughts are idling about in my head as I'm sneaking a peek at Madonna: *Truth or Dare* when something horrible happens. The director appears to have orchestrated a meeting between Madonna and a childhood friend who is lurking in a hotel lobby. The camera is on the woman, as she waits and talks nervously about her memories of Madonna, jumping on the bed together and so forth. Then her eyes light up as Madonna approaches. The two hug. Madonna is stiff but valiantly tries to be gracious—come on, this has to be awkward. The woman, in a polka dot dress, can't take her eyes off her old friend, drinks her in. Madonna has perfectly round sunglasses on so I can't see her eyes. They talk and smile and stammer. She asks Madonna to bless her unborn child and make it be a girl, as if Mad has any particular influence with the sex assignment gods. So Madonna jokingly blesses. The woman says she wants Madonna to be godmother to the baby. Don't worry, it's not religious, just spiritual, she says. Uh-oh. Madonna, sensibly, doesn't commit, says to be sure her assistant has all the right phone numbers, says she will call soon, promise.

She backs away, but the woman stops her and gives her a gift of a painting she has made, an abstract Madonna and child. And the cameras roll as Madonna takes the painting and goes off down a hall. "I love you, Madonna!" calls the woman. "I love you too," says Madonna, briskly hustling herself and her Alpine fame away, disappearing into a doorway. And this settles it. Any remote subparticle of a desire I may harbor to seek Maddie out in any way gets zapped with a ray gun. Well, at least I don't have to think about that any more!

I rarely have nightmares, but that night I wake up crying. I'm not frightened as much as deeply and profoundly sad. I have been dreaming about Madonna, but for some reason, the plot is too hazy to grasp; I just know she's there somewhere, lurking about in a wash of runny images, smiling down on the scene with red, red lips.

My children are at their dad's, Yuri's room is in the basement at the other end of the house, so I'm all alone and I just cry into my hands for about ten minutes. What has made me feel this way? I get up, get a drink of water, and splash some in my eyes. Usually, the wet cold on my face will pull me insistently into reality but tonight it doesn't help much. I go back into my room and sit in my bed with the covers pulled up to my neck. I don't want to lie down yet. If I lie down, I might fall back into that feeling … of what?

What I am feeling is a bottomless, sharp jealousy and ripped-offness, I think. Mixed with a terrible sense of being utterly left behind and alone. I'm pretty sure this all has something to do with seeing the Madonna movie, but what, precisely, is the catalyst? After all, I have been blessed with: two magnificent children, a life that has allowed me to create and perform, good friends, good health … why should I feel so dissatisfied? Am I dissatisfied? I think hard about what I have just seen: my old friend padding around in a fluffy, white bathrobe in luxury hotel suites, dancing confidently before thousands of screaming, adoring people, cool sets and lights and interesting costumes. Boundless money. Perfect breasts. A flat stomach. Pearls you can wear to bed.

I think back to how I felt when the film was over, and everyone was sitting around the living room talking about it. Yuri and his friends thought it was great. I wasn't so sure. I mean, when a camera is filming "private moments," are they "private" anymore? I know if I had a big old Armenian film director in my bedroom filming me as I went to sleep, I'd sure be sleeping a bit more self-consciously. And there are things in that film that make me feel very strange. Basically, it kind of scares me that the scrappy, funny, little girl I used to hang with could turn into the person in that movie. A person adorned with sycophants and flunkies. A person who shops at Chanel. A person with a handler. A person with an entourage. Someone so ... *coiffed*.

But these aren't reasons to wake up in tears. So, what's going on?

In the dim light shining from the lumberyard, I look around my room. Splintered floor, a few old rugs. Futon bed covered with old family quilts. A chest of drawers that was in this house when I moved in. My hands move across my body. I am still strong, I've always had muscles, but two pregnancies, and four years total of nursing babies have changed my earthly frame in ways that leave me wistful sometimes. I have no money. I have no health insurance.

What am I doing? Am I comparing? Am I comparing myself to her? Is this why I have been torn from sleep and tossed into a dark meadow of tears? After four years of weekly therapy I should be able to figure this out. What was the trigger? Was there one scene in that movie that rings this particular bell?

I light a candle and sit there, going through the film, as best as I can remember it, at 4:14 in the morning. Madonna standing on a Japanese arena stage plugging her ears over feedback and yelling at a sound guy. Madonna leading her nightly preshow prayers and getting teary. Madonna rolling around in her bed with her handsome, chiseled dancers. Crowds of Italians chanting, "Ma-don-na! Ma-don-na!" Madonna in the cemetery wondering what her mother looks like now, under the ground.

The cemetery. My breath stops and my mouth goes slack. My eyes fill with tears and turn the streetlight through my window to streaks and stars. This girl's face twists once again and falls into her hands. Cry, cry, cry.

In the film, between her concerts in Detroit, Maddie goes to a cemetery to visit her mother's grave. She walks alone through the headstones (of course she is miked, and there's a film crew somewhere taking it all in, but okay, it's a "private" moment). She finds where her mother is buried. "Madonna Fortin Ciccone" says the flat, gray stone. It is very simple and unpretentious. There's a quiet overdub where she remembers her mom, how feminine and gentle she was, how like an angel, how it was such a mystery when she left. And she lays down on the grave and softly blows at some lilies she has placed on the stone.

And here it is. So simple. Why I'm jealous, why I'm crying. Madonna's mother is dead. *("She's-dead-she-died," she says, too fast, and singsong—like a little kid repeating something she heard somewhere.)* But Maddie can go to her, lie down at her side, and imagine that somewhere, somehow, she's getting through, making contact. She knows her mother loved her, didn't want to leave, would have done or given anything to stay with her, with all her children. Madonna has no one to blame but death. She can yell and punch the pillows and sing sad songs. She can think of her mom and honor her and talk about her with her siblings. She can look at her picture and smile. She can remember her and the memories will be sweet.

I miss my mother too. My mother is dead to me. She does not call me on my birthday. She does not come out for Christmas. We don't have a favorite place to go shopping. She has never seen my dances. She has never seen my children, or heard their voices. If I write to her she will not answer.

I flash back to last week, Saturday morning: I was sitting on my front steps watching the forklifts amble by with their burdens of stacked and fragrant pine. The sun was warm on my face, and I was just thinking about planting something in my tiny front yard when the UPS truck pulled up in front of the house. The UPS truck never comes to my house. But the guy took a big box from the back and came down my walk with a smile.

"Package!" he said.

"Thank you," I said, mystified. What is this? A present!

I took it from him, turned it over. Strange thing was my name and address were printed twice on the plain brown cardboard: in both the address and the return, the letters printed in a bright and slightly curly penmanship, the hand of a friendly schoolteacher.

Postmark, New York City. Uh-oh.

I went inside and got a knife and sliced open the tape. Inside: the last tendrils of my childhood, tossed together like a salad. Letters from camp; my third-grade report card; birthday cards; schoolwork from elementary school ("Water: In, Around, and About!") all the way up to my first years of college ("The Wife of Bath: an Analysis and Criticism"); a program from the New York Philharmonic from 1970; a picture of Suzanne Farrell cut from a magazine. I went through it all, page by page, looking for a note, but of course there was none to be found. So I just spent some time looking at the address, and the return address, running my fingers over the place where she had written my name, trying to remember her hands. After a while I took the box upstairs and put it in the closet, way in the back.

And now I sit there staring at my closet door. I take a damp, balled-up Kleenex and throw it at the door as hard as I can, but it doesn't even make it past the foot of my bed.

If I call her … well, I no longer call. I tried calling a couple of years ago, on the advice of a therapist who felt I desperately needed "closure." I chose a Saturday. And I stood in the kitchen, my heart pounding so hard I could barely dial the number. I clutched the counter as she answered.

"Yes?" My mother does not say hello.

"Hi. It's me."

"Yes."

"I just need to know … if … if we will ever see each other again—"

And this is pretty much the end of the conversation. It gets loud, it gets frightening. I hang up. A couple of weeks later, she sends me a letter—just one and never again—in which she apologizes for screaming at me and says, for what it's worth, that all this *is not my fault* but she will not explain it further.

It's not my fault. Well, I thought not, but it's nice to be sure.

And she writes—typed of course—that if in the future it becomes "profitable" for us to make contact, she will call me.

Profitable.

So, I don't call. And I don't exactly wait for her to call. I go about my business. I love my children. I love my father. I love my friends and am loved in turn by all these.

There are times when the strangeness of my situation becomes overwhelming: when people I'm just getting to know ask me about my mom, with friendly, expectant faces. I have found that there are ever so many ways to tell people what has happened, and that none of them really meets my needs. Here are some of my most popular explanations:

1. "Oh, my mom disowned me. I'm not sure why."
2. "Oh, I haven't seen her since 1980. She's a bit of a hermit."
3. "My mom? Oh my God. Total nutcase."
4. "I don't really have a mother. She left the family. We don't know where she is."
5. "Oh, well, she has some problems. I don't see her. It's very sad."
6. "My mom? She lives in New York. We're not particularly close."

I never say that she is dead though. I have not been able to bring myself to do that.

Let me be clear. I understand why she was hurt and upset. I understood it then, and now that I have children of my own, I suppose I understand it even more. Yes, my life was derailed. But new tracks were built and I went someplace new. Has it been so very bad? No, it has not been so very bad. It is life, messy and mine, and filled with beauty. I have no regrets.

When I see my friends with their mothers, or overhear them talking on the phone, well, that stings a bit, but I just try and think about something else. By far the worst part is just not knowing if she ever loved me at all. If all the pillow notes and trips and the conversations and the stroking of the feverish foreheads were some kind of elaborate drama. Try as I might—and oh, do I try—I can't figure it out.

And so when I go to New York and take the E or F train to my old neighborhood, I stand across the street next to the florist, looking up at the window where my bed was, or the kitchen window, or the one in the living room, next to the radiator. And I know, with a smile that is still, after all these years, incredulous, that I am not welcome there.

I am jealous of my old friend, as she kneels beside her mom and talks to her, touches the grass. My mom is alive to everyone but me. My mom walks the earth. She eats and sleeps and travels. She is a hard worker. By all reports, she is still a good person. She volunteers. But to me, my mother is as gone as yesterday.

The Value of Their Hard Work

In 1993, the National Endowment for the Arts publishes the results of a study that examines the lives of American choreographers. It's free to anyone who requests it so I call for a copy.

It's very interesting.

I've considered myself a professional choreographer for almost ten years now. My company has grown, struggled, rallied, triumphed, waned, disappeared, reappeared, and so on, in response to the whims of granting agencies and the national economy. We have many wonderful supporters by this time, folks of all ages and backgrounds who come to our shows, respond to mailings, and supply us with in-kind donations like cheesecakes for afterglow receptions and bagels for board retreats. The press, including *Dance* magazine, has said lovely things about my work and the people who perform it. I get a few outside commissions per year. Plus I teach, teach, teach. All this, along with the hack writing, makes a meager but honest living for this American choreographer and her two wide-eyed, tow-headed bambini. I mean, this is all I've ever wanted: to dance and make dances. I guess I'm doing it.

I just never dreamed that after all this time it would still be this hard. I never expected to make a lot of money, but this? Can this be right? I suspect that living out here in between official coasts (where, as we all know, all the *real* artists live and work), I have no sense of the bigger picture and where I stand in it. Perhaps the NEA study will tell me what I want to know: am I a success in my field?

When it comes, I settle into my old green velvet couch, click on the light next to me, and tear open the envelope. The foreword includes these words:

"Choreographer" is what we call someone who makes dances, a dance maker. Just as composer is what we call someone who makes music, "makes" in the sense of creates or calls into being.

In numbers, choreographers are among the smallest of this country's population of professional art makers. But their work is acclaimed worldwide and seen by millions—on concert stages, in musical theater, in operas, in the movies and on television, and in music videos…

The life of a choreographer is beset with difficulties, beginning with the need for human bodies—dancers—to work with, and appropriate spaces in which to create, rehearse, and perform the dances...

This study's findings are bleak, especially as they reveal the exceptionally low economic status of choreographers compared with their uncommonly high educational levels, the lack of adequate outlets for their work to be seen by the public, and the abject lack of basic amenities that other professionals regard as entitlements, such as health insurance, a predictable income, advancement at an appropriate stage of development and achievement, and an acknowledgement of the value of their hard work.

Tears fill my eyes. "... *an acknowledgement of the value of their hard work.*" It is amazing to read these words. And then this:

Our choreographers turn out in the main to be women in their midyears who cannot look forward to a better life ahead.

And I realize I'm going to have to read this study in little fits and starts. I get in the car and go get a root beer float from the Washtenaw Dairy, just on the other side of the railroad tracks, then come back home and sit down to read more about my life.

Of course, no one asked them to be choreographers, the foreword continues. *It isn't as though being a choreographer in the United States were valued, by and large. It isn't a common career choice. Nor is it written anywhere that choreographers should expect to make a decent living from making dances. Nonetheless, the Arts Endowment believes that choreographers perform service of the highest public importance: the fruits of their work make visible the strivings of our people, our dreams and hopes, our nightmares and disillusions, our times and the times and values of those who preceded us. Perhaps only at such time that our society values art and artists more can choreographers look forward to a decent standard of living from their professional calling.*

And so on. I skip ahead to the section on finances because I'm suddenly burning to know just where I stand in the scheme of things. I learn, among other things, that an American woman choreographer like me makes about $4,700 a year from her work, including grants.

This means ... I am average. Some years, I am slightly better than average. I am thrilled and proud. I never dreamed this. All this time I have been under the impression that my poverty has been due to some intrinsic artistic mediocrity. All this time, I have been in very good company. So I strut around the house for a while reveling in my averageness as an American choreographer, tossing off the ancient mantle of failurehood I have worn so long, until something stops me in my tracks.

$4,700 a year is average? This must mean that those at the tippy-top of my chosen profession must be making, what? $15,000 a year? Hmmm. And then I see something truly startling. Check this out:

Survey data show that the average income from choreography for men is about twice that for women, whether or not grants are included. (Grants to men average about 50 percent more than grants to women.) There is no obvious explanation for this; the female respondents were more highly educated than the males and about as experienced ...

My field. My career. My art.

I suppose I could spend a lot of time muttering about inequity and going "grrrr," and thinking about how rich Madonna is and how with one swipe of her feathered pen she could endow a whole new nonsexist arts funding organization, but in fact, that never occurs to me until just now. In fact, life just goes on. There are people who think they can change the world and I applaud them. There are people who do change the world and I thank them. And then there are people like me who just live in an untidy world where not everything is fair.

I've never been particularly political—probably my biggest personal flaw—and for that reason, I don't think I have much right to do any serious whining. The information from the study does affect me somewhat; it pisses me off. It doesn't make me give up, but I do notice myself casting about for other outlets. Monologues? Music? Just in case I might want to teach full-time in a university, I go get a Masters in Performance Studies. Might come in handy.

There's always midwifery. My fascination with baby-having has grown more or less continuously since that long-ago evening crouching on the floor of Laco Books on South University reading *Spiritual Midwifery* for the first time. How many births have I been to by now? Maybe twenty? There's a quiet community of midwives in town, and I make it my business to get to know almost all of them. They know that if they're ever in a situation where they need an extra pair of hands, they can give me a ring. If I'm not onstage, I'll be there.

Helping a woman have a baby is like improvisation, but with a thick and practical meaning. So much of midwifery uses the same skills I've developed as a performer, teacher, and choreographer: listening, reacting, respecting, touching, and, most important of all, learning the value of doing very little at all. As any midwife will tell you, each birth is a miracle—every, every time. And as an artist, I want to see as many miracles as I can. They feed me, inspire me.

One night, at about 10, my friend Theresa calls me. She is a gorgeous dancer who performed for Alvin Ailey for many years. Now she's teaching at the U. She has one son; her second baby is due any day. Though she's planning a hospital birth, I've agreed to help her out at home until it's time to go. Then I will accompany her and her partner to the hospital and be there for the birth. Now, I don't normally help out at hospital births because I feel useless there, but Theresa is a homebirth girl—her firstborn came out at home. She has to have this baby in the hospital because her insurance will cover it there, but not at home. And of course on the salary of a dance professor, she has to take the cheaper option.

"Whitley ..." she says. I can hear her smiling. This is a woman who is smiling or laughing at every opportunity. "Baby's coming ... I just got Milo to sleep. And John's out somewhere. I can't reach him. Can you come now?"

I tell her I'm just getting my kids down for the night but I'll be over as soon as the sitter gets here. I can hear her breathing, but she's still talking through contractions, so I'm not worried. I hang up and call the girl next door. Of course, my kids sense that I want to leave so they require three or four extra James Taylor songs before they're sleeping. I grab my supplies—gloves, a new bulb syringe, and a fetascope—just in case, and jump in the car.

Theresa lives right near campus, right across the street from the

Arb where I used to go tramping about attempting time travel back in the Madonna days. It's dark in this part of town and I almost miss her driveway. I feel my way around to the back of her building, a big, old classic Ann Arbor house cut up into a warren of apartments, and climb up the rickety wooden stairs to her apartment.

I knock and peer in the window. No answer. I try the door and step inside. Silence. No—not silence, a rhythmic breathing/moaning coming from the other room. I step over piles of kid toys, books, and boxes into the hallway where a light is on.

Theresa is lying on the floor at the entrance to the bedroom, her legs spilling into the hall. Her gown is pulled up to her belly and a baby is very close to being born.

"The baby's coming, Whit. We've got to go. We've got to get to the hospital."

I'm not sure whether that's going to be possible. I put on a glove and tell her she's going to feel my fingers. My fingers don't go far at all. In all my births, I've never been quite this hands-on, but I feel very calm and in control.

"Listen, Theresa, this baby's right here. I can't possibly carry you down those stairs, and I sure don't want you to have the baby in the car while I'm driving anyway. Listen to me: do you feel like everything's OK? Is there a problem? Do you feel safe?"

"My baby. My baby's fine. No, there's no problem," she pants, looking me right in the eye.

"OK. Listen. Let's just have the baby now, and then we'll get help. But here's the thing. I want to get someone else to be here, just in case I need help, OK? Is there anyone else in the building?"

She thinks. "Downstairs. Right in front of the parking lot. There's a guy in there who might be home. His name is Larry. I think. Hurry, OK?"

I tell her I will be right back and run for the door. Where the hell is John, I wonder as I streak down the stairs. I fumble my way to Apartment One, take a breath, bang on the door, and ring the bell.

"Yeah?" comes a muffled voice.

"LARRY. LISTEN. THERESA UPSTAIRS IS HAVING HER BABY AND YOU NEED TO COME WITH ME NOW," I say through the door.

I don't yell as much as command.

"Oh. OK, just a minute." The door opens. Larry looks like a man who rarely goes outside. He only has his boxers on and I turn my head while he throws on a pair of sweats. "What … what do you want me to do?"

"I just want you to be there in case of a problem," I say, as we go round the back of the house again. "In case we need to move her or you need to call an ambulance. I just want another pair of hands. Don't worry. It'll be fine."

"Are you a … doctor?"

"No, but … just don't worry, Larry."

We get inside the apartment. From what I hear from Theresa, we've got to move quick.

"Larry. There's the bathroom. Go in there and find me every clean towel you can find. And some dental floss or thread."

I swear. It's just like in the movies. Except for the boiling water part. I don't ask for boiling water.

I kneel in front of Theresa and try to connect with her. I cup her knees in my hands. They are cool and soft, shaking slightly. Larry throws me some towels, old but clean. I hand the phone to him and the pager number of the midwife at the hospital. If I'm catching this baby, I want that midwife on her way here to do the placenta. I have my limits.

"OK, Theresa, I'm here, everything's fine. You don't have to hold back any more. How about on the next contraction, you just do what feels right?"

And she does. The baby's been right there for a good, long time, so she's all stretchy and pliant. She unfolds like ripples of water and a circle of baby head gets bigger and bigger. I support her, just as I've seen midwives do, but I'm really just responding to her. It is the most intuitive, natural, and beautiful duet—or trio—that I've ever done. Another push or two and the head is out. I quickly check for the cord, and tell her to go ahead, push your baby out. I toss a towel up onto her chest, then guide her second son out and up into her waiting arms. I cover him quickly and watch between her legs for any undue blood, but all is well.

The phone rings and I hear Larry answer it. It's the nurse-midwife from the hospital. She's on her way. Larry hands me the phone and she talks me through what to check for, placenta-wise. She tells me I've done a good job. Theresa coos to the baby who looks up into her face.

Across the room, in his bed, four-year-old Milo has slept through the whole thing. The midwife arrives. John arrives. They don't bother to take Theresa to the hospital; what's the point now? Mom and baby are nursing away like pros. Best part is Theresa has had a homebirth that her insurance will pay for because it was unintentional. Larry goes back downstairs with a story for his grandchildren. And I go home.

In their rooms, my children sleep. My daughter lies on her back, one arm thrown back over her head, her face lightly blushed with color that I can see even in the dim light from the hall. My little boy is curled on his side, clutching Snuffles, the blue elephant. And I am so tired. More tired and more alive than I think I have ever been, as if I have been dancing for hours and hours and hours.

VH1

My new house is an old house.

Some lady and her husband built it a hundred or so years ago and lived out their lives here. I once spent several hours in the public library poring over old records, trying to find clues to who they were, whether they had kids, whether they were happy here, but I found nothing more than their names. The man died in the '30s, and according to the records, the woman lived here until the mid-'60s, when, presumably, she died. Through all those years, the City Directory indicates a series of other people who lived here too. Boarders. Roommates. Single women whose names blip across these never-read pages only to disappear on the next page. Madge, Mildred, Elizabeth. In the 1977 Ann Arbor City Directory, I find my name, and Madonna's, and our address at University Towers. I remember our phone number.

Then, a flurry of activity in the house's ownership. It moves from hand to hand, every few years. It's a bargain in the '60s, that's for sure. The neighborhood archly known as the Old West Side doesn't yet have the cache it will in another decade. There are lots of the old German families left, and renovation-chic hasn't quite hit. This house becomes a haven for students at the University, the ones with cars who don't mind not living on campus. You could still park pretty much anywhere in the sixties, I imagine. These streets were far from the riots and the hemp. These streets were quiet and properly boring. Dogs, lawns, a bit of the old world.

My new house stands in a line of six similar houses, tall and pointy-topped. Whoever built them put in huge attics, which have, in my case, and in most of the others, been converted into third floors. I wish I could have seen the attic, before. There must have been an old trunk, some old boxes, a clue to who lived here.

Actually, there are clues all over the house. Out on the big front porch, where we lounge in the summers on our old, moss-green velvet sofa, I can see a name carved into the painted, wooded porch-post. Gay? May? Probably some student. Mr. and Mrs. Stein wouldn't have done that. I bet Mr. Stein screwed in the flag holder, though. It's dangling now, painted over so many times. Maybe it's brass underneath. I ought to dip it in chemicals and see.

When we moved in, I dug a garden in the side yard and unearthed lots of good stuff. Best of all was a tiny, green metal car—sort of a Matchbox precursor—a De Soto or something. I could still make the wheels turn. There were lots of bits of really old plastic, the kind you don't see anymore. Nails, of course, and other junk. I almost went to archaeology school instead of dance school. Who needs archaeology school when you can dig in your yard and find good stuff?

Sometime in the '70s, someone aluminum-sided my house. I'm dying to know what's underneath, how the clapboard is holding up under there. Loretta, the old lady across the street, says she's been here since '75 and our house was already sided. I love Loretta. She sits on her stoop and greets the world. She has a gold design built into her front tooth, she listens to the blues, and nothing gets past her. She watches us every day, our comings and goings, and knows more about us than we do ourselves. She's the neighborhood gargoyle/wisewoman. Kids tumble over her like puppies, grownups stop to chat and stay an hour.

Guess what? I'm married. I have married my piano teacher.

About four years into my morass of pitiable singlehood, while still living practically in the lumberyard, I went on a bit of a self-improvement binge and decided to take up the piano again. Now, I played a lot of piano in my youth: "Up in the Swing," "March of the Wee Folk," "The Wild Horsemen," Clementi, Scarlatti, Kabalevski, Chopin ... but wasn't feeling very classical any more.

Things had not been going well. Divorce led me on into a string of unworkable relationships, each of which left me flapping about like a landed bass. In every instance, I readily delivered my heart nigh unto the realm of impossibility (remember, I love easily, goddammit), sat back, and waited for the payoff, which of course, did not materialize. I wanted to be married again. I HATED being single. Being single is lonely. It's boring. You have to do all the garbage and recycling by yourself in bad weather. And sometimes, late at night, when the train rumbled by, and I tossed about on my lumpy futon, my once-mother's breathy words bounced from one side of my head to the other: "You don't need men, my daughter. You don't need anyone ..."

Oh, not true.

The scary part was, the further I got from the Rex experience, the more I realized what I'd been *without* for my entire adult life: partnership, good-natured teasing, a sense of shared adventure. Fun. Surrender. Trust. And I pulled the covers over my head and wondered what nine years of marriage meant. And why a girl with a good education got herself in this situation. And what's the difference between brains and wisdom. And where common sense comes in.

Sometimes, as hard as it was to admit, and despite the embossed paper and the ceremony, I began to wonder if I'd ever really been anyone's wife.

And so I dated and flailed and dated again. Don't get me wrong—these were entirely good men, just ... impossible in their own special ways.

All this while trying to achieve single-mom perfection in the battered, asbestos-sided house. I wrote and choreographed and taught dance in nearby universities and had phone conversations with gentlemen who said things in escalating volumes like, "We gonna repo you car! WE GONNA REPO YOU CAR!" And in the car in question—which required a quart of oil every week—I drove my son and daughter to school and sleepovers and youth chorale and baseball practice.

We actually approached food-stamp status, but when I met with the county social worker, she talked to me like I was someone who'd never taken her kids to the doctor, someone who needed checking up on. So I shook her hand and smiled, and when I got outside of the grimy building in Ypsilanti, I threw the forms in the trash and drove home.

To top it all off, there was this guy I came to call Batman, who followed me around and slammed me in my lower back with an old wooden baseball bat when I was least expecting it. By this I mean to say that I developed some problems with my sacrum. The body-workers all hinted that it was due to stress—you know: carrying the world on your *back*, the straw that broke the camel's *back*, and so forth. As if I had time to sit around comparing my life to the maxims of the English language and wondering how to manifest my dissatisfaction in the form of blinding and disabling pain. To be fair, maybe there was something to it. But maybe this was just something to be expected when you'd spent the last fifteen years doing things to your body—leaping, jumping, falling, twisting, getting dropped on the floor—that most people tend to avoid.

And so, each time "Batman" visited me I spent weeks lying around on ice waiting for the S-curve in my spine to straighten out so I could get up, get dressed, and be stressed again. When Batman visited, I did not teach, rehearse, or even write. All I could do was lie in bed getting slowly broker and waiting for things to calm down back there. When Batman visited, the kids would come and stare at me from time to time, but mostly they would just argue bitterly with each other off in the distance, ignoring me when I yelled from my bed for them to *cut it out*.

No, I was not feeling particularly classical. In fact, it finally occurred to me that it might be time for this white girl to play the blues.

So one night, I was sitting on the floor in my bedroom. The kids were snoozing away in their little muraled rooms (*Swan Lake* for my daughter, a volcano scene with "red-hot lava" for my son). And out of the blue I decided to call up my friend Shari, herself a working blues musician playing festivals all over the world. Shari has long, long hair and is very earnest. When she plays guitar she sounds like an old black man on a porch. I had two questions that Shari might be able to answer.

And I said, "Shari, who should I go out with?"

She didn't miss a beat. She told me who I should go out with. I didn't miss a beat. She'd been mentioning this guy every time we talked. "Nope, no way. I'm done with musicians. Never again."

And indeed, it was true. I had in the past responded to the widely held belief that musicians are cool, sexy, dangerous, bad boys. Good God, how tiresome is that myth. I had explored that territory and found it wanting. Never again. No artists of any kind, in fact. I wanted me a lawyer. A computer guy. Somebody in sales, maybe? Whatever that meant. Oh, but not the Willie Loman kind, with a suitcase, that wouldn't work for me. Somebody in sales management, maybe? Corporate sales? Again, I'd never quite been sure what this meant, but had decided that I was officially willing to find out.

"Oh, come on, Whit. He's great. He's so talented. He's got a kid. He's beautiful. He sings great."

"Nope. I'm sorry I asked. But answer me this: I want to take piano lessons. Who should I take with?"

She told me the same name as before.

"I thought he played guitar."

"He's the best blues piano guy in town. Everybody knows it."

"What are you trying to do, Shari?"

"Just take some piano lessons, OK?"

And there didn't seem to be any harm in that.

I called him up and he was very friendly. He lived about three blocks from the lumberyard. I made an appointment for a lesson. His name was Al.

Within three months, I was playing *Chicken Shack*, a slow blues in G, and the beginning form of *Tippitina*. Al was a good teacher and my five years of childhood piano and theory came flying back into my hands. My half-hour lessons stretched into two-hour marathons where we did a lot of talking about our lives and our kids, and music and Ann Arbor townie gossip. He was ever so nice. One night we even went to see Beausoleil, the Cajun band, but it was not a date in any way because, you see, I was done with musicians and anyone remotely associated with the arts.

One winter afternoon, I was at my lesson playing dispiritedly through my little blues repertoire while Big Al sat to my left and tapped his foot in time. I should have canceled because I had a rude headache. I stopped and rubbed my eyes.

"I'm sorry," I said, "I have a rude headache."

And Big Al did something entirely unprofessional. He reached around me and started rubbing my neck and shoulders with his big, old right hand. I closed my eyes and my hands fell from the keyboard. He stepped behind me and placed his hands on my shoulders and pressed gently from my neck on out. I did not know such gentleness could be. It wasn't sexy, just loving and simple. And I couldn't remember the last time someone had rubbed my shoulders, someone I had not paid to do it. And I lied before; it was very sexy.

And so I did something entirely inappropriate and intrinsically damaging to the student-teacher relationship. I said, "I think I'm going to kiss you." And he sat down beside me on the piano bench and beat me to it.

So much for learning to play the piano. I learned a whole lot of other things instead.

Al courted me in unusual ways. He did not ply me with gifts; he was as broke as I was. He did not dazzle me with his wardrobe. In fact, the first time we officially went out, he looked like a waiter in a Greek restaurant and good-naturedly endured an evening of well-deserved mocking. He did not drive up in any kind of status vehicle. He had a maroon Toyota pickup packed with amps and keyboard cases, but with no radio.

But he had a most endearing habit of singing Otis Redding songs softly into my ear, so softly that they could barely be heard, until I fell asleep. He courted me with newspapers and the lack of conversation, for we discovered we had identical needs to sit quietly, with coffee and newspapers, for a certain portion of the day. He courted me with the way some inspirational sports features in the Detroit Free Press made him tear up. He courted me with funny voices and stories of his naughty boyhood and his wild druggie days, which apparently had only recently ended. And with the ways he played piano. And the way he wasn't sure about everything in his life. And the way he picked up his old cat.

And how could I ever have thought I'd want a lawyer?

The following Christmas Eve, my kids were upstairs asleep finally, and Al came over to give me my present. I had to close my eyes and hold my hands out real far. He put a brand new Seagull guitar into my arms, and the guitar was a key that unlocked something deep inside me. My long-ago axis shifted monumentally and I started writing songs.

Songs. Now, I'd been singing for a long time, but had just automatically assumed that I could not write songs. I had tried a couple of times, but not very hard. It was easy to justify this failing of my otherwise robust creativity. I did a lot of things. If I did not write songs, well, that was okay. But then the Seagull took over and I started running into songs in vapor form everywhere I turned: the grocery store, the corner of William and Fourth Avenue, in my bed, driving to East Lansing.

Are you familiar with the vapor principle of songwriting? No? Well, the vapor, according to studies, osmoses through hair follicles at the top of the head and makes its way down into the heart where it replicates rampantly until sections of it—lines of text, bits of melody, intense, undeniable feelings—come burbling to the surface and make the subject grab her guitar and lock the door. This has been proven.

I found the whole process to be quite mysterious and pleasurable. For one thing, NO physical pain was involved. Well, after marathon writing sessions, the tips of the fingers on my left hand got a little tender, but that was all. Writing songs did not hurt my back, wrench my neck, split my feet open, or leave bruises. And an added boon was the privacy of the process. I didn't need to book studio space. I didn't need to call dancers with a tentative rehearsal schedule, then call them all back because three out of the five dancers couldn't make that time, then set a new time, then call again because I forgot I couldn't make that time.

So I sat in my sweet house and wrote songs—country songs that reminded me of my grandfather. Songs about crop circles and imperfection and buxom, lady traffic cops. Songs about being left by someone you love. And these confused me—I'd had some bad relationships, but hadn't been classically dumped in a long time—until Al reminded me whom they just might be about. And the reminding made me cry and miss my mom for the first time in a long time.

My mom. One day, while we were visiting out East, Al and I took the train to her place of employment, a busy art gallery just outside the city. We stood across the street as I prepared. I pulled my hair about my face and put on dark glasses. There were some false starts. I had him go and look in the window, to see if she was really there. He came back. There was someone in there who fit her description, he said softly, with his arms around me. My heart charged and retreated. I was not here to confront her. There is nothing left to repair. In fact, I was not sure why I was here, only that I had to be. We crossed the street.

Inside we walked around, looking at the fine *objets d'arts*. She was at the other end of the gallery, helping a customer, speaking in her soft, civilized tones. I stood by a rack of cards and listened hard, glancing when Al said it was safe to look. Her hair was straight now, pulled back into a bun. She was fashionably dressed. On her wrist was a bracelet of thick silver and turquoise. Suddenly, without warning, she walked right over to where I was and stood behind me, her back to mine, talking to the customer across the room. I could have touched her, but I did not. I stood very, very still. And so we stood there for fifteen seconds, perhaps, before she moved away and went behind the counter. Al bought some note cards from her. They made small talk. And when we left that place, I felt remarkably strong and clear.

One summer day, Al and I were out walking on the railroad tracks outside of town and we stopped on a bridge to watch a fly fisherman arcing his line over and over into the coppery Huron. The trees were lush and swaying. The sky ached with blue. The air smelled sweet with pine and moss and faint creosote. We heard the bells start to ring at the railroad crossing about a quarter of a mile into the sunset, and quickly dug out all our pennies and put them on the tracks. The Amtrak from Chicago came screaming by and we yelled and waved. It was gone in an instant. We searched for our pennies. They were warm. The silence returned. The fisherman had moved further down the river in his big black waders, but we could still see him as he tossed his line, and tossed it again. He made a rhythm the whole scene could sing along to and when I said this to Al, he understood. I thought to myself: I can have moments like this for the rest of my life with this man. I grew breathless, turned him toward me, and said, "Ask me now."

In a year, we were married in the Michigan Theater, the old vaudeville movie palace Madonna and I peered into that first day we were friends. It was a pretty big affair; everybody we know came. My mother did not come, but both my aunts flew up from the south and two of my cousins, and of course my dad, so I felt more than adequately loved. As a prelude to the ceremony, we showed an instructional film from the '60s called *Engagement, Romance, and Reality* and a whole bunch of vintage wedding cartoons—we were, after all, getting married in a movie theater. Then the screen rose and Shari, the one responsible for all of this, played guitar as we walked down the aisle with our three beaming children. The mayor of Ann Arbor married us on the stage. She looked at the wrong notes and mistakenly referred to us as a lesbian couple: *"Ladies and gentlemen, when two women come together to pledge their love …"*—which was confusing for a moment, but this was, after all, Ann Arbor, where one must be prepared for anything.

Which brings us back here to the new old house. Our home together.

It is too good, too big, too perfect for me. My new husband and I wander through it and wonder how we ever got to buy it. If you ignore the incursions of decades of landlord-style decor, you can see the eccentric grace of the building. Nothing fancy—it's a workman's house, back when workmen, whoever they were, expected a bit of grace where they lived. The angular twists and turns of the winding staircase all the way up to the third floor, and from which my son drops parachute guy after parachute guy. The strange, globular lighting fixtures, the secret staircase that winds down from my daughter's tipped-ceilinged room at the back of the second floor. A long time ago, someone paneled much of the main floor, then painted the paneling. We haven't gotten to this project quite yet. The gracious, arched doorway to the dining room was blocked in years ago to create another bedroom. The chandelier remains, swinging gently, as it did over the Stein's sauerbraten.

You're probably wondering why this chapter is called VH1.

All of the above is simply to make it clear that I am very busy just now, involved, as one is prone to be, in the immediate pleasures and distractions of life, when there is a sudden flurry of activity on the Madonna front. She's apparently going on an important tour and this trickles down to me in the form of interesting encounters with my media friends. Yes, after several years of practically no interest in my valuable status as M's ex-roomie, assistant producers all over the world have pored through the archives and discovered me afresh. I'm in the phone book and perhaps have uncovered some previously blocked memories that I might be willing to share.

See, Maddie's gotten all maternal and yogic and domestic and British at the same time. Her marriage to a handsome and edgy young director (I read about it in *People*, I think, while I was waiting at the eye doctor's) has made the world start thinking about her in new ways. Again. And that means my phone starts to ring. And in the words of my friend Linda, who took a million photos of Madonna back in the day, and is now living in the south of France, "Hello, new sofa!"

It starts with a lovely gent from the *London Mirror*. I tell him that I only do interviews for money and we quickly reach an agreement. He comes over just before Christmas with his friendly photographer. The tree looks so pretty twinkling in the corner as we drink tea (I love how English people get all misty when Americans offer them tea) and homemade biscotti and talk about ancient history. Then my son comes home, the conversation shifts, and we talk for hours about jazz and alt-country music. A few months later they send me the article, and it's actually pretty good. My photo isn't horrible.

Journal Entry, next day:

I dreamed that I was interviewed by the New York Times Magazine. *They published a picture of me taken sitting on a toilet in the bathroom of a diner, with the head of a five-pound bass perched on my head like a crown. I'm not sure what to make of this.*

Then, the big guns. Bio-maven Andrew Morton leaves me a couple of caring messages on my machine. He's coming to Michigan and would very much like to talk to me. We finally settle in for an introductory phone chat and of all things, I discover in him a new friend! I almost get to reminiscing right there intercontinentally—he's such a good listener—until I catch myself spilling details and start talking money. Truthfully? I don't really feel like getting interviewed by this guy. The *Mirror* bloke was one thing, but I have a feeling Morton's got some kind of alien chip implanted in him that will make me deliver up some kind of scandalous dirt on Madonna, dirt that doesn't even exist. What if he hypnotizes me and gets me making stuff up? I shudder to think. In my mind I try to put a price on my disinclination.

So, at the crest of one particular wave of nausea, I tell him I'll talk to him for $5000. He doesn't bat an eye, says he'll bring cash. Shit, I should have asked for ten.

The *Sunday Mirror* guy and I have struck up a bit of an e-mail friendship and I tell him what's going on. He writes, "Let me know how it goes with Andrew Morton, who's quite a celeb himself. In fact, you might care to remind him about a rather amusing *Sunday Mirror* story in which he was caught having sex on his balcony with his secret lover … Naughty boy!! Keep smiling …"

But then the pace quickens. One spring day, this telephone exchange:

Whitley? I don't know if you remember me. This is Chirpy Puppy (or some such), and I interviewed you a few years back for *Back Before They Lived Lifestyles of Rich Rock Stars*. Do you remember me?

Hmm. It wasn't a segment on Madonna, now was it Chirpy?

(Giggle) Yes!

Sure, yes, how are you? (I rifle through papers, phone wedged between shoulder and ear, searching for a first draft of article on the Ann Arbor Convention and Visitor Bureau's August Golf Outing, a lucrative new freelance gig.)

Oh, good, I'm fine. Well, guess what? I'm an assistant producer for a new show that's being taped in Chicago? It's a *What's My Line?* kind of thing where people come on and our panel of celebrities tries to guess why … well, why you are "of interest." You know? What's special about you? And we were at a meeting and I suggested you? Because you were Madonna's roommate? (Giggle)

(Oh my! I am, apparently, of interest!)

Uh, and here's the best part! We pay your travel. To Chicago!

Chirpy, I can drive to Chicago in four hours.

Oh! Well, even better! That's great! Well, we'll pay your hotel and here's the best part. For every celebrity you stump, you get $200? And if you stump all four, you get $1000!

One thousand dollars!

Yes! A Grand—if you stump all four!

So, Chirp, let me get this straight. I go to Chicago and stay in a hotel and tell some B-level celebs and the rest of the world that I knew Madonna and you might give me a thousand dollars.

Uh, yeah ... (aborted giggle).

I tell Chirpy I am very busy with some other projects just now. But I thank Chirpy for thinking of me.

Chirpy, incredulous, asks me if I am sure. I tell her that I am sure, and I thank her once again for thinking of me.

After I hang up, my hand snakes to the top of my head and feels around up there. Just checking.

On a blistering day in the middle of July, when my tomato plants are starting to make me proud and I'm consumed with details of a trip to visit my daughter who is in college in Vermont, I get calls from both VH1 *and* HBO. VH1 comes first. It's on the machine.

"Uh, hello Whitley, you don't know me. My name's Beth and I'm a producer with VH1. I'm working on the new version of *Before They Were Rock Stars* and I understand you were Madonna's roommate. We're coming out to Detroit and would love to talk to you. We'd really like to hear your Story, so call me back when you get the message." Phone number, niceties, phone number again. "Bye!"

She really seems to like me.

I go back to what I'm doing. About thirty minutes later, the phone again. I answer. The HBO lady's equally perky. I swear she really cares about my well-being, really wants to "hear your Story—it's all about the Story," but I'm suddenly in a very bad mood and so is my Story. I tell her I understand but that I'm really getting tired of reliving all this stuff. I tell her I only do interviews for money, that I'm very expensive, that that's one thing I learned from my ex-roommate. I tell her I'll think about it and she can call me back next week. I am not habitually a rude person but my tone flirts with pissed-offness. I hang up and immediately feel guilty for snapping at poor Julie/Steffie/Misty.

And then I go back to what I'm doing. Maybe the whole thing will go away.

HBO goes away, but VH1 does not go away. Beth keeps leaving messages. I actually call her back and leave a message for her. She is very perky on her outgoing message. She sounds like she has been expecting me to call. We go back and forth for a couple of days. I agonize about what to do. My friend Charmie has a great idea.

"Whitley, I'll do it! I'll pretend to be you; they'll never know. Just tell me a bunch of details and I'll just make up the rest. I'm free next Wednesday."

It's actually an excellent idea. I come very close to agreeing. But no. I don't want any trouble with the law.

"Mom," my son grumps to me in his deep teen voice. "That Beth lady from VH1 called again. You've got to call her back. I've talked to her, like, six or seven times. She knows my sleep schedule. She knows everything about me. Call her back OK? God!"

I kind of forget to call her back, so someone named James calls me. He's the segment producer. He is so incredibly enthusiastic about this show. "This isn't anything like anything you've seen before," he says in a hushed and beatific tone. "It's going to be very artistic." I wonder silently exactly what that means. "I mean, these interviews are all about the Story—about Madonna before she went off to New York. It's very simple, very classy. The people we interview are going to be up against a black background."

Oh my. A black background.

I tell James that I will only consider doing the interview if my background can be black *velvet* but he doesn't laugh. I tell him that I don't do interviews for free and that I'm very expensive and that I'm pretty sick of the whole bizness and who actually cares after all this time and all these documentaries with people up against black backgrounds talking about famous people who hate the fact that they're being talked about. (But probably actually secretly like it.) I tell him that I will think about it and to call me next week.

I go to Vermont to visit my daughter. She is flourishing. She has friends, admiring faculty, and a room with a view. Her roommate is a nice girl. Mountains, sunsets, rivers, U-Pick raspberries. I fly home to a whole bunch of messages.

"We're really different," James says when I finally call back. "This is a different kind of show. Nothing sleazy, we're not looking for scandal. We just want the Story." He pauses, then moves in for the strike. "You see, it's really about *you*, Whitley, your Story."

My lips form a smile. My heart races. "Oh, no, James," I say. "I have no illusions about who this is about, but let me explain, or try to. This is complex …"

A few days earlier I was lying around with my husband, trying to explain this very same thing to him. As I've already noted, my husband is a musician. A real, bona fide, dyed-in-the-cloth, no day job, lifer, American R & B and blues musician. We make a good married couple for we have done our work in this country, had children while young and ill-prepared, struggled our struggles, and been true to ourselves for the most part. The occasional sprinkles of regret and bewilderment are easily talked and kissed away. In the main, we are proud of what we've done in our little corner. I long ago stopped believing that it's the amount of people you reach that counts. The measures just can't be the same. Still, the lure of "distribution" is heady and ever-present.

"Imagine," I tell him, "that you get a chance to be seen by millions of people. But you aren't allowed to sing or play a note. You can't even talk about what it is that you do, the songs you've written. In fact, all you get to talk about is some sandwich you once ate, or some car you used to drive. Something you really don't think about very often but for some reason the world is desperate to learn about—every, every detail." Al sighs then gets up and goes in the kitchen and makes a tomato sandwich. He comes back in the room. "I don't think it would bother me to talk about a sandwich or a car," he says. "Especially if they paid me well."

"OK, well imagine that a long time ago you crossed paths with … with someone you really admire in music. Robert Cray—no, he's not famous enough—Al Green, yeah, Al Green, and for the rest of your life you were widely quoted, in *Rolling Stone,* say, and on MTV, talking about Al Green, but you never got to talk about yourself, or your life, or your music."

"I see what you mean," says Al, "but it's really not the same thing. "For one thing, if I had been roommates with Al Green, you can be damn sure I wouldn't have lost track of him. I'd have been in his band, then gone out on my own, and we'd have a better sofa to lie around on."

I think I'm figuring it out.

"OK, but how about this: suppose that a long time ago you were roommates with Michael Bolton. Yeah, you were really good friends, you even sang together a little bit, and then what happened happened, and he got huge, while you just kept on playing and writing and making sure you stayed in the same town as your kid, and gigging and having a good, somewhat bohemian, definitely OK American life. And then, whenever it seems like you're at a new pinnacle of struggle, you get asked to go in front of a rapt and attentive, supposedly music-savvy audience to talk about your ancient history with Michael Bolton. But you can't sing or play—nor would you want to 'cause it would look so forced and pathetic in that situation."

He opens his mouth to say something but I interrupt.

"And they pay you money when you're sickeningly broke and you need the money for an operation. Yeah, your kid's operation. Or to make a CD. A really good CD …"

Al seems to understand this analogy slightly better, but we both know it's not perfect, because I don't have the same rabid feelings about Madonna and her music that my husband has about Michael Bolton and his. I don't hate Madonna's music, I just don't care about it one way or another. It doesn't move me in any particular direction. The early songs were poppy and fun and catchy and I sing along to them like every other proper American, but when things get self-serious, slick, and overproduced, I kinda fade out and go listen to Chopin or Lucinda Williams. One slight exception is that cowboy song in which she gets all dusty and wears makeup that makes her look like she isn't wearing makeup. I like the dancing in that. I saw the video on TV once. I do admire Madonna in a distant, glassy kind of way, not so much for the music, and certainly not for the films, as much for her ability to make the world her willing playground.

In truth, I don't think much about her work. She was just my roomie and good friend, my Little Bowl of Bear Mush for a little while, long ago.

I just don't feel like talking about it anymore. Anyway, this is the kind of thing I try to express—badly, no doubt—to James from VH1. He attempts to understand my inner conflict by saying, "Awwww" in a sympathetic way that about makes my teeth fall out. We begin to haggle about price. I tell him that my most recent offer (from Andrew

Morton, whose name I do not mention and whose offer may in fact have fallen through) is $5000. He gasps (I mean, HOW will they pay for that? Greedy me ...) then says that he will plead my case to the powers that be but that they at VH1 *never* pay for interviews. I say that's fine 'cause I don't want to do it anyway.

A day later he leaves me a message and offers me half that. I accept. It is all, completely and totally, about the money. I will be a big girl and give the stylish New Yorkers their interview. I will be on TV. My kids will be happy. My friends will ask me all about it, how I feel about it. I will be gracious and evasive.

As soon as I agree to do this interview, a combination of genetic, environmental, and doubtless emotional factors come together for a meeting in the middle of my chin. The factors decide that this is the time to collaborate on a project of great importance—a zit of unparalleled artistry and magnitude. Never mind that I eat well and wash my face. Never mind that I have never had any problem with this sort of nonsense since junior high school. It is decided. The interview is a full week away, but perfectly timed. My magnum opus will need every moment of this time to prepare.

I spend much of the week looking at my chin in the mirror and applying hot, wet compresses. I think of canceling, but do not.

Okay. The day James and his Detroit-based crew come to town is so hot I just want to go in the basement, wipe off a metal bookcase, and lie down on it. The good news is my first tomatoes are ripe on the vine. The other good news is my daughter is home from Vermont and has agreed to do my makeup (eyeliner, lipstick, zit concealer), and my son is having fun in New York with my dad. So there's not really anyone to worry about other than myself.

We meet at the University of Michigan Dance Department. It is exactly the same as when Madonna and I danced there. Same orange and gray carpeting that we padded around on barefoot, same orange and gray locker room. I lead the crew upstairs and we stand at the doorway of Studio A.

Anyone who dances knows that feeling of *threshold*, of pit-of-the-stomach possibility, as you stare into an empty studio. There's a word

I learned in grad school a few years ago. I think the word is *liminal*. It has to do with being at the brink of something, between states. I love that word, that state. While the camera crew crowds past me and stomps onto the floor in their big, dirty shoes, I stand and think about this large, quiet space. It is a beautiful studio, the best in the building. It's like a pool where you can breathe anywhere you go, up or down. I have been dancing here for half of my life. I flash on a wintry Sunday twenty-something years ago, Madonna doing her pliés at the window by the barre, a silhouette against a grey and white chaos of snow. Flash on bare, bony feet on bare wood, sweat and rhythm and bruises and nerve. Quick, secret smiles transmitted like a delicate telegraph from one side of the room to the other. Me to her. Her to me. Over and out. I stand and look at the room, heels on the metal doorjamb, toes on the smooth wood. Heart and mind stretched back in time, a reluctant arabesque, spanning the decades.

A half hour later, they're all set up and James is there, shaking my hand, looking earnest and eager to begin. My daughter deftly pancakes the Vesuvius that is my chin, applies thin eyeliner, and I root around for some kind of non-linty lipstick. I pull my ponytail holder out and comb my hair with my fingers. I take a few cleansing breaths and resolve to be nice and as helpful as I can.

James: How did you meet Madonna?

"It's funny that we're taping this in this room," I say, "'cause the first time I saw Madonna I was standing right there peeking through the door into the next studio where she was taking a ballet class." (This is really true, which is not to say that the rest of the things I say are not true; it's just a really vivid, snapshot-type memory.) "I saw her at the barre. She was in the middle of a developée to the front—that's a slow leg extension—and I remember thinking 'I can't possibly live with someone that thin whose front extension is higher than mine.'"

I tell him about her coming to check out the apartment, about how the guys seemed strangely hypnotized, how I didn't much like her at first, how she, mid-gum-snap, poked me with her baby-greens and said, "What's the matter Whitley. You don't look very happy right now." How she moved in the next day.

James is looking pleased. We take a break so the camera guys can change tapes. "I'm looking for *nuggets*," he says. "Everyone I've talked to today has given me a little nugget, you know, something special and new that hasn't been said before. Her guidance counselor at her high school? We talked to her today—nice lady!—and she had a great nugget about Madonna's transcript. You've already given me some good stuff. Just keep those nuggets coming." Then he reaches over and pats my knee and says (because he cares about my well-being) "See? This isn't so hard!"

I wonder silently if James can tell that I am imagining putting those nuggets in a special hiding place he has. Why do I hate this so much?

"Was Madonna a hard worker?"

I tell him she was a hard worker. I tell him that after a night out at the Rubaiyat, drinking juice and sweating and dancing and flirting and a long walk home, she'd be up at eight and off to the studio to work out on her own.

"What was the most outrageous thing she ever did in the apartment?"

I have no answer to this. We were hardly ever in the apartment and when we were, well, what can I say? Not every moment was devoted to peculiar and highly original and outrageous antics. She sat around like the rest of us. She read books. She took showers. She dried her hair. She slept. Thought: could her corporation sue me for revealing this potentially damaging tidbit?

"Well, alright, what was the most outrageous thing she ever did during the time you knew her?"

I want to say that in a department of dancers, alive, well, and horny in the late '70s, Madonna had plenty of competition for the crown of "Most Outrageous." But, bearing in mind that I am the ONLY person being paid for an interview in the creation of this masterwork of Storytelling, I try to be accommodating. I tip my head back, stroke a goatee ...

Oh, I know! I'll tell him about Madonna punching me in the nose at the Rubaiyat! I offer up a particularly colorful recollection and it works; James appears to be having some sort of seizure, his hands flapping back and forth, whimpering with satisfaction. I have delivered. All hail James, midwife of nuggets.

I tell James about Millers. How Madonna and I actually scored those jobs.

We each were interviewed by a large and gruff woman named Barb. She informed me that I was hired BUT—and this is a very big BUT—I had to agree to wear a bra at all times. As someone who was a card-carrying member of N.O.W. as an adolescent, I was not sure what to make of this. Madonna came back from her interview and we compared notes. She too had been told in no uncertain terms to contain her unruly womanhood and we had a long conversation about what to do. The outcome of this conversation has unfortunately been lost to history.

Again, James appears pleased with this recollection. Then he starts in with the heavy stuff. The meat and potatoes. The twist of the knife. Ooh, James. He leans forward, narrows his eyes.

"What do you think drove her to become so famous?"

I spend a long time gazing over James's right shoulder, taking my time, letting the tape do its circular dance. I wonder how much of VH1's tape I can waste by pretending to think?

"Well," I say, "I think it has to be an extra chromosome, something like that, that makes someone have that kind of drive, don't you think? When it's that extreme, the need to be seen, to be loved and hated and noticed, I think it comes from a cellular level."

I have, of course, no scientific data to back this up, but it is what I think, for the most part. I talk about Christopher Flynn, what a wonderful man he was, and how important he'd been to her, how he opened a door for her, showed her something of art and the world.

"I mean, what would have happened if she'd been born, say, in an Amish community and had never had a chance to do and say and be all that was inside her? She would have combusted maybe, or imploded."

James nods sagely.

Later that night, lying in bed, I think of what I should have said:

"Yeah, Madonna Ciccone comes down from her karmic resting place, heading for the Motor City, but takes a wrong turn and winds up in Iowa wearing a bonnet and a brown dress without even any buttons. How to proceed? She bakes some really exemplary pies. Her quilts win prizes. And all the while, she's outdoing every other girl with her extraordinary "plain"-ness, attracting so little attention to herself that she eventually turns into a line drawing of a glass of milk, and tourists come from all over the world to witness the miraculousness of it. Man, she would have been *some kind of simple* …"

Calumet

February in Michigan is like a slow flu that you aren't sure you have. You'd think that after living here all these years, I'd know what to expect, that I'd have clued in to the fact that February in Michigan, short though it is, lasts forever. It's cold, too. Cold as hell.

This February I have a gig. The thing with the word "gig" is that when you say it to people who don't have "gigs" they think you're tossing arts jargon around even when you're not trying to. It's a certifiably stupid word, but I use it sometimes. I have a gig in Calumet, Michigan. In February. I am thankful to my management for getting me this gig, and at the same time, I note the irony. Calumet is just about as far north as one can go and still be in the United States. And again, we're talking February.

I no longer have my company. I have handed it off to a talented and driven friend who actually wants the ten thousand headaches involved in running a dance company and has stronger sacral ligaments. I miss my dancers, but they are still my friends. Whenever I want to choreograph on other bodies, I just make a few calls, find a venue, and get it out of my system. But for now, I am, officially, a soloist. I have been asked to perform at the Calumet Opera House: two shows for kiddies (my monster show where I play every part and work up quite a sweat), one show for adults (solo dances and monologues), and a master class for the community. Sounds great. Good money. Appreciative folks. My husband and I will call this a working vacation. I have hired him to accompany me, to drive all the way there and back, to help me backstage and provide general support. It will be beautiful and we will have fun at the bed and breakfast. Oh, my management informs me: they want me to do the Madonna piece.

The Madonna piece.

Years ago, when my company was flourishing, I decided to dive in and give everybody what they wanted. We had our annual March season coming up, and I was looking for a way to lure the bodies to the seats. This was sure to do it. The local press went nuts, people showed up in droves. I did the simplest, dullest Madonna piece I could think of, and got on with the real work. People ate it up. Since then, it's been a staple piece that I pull out when I have to assure the presenter that people will come, and when I need a piece that doesn't make me sweat. Physically.

In early February, I start packing. I make many calls up to Calumet. The presenter is a very friendly woman named Jackie. The tech director who will be doing my lights and sound is a Finnish man named Sven. I can barely understand him when we talk on the phone, but Jackie assures me that he will fully understand my cues and not let me down. Sven tells me that the theater has a rudimentary light system at best and that if I want specials, I'll have to bring my own. I pack sixteen instruments, about fifteen cables and extension cords, three dimmer packs, four trees, and my trusty little Leprechaun light board. I pack two suitcases full of costumes, an antique wig stand, my antique jester's hat, six huge monster masks, a gigantic foam-rubber tyrannosaurus tail, a tape player, all my tapes, all my backup tapes, my prefab cue sheets, a bag of my own clothes, and my guitar. I rent a white Chevy Blazer, we say good-bye to the cats and head to a hardware store where we buy ten bungee cords and spend about forty-five minutes lashing the light system to the top of the car in 5-degree weather. The kids are with their dad.

I have forgotten to mention the weather. February, normally cold, is pulling out the stops. We are in the midst of a cold snap, which has paralyzed the United States, killed hundreds of people, and shows no signs of abating. This is cold beyond the pale. As the sun sets, we head north. Really north.

US23 snakes out of Ann Arbor and turns into I75. It's a nice enough highway and we know it well. But it could be a dirt road with mud and potholes for all we care 'cause we've stopped in at Zingerman's on the way to the ramp, and the Blazer is fragrant with the smell of hot pastrami sandwiches, pickles, and cream sodas. Let's look at the situation clearly: *heading north in bitter cold to work my ass off for four days* goes on one side of the column. *So in love we're pathetic, getting out of town with pastrami, and gonna be paid to dance* goes in the other column. Not a problem.

An hour later we drive through Flint making up stream-of-consciousness blues songs. The goal is to get over the Mackinac Bridge and find a hotel for the night. Four hours later, we're close. The wind outside the Blazer is like a sheet of devils and there's an advisory posted on the signs leading to the bridge. This is a nice way of saying that if you go on the bridge you might get blown off into the Straits of Mackinac, which of course would make us late for the gig. We get off the highway in Mackinac City and stop on a side street to figure out what to do. Snow is piled everywhere and makes Mackinac look like abstract art. We pee at a rest stop and decide to make a go of it. We drive real slow, the five miles across the bridge. I'm not good with heights and windy bridges in the dead of night, but I peek through my fingers and see strange, shadowy shapes in the water below—the wind and the currents have carved the ice into eerie floes. The heater's on full blast and it's warm in the car. You know that Melissa Etheridge song, "Baby, You Can Sleep While I Drive"? I love that song.

On the other side of the bridge is the town of St. Ignace. It's about midnight and no joke, it's 25 below. When we find a motel and walk up to the office, our nose hairs are instantly frozen. Any exposed skin burns with cold. The guy in the office is real nice. Tells us where to go to eat. Tells us about a twenty-four-hour casino, run by Native Americans, we could check out. They even have a shuttle service. We say we'll think about it, and go back to pull the Blazer up to number 12.

It's about 40 degrees inside number 12, so we pump up the thermostat and go out for pizza while it warms up. Later, as we curl around each other in the less lumpy of the two beds, we channel surf: Shopping Network; Weather Channel ("cold, very, very cold "); a Western; a Christian man with jowls relating a parable; some too-orange eighties-style people on a beach; Madonna running around a bullring chasing a good-looking matador. Hi, Madonna. When we turn it off, there's deep silence in the room, but outside the air itself shatters with cold. This we can hear. We thaw together, softly, nearing sleep.

One afternoon in the waning days of the sixties, I ran in the downstairs door of my apartment building and stuck my tiny mailbox key in the lock. It was there: the latest issue of *Mad*

magazine. Alone in my tiny home, on the third floor, at the corner of First Avenue and Fifty-Second Street, with the endless current of cars and cabs flashing their colors on my living room ceiling, with the endless symphony of car horns and growling buses, I sat in the kitchen eating buttered Pepperidge Farm toast and slathering the sweet sarcasm of *Mad* magazine all over me. That day, the theme of those stupid song spoofs was food. They'd turned "Downtown" into "Ground Round." ("When you eat meat but hate the meat that you're eating, then you always know: ground round. It's so unnerving when they're constantly serving in a restaurant, ground round …")

And what do you know? Halfway across the country, in Ann Arbor, Michigan, while hippies were screwing publicly on South University, my future husband was sequestered in his room with his copy of *Mad*, singing "Ground Round" just like me.

❦

And this we discover entwined in a Saint Ignace motel room. After we stop laughing, he sings me "That's How Strong My Love Is" right in my ear and I'm out like a light.

The morning's white is everywhere and blinding. We feel post–eye-doctor-visit, the kind where you get drops in your eyes, but it's only more snow than we've ever seen. We stop at a gas station for muffins and tea (and gas, we're using up a lot of gas), then hop on the road, heading west along the southern coast of Michigan's Upper Peninsula. Lake Michigan is on our left for the first hour or so, an endless field of ice and wind. We pass ice cream stands, whitefish shops, motels—all boarded up for the winter. We pass the famous Mystery Spot (closed for the season). We pass high forests of pine trees. At a gas station, there's a thin coating of ice in the toilet water. It is minus-15 degrees. I go inside to pay. A radio somewhere in the back is playing "Borderline." Well, hello again.

We jog north and hit Lake Superior where we eat fish sandwiches for lunch in a town rendered strangely shapeless by snow. By 3 PM it's already getting dark. We drive and drive and drive. We are ten hours from home, twelve hours from home, thirteen hours from home, and we're still in Michigan, happily dissecting Joan Osborne's CD, which Madonna had something to do with, didn't she? We like it pretty well, and some of it a lot. We talk about the program order of the show I'm about to do. My husband asks me about the Madonna piece.

"You've seen it," I say.

"No, I haven't," he says.

"Yes, you have."

"Well, alright, then. Why don't you tell me about it, just for kicks?"

"There's nothing to tell. I just do it."

"Do you dance?"

"Not a bit of it. I just sit in a chair and answer questions."

"Whose questions? Are they on a tape?"

"I answer questions from the audience."

"That's all?"

"I read out of the journal I kept when I was living with her. Then I answer questions, then I read a bit more, then it's over and out and onto the good stuff."

"The good stuff?"

"The real work. The real pieces. The pieces that mean something to me."

"Doesn't it mean anything at all to you?"

"Sometimes it does, if I get a laugh when I want one. One time somebody asked me what Madonna was like in bed. I said she was very still and everybody laughed. And sometimes the conversation gets going and I'm asking them stuff and the whole performer/audience thing gets all shifted. That's fun. But mostly I just don't like doing it. It makes me feel cheap and unsuccessful and desperate a little. Nah, that's overstating it."

There is a pause. Then he says, "Do you really feel that way? You? Ever?"

"No ... like I said, that's too strong. But it makes me feel uncomfortable sometimes because ... because people—audiences, people at parties, whoever—*expect* me to feel that way. There's always this unspoken assumption that because she's a performer and I'm a performer that I must be all bitter and resentful and mad at the world because of ... the sheer stratospheric-osity of her success. Is that a word?"

"Is now. Well, are you? Mad at the world?"

"Gosh, I don't think so. Certainly not about that. I wouldn't have a right to be. I've always liked that the whole concept of fate is a bit of a mess. That there's no figuring it out. Do I ever wish I had what she has? Only a teensy bit of her drive maybe. I could have done better for myself and the kids maybe, if I'd just pushed a little harder... But I'm too friggin' dainty. I hate that side of performing: selling yourself, getting the word out, knocking on doors, never taking 'no' for an answer. Yeah, I do admire her drive. But kind of in the way you admire ... I don't know, a *lava-flow* or something. It's gorgeous and undeniable, but kind of terrifying too. I guess I admire how she can do whatever she wants. She wants to make a record, she makes a record. She wants to get naked in a book, she gets naked in a book. She wants to be in a movie, she's in a movie. But shit, what a trade off: to not be able to take a walk, to never be anonymous ... I'm too shy for that."

"You? Shy?"

"Yeah. I am shy. I want attention, I want an audience, but I want to see their faces, and to ask them stuff. And I don't want there to be too many of them. It has to be just right."

We drive in silence past a sign for the World's Largest Crucifix.

"So stop doing it," says Al.

"Doing what? Was I biting my nails again?"

"No. The Madonna piece. Stop doing it if it makes you uncomfortable."

"Oh, I don't mind really. It's always the least interesting piece on the program, which is the way it should be. That's the point, really."

"Oh. Got it."

There's a nice sunset going on. He pops in a tape for accompaniment and rubs the back of my neck. Score, I think.

It's certifiably dark when we pull into Calumet. The snow is piled so high that all you can see are the peaked roofs of the houses. We drive around until we find the Calumet Theater, where I'll be performing for the next few days. It is a beautiful thing, one hundred years old, perfect acoustics. Then it's off to the B & B to unload and fall into a magnificent carved antique bed. I curl up with a book about nuns and learn many interesting things. Did you know that nuns-in-training are warned about the dangers of having "a particular friend"—a bond with another girl that becomes exclusive and all-consuming? Hmm. Somehow it doesn't snow all night.

In the morning we move into the theater. Sarah Bernhardt played here once. If you stand exactly center stage and look across the audience to the furthest wall, there's a small picture of her there. The tiny stage is soaked through with the essence of more than a century of plays, speeches, musicals, operas, graduations, and sermons. Thick red velvet curtains hang to the side and the walls and the front of the balcony are alive with painted carvings. It simply doesn't get better than this.

Sven, the lighting guy, is as together as promised. He unloads the instruments and cable I've brought up with me and starts patching them into the in-house system. My show is simple, but light is important to me and there are certain cues I have to have: the long, low diagonal swath in *Jester*, the strategically placed colorless sidelights in *I, or Someone*, the pinspot on the skull in *This, Uh, Head*. In nonunion situations like this, I jump in and help all I can, plugging and unplugging, moving the rolling ladder about the stage, shouting up to the grid. Even with the lights I've brought with me, we have barely enough, and we spend hours changing or eliminating cues. But I don't care. I love this theater, and besides, I'm being paid to dance.

Perhaps more problematic, the theater's furnace is working overtime, but the weather is extreme, even by Calumet standards—the temperature onstage is in the low 50s. I'm not sure what will be harder in the cold, the rigorous dances or the stock-still monologues. I'm also worried about the receptiveness of a lightly frosted audience.

Around five, area dancers show up for a master class. There are about twelve of them, from Calumet and Houghton, a university town we passed through getting here. Levels are mixed, but we warm up as best we can and spend an hour playing sound and movement improvisation games, which they eat right up. Then we get down to business. They are going to be in a dance.

I learned a long time ago that for the most part, Americans hate what I do, if they even know that it exists. If it's not ignored, it's often despised, and I have to say I know why. There's a lot of bad, hackneyed modern dance lurking about, created by people who just want to express their feelings and to hell with craft or the existence of an audience that presumably might want to connect with what they're seeing. I've made my share of clunkers I guess, but I do think a lot about the audience. Probably too much.

And I also learned a long time ago that in the world of minor-league, farm-team, hinterland modern dance touring, where I for the most part reside, if you want to lure an audience, savvy or not, to your shows, it's a good idea to involve members of the community where you are headed. For this reason, I have a tried-and-true group piece, which I can teach in about an hour to dancers of all levels. All they have to do is be able to count to eight, move in time with one movement of a Handel concerto, and remember a few simple, gestural combinations. It works every time. The local dancers bring their moms and dads and friends and goodwill is fostered. And instead of selling 64 tickets and losing about $1,500 to bring me to their community, the sponsoring arts organization sells, gosh, nearly 100 tickets and loses only maybe $1000. It's a good feeling.

Anyway, I teach the sweet young Calumet/Houghton dancers how to do the piece and we have fun on the cold stage. Then it's a dinner of pizza in a local bar and back to reading about nuns, and other pleasant activities in the four-post bed as the wind screams outside and the temperature drops to 45 below.

The next day I am scheduled for two performances of my monster show for area schoolchildren. We show up at the theater by ten. Al will be backstage acting as my "dresser" for there are many quick changes in this multicharacter show in which I dance all parts. Here I am, a mature mother of two dressing up like monsters and jumping around in front of children. I would look askance at myself except for the fact that it is so very fun. I get to wear gorgeous, handmade masks, crafted from hockey helmets, chicken wire, window screen, and *papier maché*. My Suess-like story-poem about the monsters who live next door to me is punctuated with music—an Argentine tango, Etta James's "At Last," the Beatles' "Can't Buy Me Love"—performed by barking dogs—and a sweet Ravel piano solo to finish. The dancing is hard and fast and relentless. I lose several pounds of water each time I perform it, and by the time I remove the final mask at the end of the show and step forward to take questions from the kids, my face is flushed deep, deep red.

I'm ready to go, but there's a problem. The first show is canceled. Even Calumet cannot function in this cold; the school buses simply won't start. By afternoon, however, God has doled out a few more degrees to the Upper Peninsula of Michigan and the theater is filled to the top of the balcony with squirming young things. After the show I make them all smile and I take their picture with my Polaroid.

Next night is the real show, for adults, and I couldn't be more ready. I'm at the theater by 6 for an 8 PM hit. Temperature onstage still hovers in the low 50s and I go for layers: long underwear, sweats, several pairs of massive socks. I lay a blanket on the stage, lie down, and begin rolling around. A dancer's warm-up is a deeply personal thing. Over the years I've developed a series of physical tasks that simply must be done prior to performing. One of these tasks is rolling slowly on my butt, with my knees in the air, allowing the stage to press carefully into the crest of my pelvis. Sometimes I use tennis balls, or my fists, to go deeper into those vital but temperamental connections between my back and my hips. This is the single most imperative preshow ritual. After about five minutes of this, I can continue stretching, doing pliés, tendus, battements, a few jumps, and the more weight-released modern stuff. I run through a few lines. I sing scales and songs. I try valiantly to work up even a gentle sweat but I'm just too cold. We do a quick sound check for good measure, then it's time to open the house.

I stand exactly center stage and stare out at Sarah's picture. I wave at her, then go backstage. The curtain drops. The house opens.

Again, it's gotten so cold that the automotive batteries of Calumet have given up the ghost. At 8:05 there are about fifty people in the audience, bundled in everything they own, but laughing and talking and good-natured. I peek out at them. I have performed many, many times, but not so many that this moment has lost its power over me.

It's heady, addictive. Fifty people? I love them, each and every one.

First piece is *Letter to Annabelle*: cowboy songs, me in boots with a fake campfire, and a text about a surreal cattle drive over a remote Colorado pass, littered with dinosaur bones and the skeletal remains of a Conestoga wagon. Next is *Jester*, which I've performed for many years. It's based on the character Feste from *Twelfth Night*. I get to wear an antique harlequin hat tipped with tiny bells. It is one of my favorite pieces. *I, or Someone* and *Appliance Boxes/Wind* are performed back to back, and based on dreams. I use two local women for one of the sections. They cross slowly from one side of the stage to the other, in '50s-era one-piece bathing suits while I tell the audience about swimming at the Y, lap lanes covered in orange carpeting . . . oh, forget it. You have to be there.

Next comes the group piece. The local dancers are beside themselves with excitement. I have them wearing office clothing: skirts and blazers, silly, scarfy neck bows, sensible pumps. As the Handel soars to the rafters, they clomp about the stage, sitting on and otherwise interacting with simple folding chairs, performing eight or ten short gestural phrases of movement in any order they choose. This may be the first time they've ever allowed themselves to be funny onstage. If I can get them over this hurdle, then I've done my job. They get the loudest applause so far, hoots and hollers from their friends. Yeah.

After intermission comes *This, Uh, Head*, a thirty-five-minute monologue set in rural Mississippi during the 1940s and peopled with characters from *Hamlet*. It is my best work, and I guess I'm more proud of it than anything I've ever done. I forget the cold and dive into southern sun, and the texture of the dirt in the fields, the skull of Yorick, and the voices of young "Felia" and her family. The state of Michigan commissioned this piece, along with five other dance and theater works based on nonpivotal characters in Shakespeare. The state of Michigan is duly credited in the program.

I am a quiet person at heart. My songs are quiet, mostly, and my dances, even the big ones, even the funny ones, have a quiet core. Performing is like a friendly, willing kidnapping. And when I purloin an audience and bundle them off to a place where my young, long-ago mother can throw Yorick's skull into the Tombigbee River and you can still hear the nightbirds sing over the splash as it hits the water, well, that makes me very happy.

I change out of my Depression-era farming togs, grab my guitar, and walk to the center of the stage. Big Al joins me at the side with his Telecaster. More and more I find myself singing at my performances, preparing for the day I can no longer dance.

We do five songs, then it's time for the closer.

Wearing a red wool, Jackie Kennedy-style suit with a black fur collar and high heels, I grab my actual college journal and a folding chair and walk out onto the dark stage. I find my glow-tape mark, open up the chair and sit down, staring hard where I know Sarah B. will momentarily appear. My roomie's voice swells in the blackness.

"Come on, girls! Do you believe in love? 'Cause I got something to say about it! And it goes something like this! Don't go for second best, baby! Put your love to the test! Youknowyouknowyougotto make him express how he feels. And then you know your love is real …"

It is quite a change in mood.

The music fades out and I just smile at everyone for a minute. Then I start talking fast.

"OK," I go, "If you've read your program, you will know by now that Madonna roomed with me back in college. I do this piece simply to get people to come to my shows." I let that sink in. Again, there are only fifty people here.

"Here are the rules: I will read a section of my journal, about the first time I met her. Then you can ask questions and I will answer them, and then that will be the end. OK? OK."

I read the section about the day Madonna sat on the sofa opposite me and said, "You don't look very happy, Whitley. What's wrong?" The day I said she could live with me, and Joel and Tony. Then I close the book and just sit there. Sometimes it takes a minute for people to get the idea that they can ask questions but not this crew.

"Are you surprised at how famous she's gotten?"

"Was she a good singer?"

"Was she nice?"

"What did you guys do together?"

"Are you still in touch?"

"Did you like her?"

And then, this, from a lady in the second row:

"Do you think Madonna is lucky?"

Lucky. Hmm. Never thought about it. I sit back in my chair and take a moment to think. And then I tell them this.

§2

It is a Sunday, the last day we are to live together. The spring semester—spent learning Liz's "carillon" piece and performing it outside under the Bell Tower—is over. Our lease is up on the monstrosity apartment. Tony and Joel have gone home for the summer. Tomorrow I will move into my tiny loft place on Packard full time and Madonna will move in with her sister Paula who has a house over on Ashley. She's planning on staying there for about two weeks to save a bit more money before leaving for New York. I'm bussing tables at Seva and haven't figured out yet that I'm going to the Rainbow Gathering.

"Whit-leee. Geddup."

The shins. This is the last time I will be awakened by shins. She crouches down.

"Geddup, OK? We're going to the river. Paula has a bike for you. Let's go swimming. It's so friggin' hot outside."

It is that. I sit up amid my sheets and realize that I'm already sweating. I go in the bathroom, wash my face, and come back in the room, which is filled with suitcases, boxes, and piles of clothes. Madonna is sitting on the floor, leaning up against the dresser, looking at something on the bottom of her foot. This is the last day.

"So, where exactly are we going?" I say.

"The swimming hole. I told you about it last week. Christopher says it's great. You can swim naked. Lots of people go. The water is deep there and it's really fun. And families go by in canoes with their little kids and get all bent outta shape ..."

"Is it ... safe? Is it legal? What if it's private property or ..."

"You are going, so shut up," she says. "This is simple. We're gonna ride bikes out to this railroad bridge, then climb down the side, and it's a little, short hike. I know right where it is. Don't worry."

"OK" I say, though I don't feel very okay. Despite nine months of training at the Ciccone Academy of Derring-do, I have my moments of regression. The naked part doesn't bother me but I am not sure about encounters with any kind of railroad architecture.

In honor of our last official day as roommates, we have bean-sprout omelettes at Steve's Lunch, then hike through the sunshine to Paula's.

June in Ann Arbor is the best. The temperature is still something of a novelty, and about 80 percent of the students are gone. We feel like we own the place. As we cross the Diag, I flip suddenly back to last fall, when we were walking to the farmers market, tentatively touching our friendship. It seems like a million years ago. Now we can walk in silence, or simply communicate with a glance. We are familiars.

Paula's not home but she's left the bikes on the porch, so we climb on and head north on Main Street toward Huron River Drive.

One thing that's really nice about this town is that you can ride five or ten minutes in any direction and be in the country. Farms, cows … country. For a city girl like me, this is perfectly amazing. The road snakes its way for miles and miles along the Huron, a small, but clean-looking river; we're heading slowly west, following all its twists and turns. Madonna is ahead of me, sometimes standing up on the pedals to get some speed, or coasting down the hills with her hands at her sides. I'm busy breathing deeply, taking in the greens and blues, the bridges and ducks, wondering why on earth I don't do this more often.

About five miles outside of town, on an old cement bridge, Madonna pulls her bike off the road and twists back to look as I pull in behind her.

"This is it," she says. We hide the bikes in some bushes, and cross the road to the other side, where the Amtrak tracks fly off in either direction. And about 50 feet down, the river burbles dark green over white stones.

"Uh, how are we supposed to get down there?" I ask.

She doesn't answer, just points to a concrete buttress that stretches from the tracks all the way down to the riverbank at a steep angle.

A very steep angle.

In her battered Adidas, Madonna hops onto the embankment—it's maybe a foot wide—and starts a quick and precise chain of steps to the bottom. Why is she so damn fearless? I take a deep breath and follow. Okay, that wasn't so bad. At the bottom, we sprint along a narrow, muddy path, hopping over roots and fallen trees and the river tumbles beside us, sending wafts of iron and moss. It is most intoxicating. Suddenly the path widens out into a small grassy area where five or six hippie-ish folks are sunbathing, some naked, some not. They greet us with smiles. It feels pretty wholesome. Directly across, on the opposite bank are more naked bodies. Several more bob in the water. I let my hair out of its clip and feel oh so Native American.

After a quick joint, passed amicably around the riverbank, we strip off our clothes and wade in. I may not like steep embankments but water always makes me brave. I clamber to the very center of the rapids where nature has fashioned a chute of water. You can hang on to a large branch and dangle your butt over the chute as water tugs and tugs, and you let go and slide down into a world of mossy green thunder that suddenly dissolves into a most civilized, sandy-bottomed current. Then you wade out and do it again. We stay there all afternoon, playing, splashing, and flirting with hippies. And if this is the last real day we spend together, well, that's okay—it's a good one.

The ride back into town seems much shorter, even though we're tired and sunburned. Paula's home and we hang there for a while, eating stuff. Madonna gets inspired and even starts baking bread. Somehow it has escaped my notice that Madonna bakes bread, but she's standing there in the kitchen in her shorts and bra, up to her elbows in flour, listening to Stevie Wonder. While the dough rises, we walk Paula to work. Paula—whom I barely know, but really like—works at the Earle, a fancy restaurant on Washington. She goes inside and we're just standing on the sidewalk watching the sunset when Madonna gets this look in her eye.

"Hey, Whitto, come on …"

Oh shit, now what?

She ducks into an alley, points to a fire escape on the side of the old brick building, and a ladder that hangs down, just out of reach.

"Whit, let's you and me go up on the roof. I did it last year with (she names some guy I don't recall her mentioning) and it's really fun. NO, shut UP, don't say anything. We are going on the roof. Here, help me pull that garbage can over."

Well, actually Missy, I wasn't going to say anything. I am actually perfectly happy with this plan, so fuck you. I, who grew up on the roofs of city buildings …

Standing up on the garbage can, we can easily reach the ladder and climb it to the fire escape, which teeters a bit sickeningly as we run up the metal stairs to the roof.

God, it's beautiful up there. It's Mary Poppins and Peter Pan and a Carole King song, all rolled up and smoked. The sun is a sticky orange ball; you could lick it and it would taste good. We stand at the parapet and look west. We put our arms around each other. I wish I could recall some clever but heartfelt conversation about the imminent parting of our ways, but in truth we just stand there not saying much of anything, watching the sun go down. Then we go dance on the roof for a while. We do the old Bach combination we made up on that snowy day. We do a combination from the pratfall dance.

"Hey, Madonna," I say. She's lying on the tar watching a flock of birds roll through the evening sky.

"What?"

"What do you think these pipes are?" I'm leaning against one of those weird roof pipes. I think they have something to do with furnaces or toilets.

"Shit, I don't know. Why?"

"Well, because when I was a kid and my mom and I were up on the roof of our building, I would always bring a penny and when she wasn't looking I would drop it down the pipes. I thought it was probably good luck. I would drop it down and listen and listen for the clink."

I fish a penny out of my shorts, stand on my tiptoes, and look down the hole. I slowly inch the penny to the edge and push it over the side. Clink. Far, far down.

"Oh good," I say. "I'm lucky. I'm a lucky girl."

Madonna watches the birds. She stretches one leg up to the sky, pulls it close to her chest. Then the other.

"I'm getting cold," she says, rolling to her feet.

I'm one flight down the fire escape when I realize Madonna's not behind me.

"Hey. You coming? What are you…?"

I climb back up and peek over the wall. She's standing by the pipe, silhouetted against the orange-purple sunset. Madonna is stretched as high as she can go, peering into the circle of black. Her fingers snake over the edge, drop something in. Then, quick-quick, she presses her ear to the metal. She listens. I don't ask her what she hears.

The audience in the Calumet Opera House sits quietly. The music swells up, the lights go down.

After the people trickle out, my husband and I slowly start packing costumes, masks, lights, and cable. We load the Blazer, strapping the poles and instruments to the roof with the bungee cords. It's a bit warmer, maybe zero, and the stars are a feast. Before we head out, I stop and take one final look around. "I'll be right along," I call.

And I walk to the center of the quiet stage and look across the empty seats to the face of Sarah Bernhardt glowing faintly back at me.

And I think about everyone who's stood on these splintery boards, this steep and battered stage. Not just the Divine Sarah, declaiming

Hamlet, Cleopatra, Portia before the miners and the miner's wives, but the Vaudeville hoofers, the long-ago baritones touring from town to town, the people in the local community theater, the children in their Easter plays. All of them finding their way to the center of this gilded frame, hearts tousling, words catching, then tumbling out into the wide dark. And I think about luck. And joy. And how maybe they're one and the same, and not so much found, like treasure, or bestowed, from pennies dropped, as just taken up and held close. Willingly.

I pull my coat tight around me.

"Am I lucky?" I ask the balcony. "Am I a lucky girl?"

My words turn to motes of mist in the dim light and quickly disappear. I smile and shiver. Cold as it is, I just don't want to leave.

The next morning, we eat eggs on Main Street in Calumet then head south into some semblance of sun.

Acknowledgments

Many thanks to all my early readers for their great insight and encouragement: Helen Hill, Karen Chassin Goldbaum, Jane Myers, Deirdre Knight, Penny Schreiber, John Hilton, Charmie Gholson, Marianne Schapiro Barber, Marie Frost and so many others.

Happy gratitude, as well, to Naomi Rosenblatt, Sue Havlish, Fred Ciporen, Nancy Burke, Leah Wells and all of Team NAM.

And, of course, deep appreciation to my sweet family for their patience and support: Al, Maya, Sam, Cullen, Dad, Kate and Ilya.

CPSIA information can be obtained at www.ICGtesting.com
Printed in the USA
LVOW100809210413

330133LV00002BA/43/P